ADOBE® PREMIERE® 6.5

Digital Video Editing

AGAINST THE CLOCK
mastering graphic technology

Prentice
Hall

Upper Saddle River, NJ 07458

Library of Congress Cataloging-in-Publication Data

Adobe Premiere 6.5: Digital Video Editing/Against The Clock
    p. cm. — (Against The Clock Series)
ISBN 0-13-112641-5
1. Motion Pictures — Editing — Data Processing.
    2. Digital Video — Editing — Data Processing. 3. Adobe Premiere.
    I. Against The Clock (Firm). II. Series.

TR899 .A375 2003
778.5'235'0285   2002038116

Editor-in-Chief: Stephen Helba
Director of Production and Manufacturing: Bruce Johnson
Executive Editor: Elizabeth Sugg
Managing Editor – Editorial: Judy Casillo
Editorial Assistant: Cyrenne Bolt de Freitas
Managing Editor – Production: Mary Carnis
Production Editor: Denise Brown
Composition: Erika Kendra, Against The Clock, Inc.
Design Director: Cheryl Asherman
Design Coordinator: Christopher Weigand
Cover Design: LaFortezza Design Group, Inc.
Icon Design: James Braun
Prepress: Photoengraving, Inc.
Printer/Binder: Press of Ohio

The fonts utilized in these training materials are the property of Against The Clock, Inc., and are supplied to the legitimate buyers of the Against The Clock training materials solely for use with the exercises and projects provided in the body of the materials. They may not be used for any other purpose, and under no circumstances may they be transferred to another individual, nor copied or distributed by any means whatsoever.

A portion of the images supplied in this book are Copyright © PhotoSpin, 4030 Palos Verdes Dr. N., Suite 200, Rolling Hills Estates, CA. These images are the sole property of PhotoSpin and are used by Against The Clock with the permission of the owners. They may not be distributed, copied, transferred, or reproduced by any means whatsoever, other than for the completion of the exercises and projects contained in these Against The Clock training materials.

Against The Clock and the Against The Clock logo are trademarks of Against The Clock, Inc., registered in the United States and elsewhere. References to and instructional materials provided for any particular application program, operating system, hardware platform, or other commercially available product or products do not represent an endorsement of such product or products by Against The Clock, Inc. or Prentice Hall, Inc.

Premiere, PageMaker, Photoshop, Acrobat, Adobe Type Manager, Illustrator, InDesign, and PostScript are trademarks of Adobe Systems Incorporated. Macromedia Flash, Generator, FreeHand, Dreamweaver, Fireworks, and Director are registered trademarks of Macromedia, Inc. QuarkXPress is a registered trademark of Quark, Inc. Macintosh is a trademark of Apple Computer, Inc. CorelDRAW!, Painter, and WordPerfect are trademarks of Corel Corporation. FrontPage, Publisher, PowerPoint, Word, Excel, Office, Microsoft, MS-DOS, and Windows are either registered trademarks or trademarks of Microsoft Corporation.

Other product and company names mentioned herein may be the trademarks of their respective owners.

Pearson Education LTD.
Pearson Education Australia PTY, Limited
Pearson Education Singapore, Pte. Ltd
Pearson Education North Asia Ltd
Pearson Education Canada, Ltd
Pearson Educación de Mexico, S.A. de C.V.
Pearson Education – Japan
Pearson Education Malaysia, Pte. Ltd
Pearson Education, Upper Saddle River, New Jersey

10 9 8 7 6 5 4 3 2 1

Prentice Hall

ISBN 0-13-112641-5

Contents

Purpose

The Against The Clock series has been developed specifically for those involved in the field of computer arts, and now — animation, video, and multimedia production. Many of our readers are already involved in the industry in advertising and printing, television production, multimedia, and in the world of Web design. Others are just now preparing for a career within these professions.

This series provides you with the necessary skills to work in these fast-paced, exciting, and rapidly expanding fields. While many people feel that they can simply purchase a computer and the appropriate software, and begin designing and producing high-quality presentations, the real world of high-quality printed and Web communications requires a far more serious commitment.

The Series

The applications presented in the Against The Clock series stand out as the programs of choice in professional computer-arts environments.

We use a modular design for the Against The Clock series, allowing you to mix and match the drawing, imaging, and page-layout applications that exactly suit your specific needs.

Titles available in the Against The Clock series include:

Macintosh: Basic Operations
Windows: Basic Operations
Adobe Illustrator: Introduction and Advanced Digital Illustration
Macromedia FreeHand: Digital Illustration
Adobe InDesign: Introduction and Advanced Electronic Documents
Adobe PageMaker: Creating Electronic Documents
QuarkXPress: Introduction and Advanced Electronic Documents
Microsoft Publisher: Creating Electronic Mechanicals
Microsoft PowerPoint: Presentation Graphics with Impact
Microsoft FrontPage: Creating and Designing Web Pages
HTML & XHTML: Creating Web Pages
Procreate Painter: A Digital Approach to Natural Art Media
Adobe Photoshop: Introduction and Advanced Digital Images
Adobe Premiere: Digital Video Editing
Adobe After Effects: Motion Graphics and Visual Effects
Macromedia Director: Creating Powerful Multimedia
Macromedia Flash: Rich Media for the Web
Macromedia Fireworks: Digital Imaging for the Web
Macromedia Dreamweaver: Creating Web Pages
Preflight and File Preparation
TrapWise and PressWise: Digital Trapping and Imposition

You will see a number of icons in the sidebars; each has a standard meaning. Pay close attention to the sidebar notes where you will find valuable comments that will help you throughout this book, and in the everyday use of your computer. The standard icons are:

The Hand-on-mouse icon indicates a hands-on activity — either a short exercise or a complete project. The complete projects are located at the back of the book, in sequence from Project A through D.

The Pencil icon indicates a comment from an experienced operator or trainer. Whenever you see this icon, you'll find corresponding sidebar text that augments the subject being discussed at the time.

The Key icon is used to identify keyboard equivalents to menu or dialog box options. Using a key command is often faster than selecting a menu option with the mouse. Experienced operators often mix the use of keyboard equivalents and menu/dialog box selections to arrive at their optimum speed of execution.

The Caution icon indicates a potential problem or difficulty. For instance, a certain technique might lead to pages that prove difficult to output. In other cases, there might be something that a program cannot easily accomplish, so we present a workaround.

If you are a Windows user, be sure to refer to the corresponding text or images whenever you see this Windows icon. Although there isn't a great deal of difference between using these applications on a Macintosh and using them on a Windows-based system, there are certain instances where there's enough of a difference for us to comment.

For the Reader

On the Resource CD-ROM, you will find a collection of data files. These files, necessary to complete both the exercises and projects, may be found in the **RF_Premiere** folder on the Resource CD-ROM.

For the Trainer

The Trainer's materials, available online, include various testing and presentation materials in addition to the files that are supplied with this book.

- **Overhead presentation materials** are provided and follow along with the book. These presentations are prepared using Microsoft PowerPoint, and are provided in both native PowerPoint format and Acrobat Portable Document Format (PDF).

- **Extra free-form projects** are provided and may be used to extend the training session, or they may be used to test the reader's progress.

- **Test questions and answers** are included. These questions may be modified and/or reorganized.

Chapter openers provide the reader
with specific objectives.

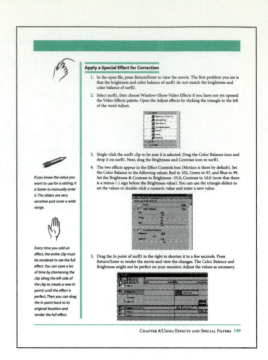

Sidebars and hands-on activities
supplement concepts presented
throughout the book.

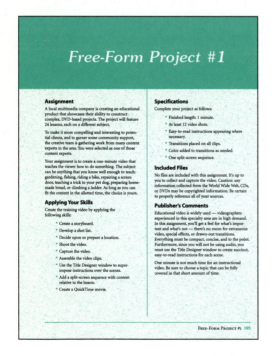

Free-form projects allow readers to
use their imagination and new skills to
satisfy a typical client's needs.

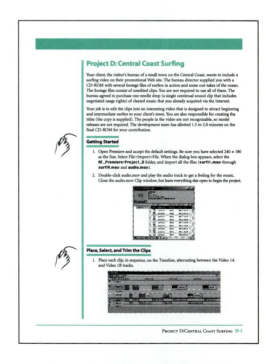

Step-by-step projects result in finished
artwork — with an emphasis on
proper file-construction methods.

Project A: The Monkey Movie

This project will help you learn how to create a real-world video production. You will produce a basic video, featuring monkeys at play, that will be used in a promotional fund-raising campaign. You will import a number of short video clips and then build a basic project. Next, you will add transitions and generate a final video. These basic videography skills are at the heart of virtually every movie you will create during your film-making career.

Project B: Making Spaghetti

In this project, you will work on a multimedia cookbook that includes a series of videos illustrating some of the finer techniques used to prepare tasty dishes. When complete, your movie will teach the viewer how to make spaghetti. You will add transitions, credits, and titles to make your presentation more interesting and informative. This video is a team effort; while you are completing this segment of the video, other editors will be creating additional cooking tips. It is important that you precisely follow the directions so all of the final segments have the same overall appearance.

Project C: The Gold Rush

Your company is creating a series of multimedia CDs that travel agencies will use to promote summer vacation destinations. This particular CD will showcase vacation possibilities in California and Alaska, including a cruise to Alaska with a stopover at Skagway. To promote this stopover and generate interest in the cruise, you are producing an "authentic" old-time movie about the history of the gold rush and a train journey along the Yukon Trail. You will use some advanced editing techniques to create moving images from still pictures, and semi-transparent images that display over a solid background.

Project D: Central Coast Surfing

Your client, the visitor's bureau of a small town on the Central Coast, wants to include a surfing video on their promotional Web site. The bureau supplied you with several clips of surfers in action, some additional out-takes of breaking surf, and a sound clip. They gave you a rough sketch of the order of the clips (they are numbered), but you are not required to use all of the footage. You are also responsible for creating the titles (the copy is supplied). The development team allotted 1.5 to 2.0 minutes on the final CD-ROM for your contribution.

Acknowledgments

I would like to give thanks to the writers, illustrators, editors, and others who have worked long and hard to complete the Against The Clock series. And special thanks to Gavin Nagatomo, Project Manager, and Dean Bagley, Production Manager, for their hard work and dedication to our team.

Thank you to Debbie Rose Myers, of the Art Institute of Fort Lauderdale, for all of her work on the previous version of this book, *Adobe Premiere 6.0: Digital Video Editing*.

A big thank you to the dedicated teaching professionals and industry professionals whose comments and expertise contributed to the success of these products, including Eric Holm, Gary Powell of the Detroit Public Schools, Collin Pillow of Arkansas State University, and Doris Anton of Wichita Area Technical College.

Thanks to Laurel Cucchiara, copyeditor, and final link in the chain of production, for her help in making sure that we all said what we meant to say.

A big thanks to Denise Brown and Kerry Reardon, for their guidance, patience, and attention to detail.

— Ellenn Behoriam, November 2002

Our History

Against The Clock (ATC) was founded in 1990 as a part of Lanman Systems Group, one of the nation's leading systems integration and training firms. The company specialized in developing custom training materials for such clients as L.L. Bean, *The New England Journal of Medicine*, the Smithsonian, the National Education Association, *Air & Space Magazine*, Publishers Clearing House, the National Wildlife Society, Home Shopping Network, and many others. The integration firm was among the most highly respected in the graphic-arts industry.

To a great degree, the success of Lanman Systems Group can be attributed to the thousands of pages of course materials developed at the company's demanding client sites. Throughout the rapid growth of Lanman Systems Group, founder and general manager Ellenn Behoriam developed the expertise necessary to manage technical experts, content providers, writers, editors, illustrators, designers, layout artists, proofreaders, and the rest of the chain of professionals required to develop structured and highly effective training materials.

Following the sale of the Lanman Companies to World Color, one of the nation's largest commercial printers, Ellenn embarked on a project to develop a new library of hands-on training materials engineered specifically for the professional graphic artist. A large part of this effort is finding and working with talented professional artists, authors, and educators from around the country.

The result is the ATC training library.

About the Author

Robert Howell received his Master of Arts Degree from Pepperdine University. As a Full Professor in the Department of Art and Design — Photography and Digital Imaging Concentration, California Polytechnic State University, San Luis Obispo, California, Robert teaches numerous courses in digital video production, interactive design, Photoshop, and commercial photography. He is also the owner of a successful consulting business in San Luis Obispo. Some examples of his work can be found in the permanent collections of the Corcoran Gallery and the Library of Congress. Robert has delivered hundreds of independent courses and lectures, including a presentation at the International Conference on Technology in Paris, France.

For the past several years, Robert has served as a judge at the SLO International Film Festival and other California competitions. In 2002, he was nominated and accepted for inclusion in *Who's Who Among American Teachers*. His other interests include blacksmithing, fine woodworking, precision machine work, and restoring hisoric Harley Davidson motorcycles.

Getting Started

Platform

The Against The Clock (ATC) series is designed for both the Macintosh and Windows platforms. Some features of Premiere 6.5 are platform dependent. These features are noted where appropriate.

Prerequisites

This book is based on the assumption that you have a basic understanding of how to use your computer. You should know how to use your mouse to point and click, and to drag items around the screen. You should be able to resize and arrange windows on your desktop to maximize your available workspace. You should know how to access drop-down menus, and understand how check boxes and radio buttons work. Lastly, you should know how to create, open, and save files. It doesn't hurt to have a good under-standing of how your operating system organizes files and folders, and know how to navi-gate your way around them.

If you are familiar with these fundamental skills, then you know all that's necessary to utilize the Against The Clock courseware library.

CD-ROM and Initial Set-Up Considerations

Before you begin using this Against The Clock book, you must set up your system to have access to the various files and tools to complete your lessons.

Resource Files

This book comes complete with a collection of resource files, which are an integral part of the learning experience. They are used throughout the book to help you construct increasingly complex elements. These building blocks should be available for practice and study sessions to allow you to experience and complete the exercises and project assign-ments smoothly, spending a minimum amount of time looking for the various required components.

All the files you need to complete the exercises and projects in this book are located on your Resource CD-ROM in a folder called RF_Premiere. It would be best to copy the files onto your hard drive before beginning the exercises if you have 100MB or more of avail-able space. If not, you can work directly from the Resource CD-ROM.

Work In Progress Folder

Before you begin working on the exercises in this book, you should create a folder called "Work_In_Progress" either on your hard drive or on a removable disk. As you work through the steps in the exercises, you will be directed to save your work in this folder.

If your time is limited, you can stop at a logical point in an exercise or project, save the file, and later return to the point at which you stopped. In some cases, the exercises in this book build upon work you have already completed. You will need to open a file from your Work_In_Progress folder and continue working on the same file.

Locating Files

Files that you need to open are indicated by a different typeface (for example, "Open **file.ppj**"). The location of the file also appears in the special typeface (for example, "Open **document.ppj** from your **Work_In_Progress** folder").

When you are directed to save a file with a specific name, the name appears in quotation marks (for example, "Save the file as "new_file.ppj" to your **Work_In_Progress** folder").

In most cases, resource files are located in the **RF_Premiere** folder, while exercises and projects on which you continue to work are located in your **Work_In_Progress** folder. We repeat these directions frequently in the early chapters, and add reminders in sidebars in the later chapters. If a file is in a location other than these two folders, the path is indicated in the exercise or project (for example, "Open the file from the **Audio** folder in the **RF_Premiere** folder").

File Naming Conventions

Files on the Resource CD-ROM are named according to the Against The Clock naming convention to facilitate cross-platform compatibility. Words are separated by an underscore, and all file names include a lowercase three-letter extension. You see the three-letter extension as part of the file name.

The extension for Premiere projects is ".ppj". Premiere for Windows always adds the file extension to a file's name; Macintosh users should add the extension when saving files.

When your Windows system is first configured, the views are normally set to a default that hides these extensions. This means that you might have a dozen different files named "myfile," all of which may have been generated by different applications and may consist of completely different types of files. This can become very confusing.

On a Windows system, you can change this view. Double-click "My Computer" (the icon on your desktop). Select View>Folder Options. From Folder Options, select the View tab. Within the Files and Folders folder is a check box for Hide File Extensions for Known File Types. When this is unchecked, you can see the file extensions.

It's easier to know what you're looking at if file extensions are visible. While this is a personal choice, we strongly recommend viewing the file extensions.

Fonts

No special fonts are required for the exercises in this book. If you decide to use a special font that is not included with your system fonts, you can add it to your system. Specific instructions for installing fonts are provided in the documentation that came with your computer.

Key Commands

There are three keys generally used as modifier keys — they don't do anything by themselves when pressed, but they either perform some action or type a special character when pressed in conjunction with another key or keys.

We frequently note keyboard shortcuts that can be used in Premiere. A comprehensive list can be found in the Premiere Help files. A slash character indicates that the key commands differ for Macintosh and Windows systems; the Macintosh commands are listed first, followed by the Windows commands. If you see the command "Command/Control-P", for example, Macintosh users would press the Command key and Windows users would press the Control Key; both would then press the "P" key.

The Command/Control key is used with another key to perform a specific function. When combined with the "O" key, it opens a file project, with the "S" key, it saves the file. In addition to these functions, which work with most Macintosh and Windows programs, the Command/Control key can be combined with other keys to control specific Premiere functions. At times, it is also used in combination with the Shift and/or Option/Alt keys.

Preferences

When you start Premiere for the first time, the program uses the default preferences supplied by Adobe. Thereafter, the preferences file retains the settings you used in your last editing session. To eliminate the preferences file and return to the original, default settings, hold down the Control and Shift keys when you start Premiere (as soon as the program starts to load, press both keys simultaneously). The same key combination is used on the Windows and Macintosh platforms. If you forget to do this, you can individually reset each preference after the program starts.

System Requirements for Adobe Premiere 6.5

Macintosh:

- PowerPC® G3 or faster processor (G4 or G4 dual recommended)
- Mac OS 9.2.2 or Mac OS X 10.1.3
- 64MB of RAM (128MB or more recommended)
- 600MB of available hard-disk space for installation
- 256-color video display adapter
- CD-ROM drive
- QuickTime 5.0.2
- For DV: QuickTime compatible FireWire® (IEEE 1394) interface, large-capacity hard disk or disk array capable of sustaining 5MB/sec, and FireWire 2.7
- For third-party capture cards: Adobe Premiere-certified capture card
- For Real-Time Preview: G4 processor (G4 dual recommended)

Windows:

- Intel® Pentium® III 500MHz processor (Pentium 4 or multiprocessor recommended)

- Microsoft® Windows® 98 Second Edition, Windows Millennium Edition, Windows 2000 with Service Pack 2, or Windows XP

- 128MB of RAM (256MB or more recommended)

- 600MB of available hard-disk space for installation

- 256-color video display adapter

- CD-ROM drive

- QuickTime 5.0 recommended

- For DV: Microsoft DirectX certified IEEE 1394 interface, dedicated large-capacity 7200RPM UDMA 66 IDE or SCSI hard disk or disk array, and DirectX compatible video display adapter

- For third-party capture cards: Adobe® Premiere® certified capture card

- For Real-Time Preview: Pentium III 800MHz processor (Pentium 4 dual processors recommended)

Note: During testing, there were some compatibility problems with QuickTime 6.0. If you experience problems, reinstall QuickTime 5.0 for use with Premiere.

Introduction

This book was designed to familiarize you with the fundamentals of Premiere 6.5, the standard program for creating and editing video images for computer, Web, video, and DVD presentation.

As the use of video becomes increasingly popular — particularly at the corporate and educational levels — knowing how to apply the robust set of features and functions in a product such as Premiere could prove to be an invaluable skill.

First and foremost, Premiere is used for video editing. Video editing is the process of extracting scenes (clips) from existing video, audio, and still footage, and then assembling the clips to create a final movie. Original footage can be pre-existing or created by you using digital and analog recording equipment. Premiere can also be used to create special effects and transitions between scenes, as well as titles and credits. You can combine images to create a composite image (montage) to which you may add special effects. It is easy to see why Premiere is the first choice among video-development tools.

The program provides overlay and transparency options that allow you to create completely original scenes. Using blue- and green-screen techniques, you can create virtually anything — from the real to the surreal, entertaining to heartbreaking, factual to unbelievable.

New to Premiere 6.5 is an enhanced Title Designer window that makes the creation of rolling, crawling, and special-effect titles easier than ever. Its color palettes and specialized tools allow you to create original artwork from scratch. In addition, you can control many aspects of type design including kerning, leading, drop shadows, and transparency. All of these advanced features add depth to this robust application.

Premiere is capable of making color corrections — very fine adjustments to specific colors or tones in a video clip. Few other video-production products can make that claim. The color corrections can be as minute as altering a color shift on the overall image, or as extreme as creating a posterized effect. Premiere also provides audio tools you can use to manipulate sound clips. Digitized sound can be "tweaked" to perfection or distorted beyond recognition — whatever is required for a particular production. Once you become familiar with all of the features and techniques, you will find the development process to be fast, easy, and usually quite a bit of fun.

Premiere 6.5 is also invaluable for producing graphics for new media applications. Your finished movies can be output in highly compressed formats for fast playback on the Web and new formats destined for DVDs.

Premiere 6.5 works in conjunction with Adobe After Effects to provide virtually unlimited creative possibilities. Premiere can seamlessly use many of the effects provided with After Effects; it also includes five new effects of its own. Projects created in Premiere can be imported into After Effects, retaining all of the After Effects keyframes and special effects. Movies exported from After Effects can then be imported into a Premiere project and used in your final production. You can even preview your project in real time as you create it. Premiere 6.5 can adjust video quality and frame rate "on the fly" so you can preview your movie before you render it to disk or tape.

The focus of this book is to introduce you to Premiere as a video-editing and export tool, to teach you techniques of clip organization and production planning through the use of storyboards, to demonstrate methods for capturing audio and video clips, and to teach you some basic special effects that are suitable for both production video and multimedia applications. We hope you find this book is helpful as you learn to use this powerful movie-making application.

1 Working with Projects

Chapter Objectives:

Editing your first movie can be a daunting experience if you simply start shooting footage. Through careful preparation and planning, you can make the process much easier and more enjoyable. The more you know about developing effective ideas and setting up Premiere to meet your needs, the more effective the final project will be. In Chapter 1, you will:

- Learn about and practice creative visualization techniques.

- Learn how to create a storyboard and understand why it is such a valuable addition to video production.

- Become familiar with many of the screens and dialog boxes used to set preferences for your Premiere projects.

- Learn the meaning of many terms used in video production and how to select project options to meet your particular needs.

- Understand the various editing modes that Premiere offers and when to use each of them.

- Discover the value of selecting the right scratch disk for your editing session and how to optimize your system for maximum performance.

Projects to be Completed:

- The Monkey Movie (A)

- Making Spaghetti (B)

- The Gold Rush (C)

- Central Coast Surfing (D)

Working with Projects

We all have a story to tell, or perhaps something that needs to be sold — fiction novels, documentaries, business products and services, entertaining and informative educational materials — and creative video provides an excellent way to convey our messages and our products. The most recent version of Adobe Premiere provides all the tools, effects, and editing controls you need to produce professional-quality videos to inspire, entertain, inform, and educate your audience. All you need to supply are the creative ideas, camera skills, and experience as a videographer and film editor.

As you learn the materials presented in this book, your ideas will expand rapidly, as will the complexity of your projects. Each chapter introduces new visual possibilities, and the exercises provide hands-on experience that you can incorporate into your own projects. At some point, you will experience a transition (some call it a revelation) when you realize that your videos have become more than just a collection of scenes, transitions, and effects. At that point, you are in control of the medium and ready to present your stories to the world.

Don't be impatient. Good video takes time and careful attention to each step of the process — from collection of footage to final rendering of the movie. Careful planning is a key element to your success, as well as a structured approach to learning the requisite videography skills. Read each chapter, complete every project, and don't overlook the hints and tips supplied in the sidebars. You can learn to "shoot" video in less than five minutes — you can spend the rest of your life learning how to do it better.

Creating a Project

Every Premiere project begins with an idea. It may be the result of something you saw, a conversation you had with a friend, or even a dream. How clearly you understand and define your idea has a major impact on how easily you can create your final video. Planning is extremely important not only for you, but for the talent working with you on the project. As you read through the following information on storyboarding, you should start to sketch your own ideas.

Creative Planning

Much of what you need to know about the technical aspects of video-production editing begins with Premiere, but it does not end there. In fact, great videographers need to be creative while paying close attention to the technical aspects of their work.

Practice Creative Visualization

1. Take a look at your surroundings. Take note of what you see: computers, chairs, the lighting fixtures, other people, and your family pet. Now try the experiment below.

2. Close your eyes and count to three. Now open your eyes and look around the room; but this time, look at the room in color. Note what you see. Are things any different than they appeared before? Chances are that you see things a little differently. Most people don't pay much attention to their surroundings. The creative person, however, doesn't just exist in an environment; the artist uses the environment to tell a story.

Except for a few exercises, you should not actually do the things you read about in this chapter. You'll start performing activities and completing exercises very soon. If you are running Premiere at this point, your screens and dialog boxes probably do not resemble the screens shown in this chapter.

3. Look around the room again. This time try to find the most unusual and creative camera angle. It could be looking through the legs of your chairs at floor level. Or perhaps your unique shot would be taken from the ceiling looking down at your colleagues at work. A shot looking through the light switch plate back at the others from the inside out might be interesting.

Videography is all about telling a story in the most creative possible way. We usually sit in a room without paying too much attention to what's around us; yet everywhere we look, we can find interesting camera shots. When you learn to identify these shots, you will be well on your way to becoming a great video director.

Storyboarding

One technique frequently used by videographers to plan their video productions is storyboarding. A *storyboard* is a series of sketches of the key visualization points of an event combined with audio information. It often includes camera angles, camera movement, and key phrases from the script. A storyboard can range from a series of rough sketches to a finely illustrated set of panels worthy of framing. It is important to remember that storyboards form the basis — indeed the very foundation — of all your production work. Without a good storyboard, your best ideas can become muddled and lose their continuity when executed in Premiere.

Storyboards often list dialog and possible music under each panel. This helps the director connect the script with the visuals. It's not important that the drawings are perfect or life-like; it's only important that the person looking at the storyboard understands the intent of the shots. It helps to identify the duties and requirements of the team members as the production gets underway.

Exercise Setup

The best way to learn about storyboarding is to practice creating one. In the following exercise, you produce a storyboard detailing your morning wake-up routine. (This exercise should be completed with paper and pencil, not in Premiere.)

Your storyboard should contain roughly eight panels, although you can use a few more if you feel they're important in telling the story. Add instructions for dialog or music if you feel these elements will enhance or strengthen the story.

Create a Storyboard

1. Create a storyboard that details your wake-up routine. It should include about eight panels. Allow your sense of humor to have free reign.

2. Think about and use unusual angles from which to film (view) the scenes. You could stand just outside your window, looking in. Or perhaps the camera could be placed above the ceiling paddle fan, looking down at a person sleeping in bed. The camera would show how the fan turns under the shot of the camera.

The following storyboards were created by Dan Rossi, Darren J. Brent, and D'Andrea Travis, students at the Art Institute of Fort Lauderdale. They created these storyboards as part of their coursework in Adobe Premiere.

3. To help you get some storyboard ideas, we included examples created by students at the Art Institute of Fort Lauderdale. They are fresh and original ways to complete this assignment.

Dan Rossi's storyboards.

Darren J. Brent's "Good Day Sunshine" storyboards.

Storyboarding is also used in cartooning, Web site development, animation, stage production, seminar or presentation preparation, and other situations where artists need to organize their work before actually creating it. It's similar to having a set of blueprints in hand before you start building a house. You know where you want the rooms, but without the plans, all you have is undifferentiated concrete, bricks, wood, hammers, nails, saws, and other building materials. A well-executed storyboard provides directors, actors, camera operators, and other personnel with a simplified visual overview of the entire production.

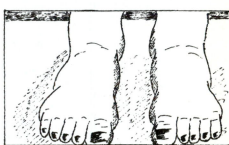

D'Andrea Travis's "How I Get Up in the Morning" storyboards.

4. The act of waking up in the morning is not inherently a very exciting event, but it can be made funny and entertaining when the proper treatment is applied to the activity. Very few people enjoy getting out of bed while it is still dark, but it is something to which we can all relate. As you find ways to tell this story in a humorous and engaging fashion, you will start to think in a new and imaginative way.

Once you have a completed storyboard, you can collect the footage you will use (film clips, audio files, still images, etc.), and then you are ready to begin using Premiere to start the creative editing process.

Project Settings

Creating a project in Premiere involves several steps, the first of which is deciding what settings you want to use. Settings depend on what equipment you have available and how you are going to use your final movie. The remainder of this chapter presents a great deal of information without a sizeable amount of activity on your part. Please read this information carefully, as it is critical to successful completion of any Premiere project and your mastery of the Premiere program.

Presets

Presets, as the name implies, are settings that have been predetermined to meet production standards. Adobe Systems supplies several presets with Premiere. If necessary, you can also create your own customized presets. You may, for example, decide to use a standard video preset, but change the quality of the audio output of the preset to meet your needs.

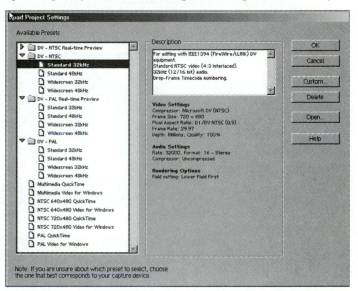

Custom Settings

Custom settings allow you to keep most of the preset settings and adjust only the features you want (or need) to change. Adjustments can be made in one or more of the following categories.

General

General settings control the Editing Mode, Timebase, and Time Display for your editing session. Changing these values can add or remove other options available in other settings areas.

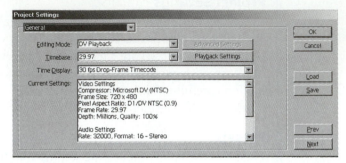

Editing Mode

Your choice of editing mode determines how Premiere displays video in the Timeline. Options supplied with Premiere are DV Playback, QuickTime, and Video for Windows. If your video card manufacturer supplied additional modes (plug-ins), they show in this list and the Advanced Settings option becomes available.

Timebase

The Timebase selection determines how Premiere calculates the exact point in time for each edit. If you were editing motion picture film footage, you would choose 24. For NTSC standard video, you would choose 29.97. For video from other sources (such as a CD-ROM), you would choose 30. Note that the options available for Timebase differ depending on which editing mode you choose.

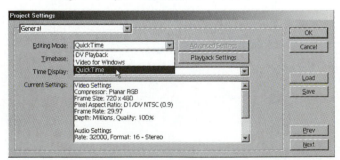

Time Display

Selection of the Time Display determines how time is displayed in your project. If you were using motion picture film, selecting 24 fps Timecode would cause the time to be displayed in frames. Selecting Feet + Frames 16 mm would indicate the current position of your video in feet and frames; 16 mm film uses 40 frames per foot.

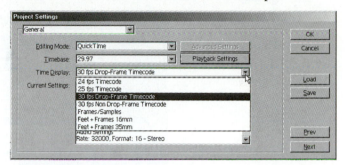

The Non Drop-Frame Timecode option is convenient and easy to understand, but it is not accurate. NTSC video has a true timebase of 29.97 frames per second (fps). Non Drop-Frame Timecode counts at 30 fps. As time progresses, this tiny difference adds up, and the timecode displayed no longer exactly matches the actual video frame. Usually, this does not present problems and the inaccuracy is insignificant.

If exact matching of timecode is important, Drop-Frame Timecode can be selected. Drop-Frame Timecode was developed by the Society of Motion Picture and Television Engineers to account for the time difference between NTSC video and a 30-fps counter. At the end of every minute (except every tenth minute), the counter advances by two numbers. The actual number of frames is not affected, but the counter is readjusted.

To determine which timecode type your equipment or software is using, look at the counter. Non Drop-Frame counters separate the numbers with colons; Drop Frame counters use semicolons.

Playback Options

Playback options vary depending on the editing mode or preset you choose. In the above example, DV mode was selected so the playback options would allow viewing on the desktop or the DV camcorder. Your choice will be based on the type of external viewing equipment available to you. If your video images are clearer on the monitor of your DV recorder, that is what you should choose.

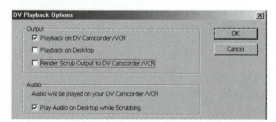

Video

Selecting the Custom Video Project setting offers choices that, again, depend on the video mode you select. The example shows that Microsoft DV (NTSC) was selected. The only option available is the Pixel Aspect Ratio. Frame Size, Frame Rate, and Quality options are grayed out because the Microsoft DV (NTSC) setting overrides these values.

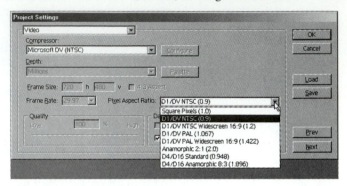

Audio

Decisions regarding the audio setting depend on the equipment you are using and the speed of your computer:

- **Rate**. The rate, in Hertz (a measure of audio frequency), determines the quality of your soundtrack. Generally, the higher the rate, the better the quality. It is important to capture your sound at the same rate you plan to use for playback. Higher rates require more computing power.

- **Format**. Bit depth (how many sound samples are taken) also affects the quality of your sound; the higher the bit depth, the better the quality. High bit depths require more memory and disk space, and tend to cause playback errors if you use a machine with limited speed and memory. The choice of Monaural or Stereo depends on your playback system.

- **Compressor**. Depending on the mode you are using, various codec settings may be available. A *codec* (COmpressor/DECompressor) determines how, and to what extent, the audio portion of your production is compressed. Several codecs are supplied with Adobe Premiere and others are available from independent suppliers. Advanced settings allow you to set specific values for a codec.

- **Interleave**. The Interleave setting determines how often Premiere must process audio. If it is set for one second, one second of audio is processed and then played in synchronization with your video. Long interleave settings require more RAM and less processing time. Short interleave values (1 frame = 1/30 second) require more processing and less RAM. This is one example of the many trade-offs in video processing.

- **Enhance Rate Conversion**. This option determines the quality of playback based on your choice of rate and format. When it is turned off, the lowest quality will be used at the fastest speed. The other two options, Good and Best, should be selected only when you are rendering your final movie.

- **Use Logarithmic Audio Fades**. Most audio gear uses logarithmic potentiometers (volume controls). A logarithmic fade sounds more natural because of the way the human ear responds to changes in volume. Linear audio fades do not sound as smooth and natural.

- **Audio Preview**. Create audio preview files if there are three or more active audio tracks. As you add audio tracks (and sound effects) to a production, the processing load on the system is increased. At some point, the capacity of the system to process sound and video can be exceeded; once that point is reached, you hear distracting noises (pops) in the sound track. When you reduce the number of active audio tracks and effects, you can clean up the sound. When Adobe Premiere creates an audio preview file, instead of maintaining individual active tracks, the load on the system is reduced.

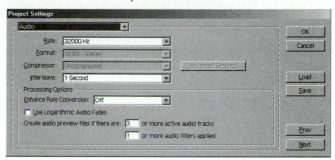

Keyframe and Rendering

Keyframes indicate points in time where changes occur (places where you have added effects to your video). Ignoring effects decreases rendering time and places less of a load on your system while you test, preview, and make final decisions about how your final movie should look.

Still image optimization is available on some, but not all, video capture cards. Instead of rendering a new image of a still for every video frame, a single image is rendered and displayed for as long as it is on the screen. The advantage is a reduction in processing load.

Another method of conserving processing power while editing is to select Frames Only at Markers. This option causes Premiere to render only the frames that contain markers that you have placed at strategic points in the video. If the Real Time Preview option is not selected, the video may play back at a slower rate than the final movie. To test effects and transitions as they will actually appear, select Real Time Preview.

The manufacturer of your video capture card preset usually determines field rendering. If your movie has a lot of flicker, try changing the Fields setting from None to Upper Field First or Lower Field First.

The Keyframe Options area allows you to select how often compression keyframes are generated. Most codecs record only the changes in a scene by comparing the current frame to a previous keyframe. By selecting when a keyframe is generated, you control how often a complete frame is incorporated into the rendering.

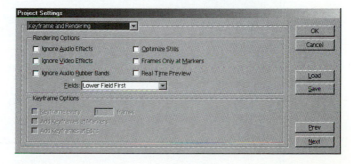

Setting Up the Workspace

Long before video became a popular choice for collecting and editing footage, 16 mm film was used. In order to create a transition between two scenes, the film was actually assembled in two strips (or rolls) known as the "A" roll and the "B" roll. The A roll contained the first scene and the B roll contained black (opaque) film equal to the length of the scene on the A roll. The second scene was spliced into the B roll while black film (of equal duration) was spliced into the A roll.

The completed A and B rolls were then printed (in two passes) onto a single, continual strip of film. Any required transitions or effects were added at printing time.

A second method was used by sports photographers, journalists, and many documentary filmmakers. Individual scenes were cut to length and then spliced together to make a single roll of finished film. To add a special effect using this method of editing, filmmakers created the effect as a scene and spliced it into the film. Very few effects were added to this type of edit unless they were made "in camera" while the footage was being shot.

Adobe Premiere offers these and two additional editing modes. They are available for selection at any time during your editing session. Before we could begin editing, however, we would have to start a project.

To begin a project, you would launch Premiere and either select a preset (to establish the project settings) or customize your settings as described above. If Premiere is already open, you would select File>New Project, then adjust the project settings to meet your needs.

Determining the Editing Mode

By default, A/B edit mode displays six tracks for footage (video, audio, still images) and an additional transition track. The tracks are labeled Video 2, Video 1A, Video 1B, Audio 1, 2, and 3, and Transition. Additional tracks can be added. The collection of clips (scenes) you are assembling is shown in a separate window.

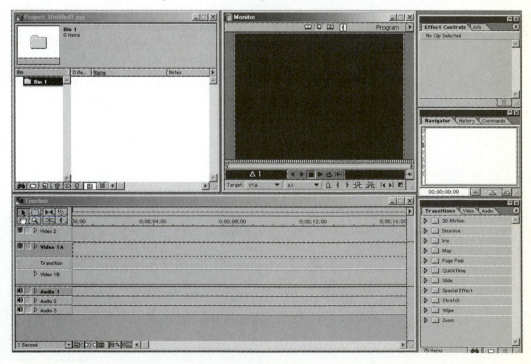

A/B edit mode.

Single Track edit mode displays two Video and three Audio tracks. Video clips are assembled sequentially on the Video 1 track and special effects are assembled on the Video 2 track.

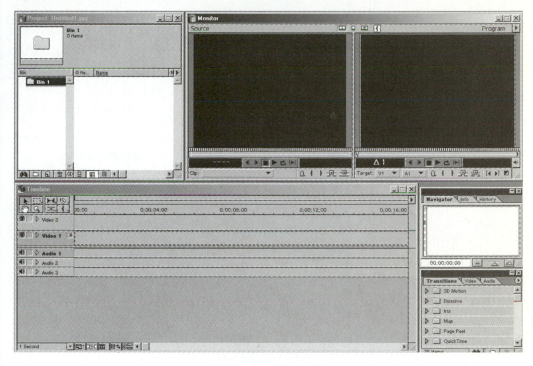

Single Track edit mode.

Effects mode is similar in appearance to A/B edit mode. It includes separate palettes so you can see included effects and additional information about audio and transitions.

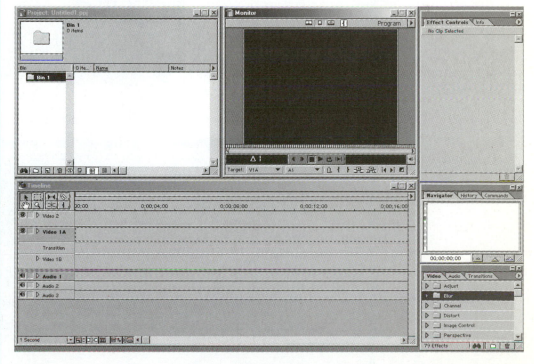

Effects mode.

Audio mode is the same as Effects mode except for an additional on-screen audio mixer.

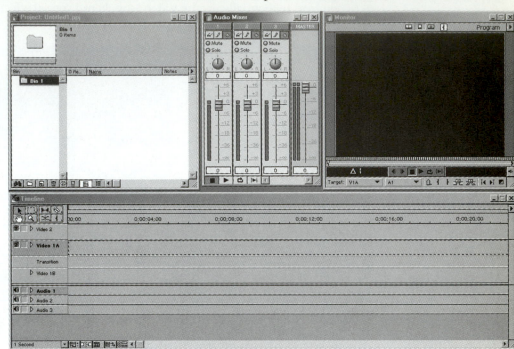

Audio mode.

Settings Viewer

To open the Settings Viewer, you would select Settings Viewer from the Project menu on the main Menu bar.

The Settings Viewer allows you to see all of your project settings at once.

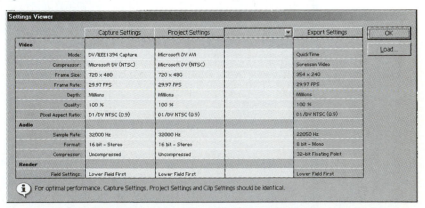

If you need to change one or more of the settings, click on the header at the top of a column. The Settings Viewer dialog box would appear.

We strongly recommend that you get into the habit of saving your project as soon as you select your preferences, settings, and mode. That way, the next time you open the project, all of the preferences will be retained and available. If you think you will use the settings in a future production, click Save in any of the settings dialog boxes. You will be asked for a file name to save the settings. An information box allows you to enter several lines of notes to remind you of the settings' functions. The file name will be added to the available presets that are displayed when you open a new project. Click on the file name, and the presets you defined will be used for your new project.

Saving a Project

To save a project, you can select File>Save (or File>Save As to save the project under a different name). Premiere uses the extension .ppj to indicate the file is a Premiere project. The size of the saved project is usually smaller than the total of the files used to create the project because the project file saves references to the footage used, not the actual footage.

Selecting the Save a Copy option saves a copy of your project, and allows you to continue working on the original project. To automatically save your project at regular intervals, you can select Edit>Preferences>Auto Save and Undo. The dialog box that appears allows you to select Auto Save options.

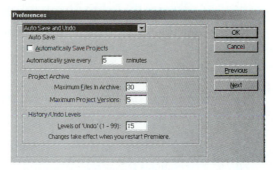

Using Auto Save options, you can select how often your project is saved, how many files are saved in the archive, and how many total copies of your project can be saved. Increasing these values requires more disk space. Decreasing these values places limits on how far you can back up if you make an error in your project or change your mind about recent edits.

The number of Undo levels determines how far you can back up through the history of your choices. Increasing this value causes the program to use more memory. The maximum number of undos is 99.

To recover a file from the Auto Save Archive, you can select File>Open and search for the file in the Project-Archive folder. Project archives are stored on the same drive as the Premiere program. Once you locate the archive file, you can double-click it to open it.

Locating Missing Files

When you rename a footage item (file) in Premiere, you do not actually change the name of the file; you only change Premiere's reference to it. If you actually change or delete a file, Premiere will not be able to find it when it is needed. Premiere alerts you with a message that the file is missing and offers the opportunity to search for it on your disk drives. After locating the file, click OK and the file will be restored in your project.

Placeholders

A *placeholder* is a file name for a clip (footage file) that does not yet exist. Perhaps it has not been captured (uploaded from the camera) or not photographed because certain elements of the scene are not yet available. Placeholders are used to reserve space during the editing process for footage that will be included as soon as it becomes available. Adobe Premiere refers to placeholders as "offline files."

Offline files are also created when Premiere cannot find footage files in the proper place on your hard drive. Any file that has been moved or renamed outside of Premiere is automatically replaced by an offline file name until the program user locates the file.

The following steps demonstrate how to create an offline file. Do not perform these steps at this time. Read through the steps to get accustomed to how the program works; you can use these steps for reference when you actually need to create an offline file once you begin to use Premiere:

- Start Premiere. Select New Project from the File menu.
- Choose Multimedia QuickTime when asked to select a preset.
- Choose File>New>Offline File.
- Enter the file name of the actual file you will include.
- Enter the length (duration) of the offline file.
- Enter the point in time (Timecode) where you want the file to begin (the In point).
- Enter the name of the reel containing the video.
- Enter the Time Format that corresponds to the original footage.
- Enter the Speed (frame rate) for the video.
- Select Has Video and/or Has Audio, depending on the clip you intend to use.
- Click OK.

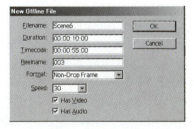

Using the Project Trimmer

When you trim a clip by resetting the In (start) and Out (end) points, Premiere retains the information from the original clip. Video footage uses a lot of memory, so it is a good idea to retain only the amount of footage you will actually use. The Project Trimmer is used to remove any extra footage that is wasting memory and disk space. Before you use it, however, be sure you are satisfied with your choices; once trimmed, the clips are permanently changed and unused clips are deleted.

To open the Project Trimmer, you would select Project>Utilities>Project Trimmer.

The first item on the Project Trimmer dialog box, Create Trimmed Batch List, only works if you have a digital camera that includes timecode and a device controller to operate the camera. Premiere creates a list of the In and Out points of each trimmed video clip and then follows that list to recapture the footage based on the new In and Out points. This is necessary if you originally captured low-resolution footage for editing and need to recapture your video for a high-resolution final film. If your device controller does not offer the option for batch capture, do not check this box.

The next item, Copy Trimmed Source Files, makes a copy of all of your clips with the new In and Out points as the beginning and end of the clip. This feature is useful if you are backing up your project or moving it to another machine because the excess footage will be removed from the project.

The Keep (_) Frame Handles option saves the specified number of frames before the beginning and after the end of each clip. Keeping a few frames at each end does not consume much memory and allows you to make small changes in the exact In and Out points.

Cross-Platform Projects

Premiere projects can be moved from one platform to another as long as the Premiere 6.5 program is available on the receiving computer. You must remember to transfer all project clips and any other supporting files. If you know that you will be moving between Windows and Macintosh platforms, it is advisable to use the 8:3 naming convention. Use a file name of eight characters or less, followed by a three-character extension (such as video1.ppj).

The first time your project is opened on the new platform, you will need to relocate all of your source clips. Remember, too, that some files do not have cross-platform compatibility. To avoid errors and development difficulty, file formats designed specifically for one platform or the other should not be used.

The Project Trimmer removes any clips that are not used in a project. If you plan to include those clips in the future, you must re-import them at that time.

Macintosh computers do not require an extension for the file name. Using it can help you identify file types when you are exploring a directory on your disk.

Using Scratch Disks

A *scratch disk* is hard disk space created and used by Premiere when available memory becomes fully utilized. Scratch disk space is used to store temporary files, previews, and other information that Premiere uses while processing video and audio. It is important to store your video information on the fastest disk drive available on your machine. It is also a good idea to regularly defragment and optimize your scratch disk. Check your computer documentation to learn how to defrag and optimize your hard disk.

Select a Scratch Disk

1. Launch Premiere if it is not already running. From the File menu, choose Capture, and then select Movie Capture.

2. In the Movie Capture dialog box, click the Edit button in the Preferences section.

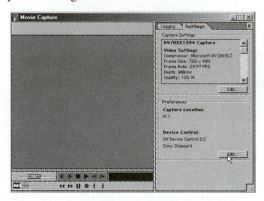

Remember to select your fastest drive for video files. Drive speed is not as important for audio files.

3. Click the down arrow to the right of Captured Movies, and then select the drive and folder where your Captured Movies should be stored. Do the same for Video Previews and Audio Previews using the associated pop-up menus for each.

4. Close Premiere. The preferences that you just set will be retained the next time you open the program.

History Palette

The History palette allows you to take several steps backward in your editing process. This function can be very helpful if you make a mistake or change your mind. You can back up as many as 99 steps.

If you plan on using the undo/History palette (and virtually every Premiere user takes advantage of it), you must remember to set the level of undos before you begin editing. The setting only takes effect when Premiere is started.

Remember that the number of undo levels is set in the Auto Save and Undo dialog box. To access it, select Edit>Preferences>Auto Save and Undo.

You can enter the number of undo levels you want to use. The more levels you choose, the less memory is available for editing. We recommend that you set it high while you are learning Premiere or if you plan to do a lot of testing with effects and transitions. Set it low after your confidence builds and when you are doing simple, straightforward editing.

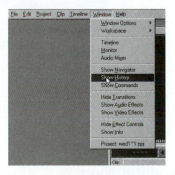

The palette itself is very easy to use. To move back to a particular step, click on that step and then continue working. All steps following that particular step will be lost.

When you delete or change a step in the History palette, you lose all the steps that follow it.

To delete all steps in the History palette, or to step backward or forward in the history list, click on the preferred option in the History palette Options menu. To display the menu, click on the arrow at the top right of the palette.

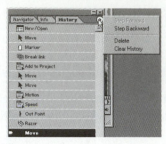

Premiere Windows

You use three main Premiere windows and several palettes while you assemble a video. The windows include the Project window, Monitor window, and Timeline window. These windows are usually left open (visible) for the entire editing session.

Project Window

The Project window is used to manage all of the footage (motion, stills, offline files, audio clips, and titles) used in your project. In addition, the Project window displays information about each piece of footage including name, type, duration, video and audio information, and how many times the clip is used. Footage files (clips) are organized in bins that you create to organize all of the parts of your production. Additional details about the Project window and how to use it are found throughout this book.

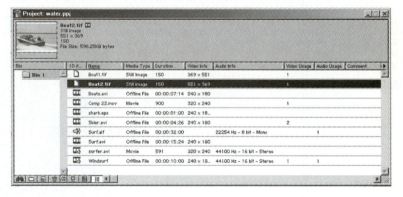

Monitor Window

The Monitor window is where you view and edit clips. Depending on the editing mode you chose when you start your project, you may see Source Monitor and Program Monitor windows at the same time.

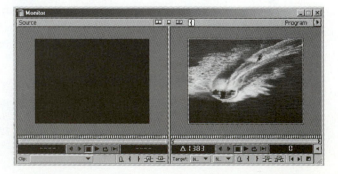

Timeline Window

The Timeline window provides a view of your production over time. The Timeline is scaled from left to right and indicates the relationships between clips, effects, and transitions. The Timeline window also permits you to edit clips and change the position of clips in time.

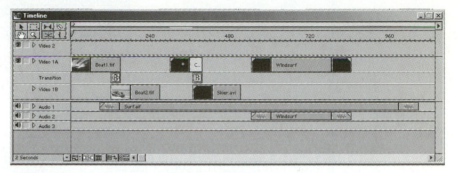

Using Bins

The key to effective video editing is organization, and one of the major organizational tools available in Premiere is the *bin*. Creating and using a bin is similar to creating and using a sub-folder on your hard disk. You might choose to create one bin to hold all of your audio clips, another to hold your video, and yet another for titles or still images. Once you have created a few bins, you can freely move clips back and forth between them. You can also create a new bin at any time to further organize your source clips.

Create and Use a Bin

1. Launch Premiere. Select Open from the File menu, and then select **water.ppj** from the **RF_Premiere** folder (refer to the Getting Started section of this book if you have difficulty locating the **RF_Premiere** folder).

2. To create a bin, click the New Bin icon at the bottom of the Project window.

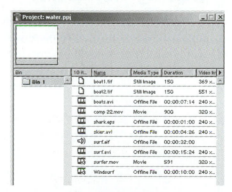

3. A dialog box opens. Enter the name "Still Images" for the new Bin Name, and then click OK.

When you access the RF_Premiere folder the first time, Premiere will ask you to locate at least one file. This is because Premiere has no record of where you placed the folder on your machine. Once the file is found, Premiere will not ask again unless you move the folder to another location.

4. The new Still Images bin appears in your bin list in the Project window; because it is new, it is empty.

5. Return to the default bin (Bin 1) and drag all of the still image files (boat1.tif, boat2.tif) to the new bin you just created. To move multiple clips at one time, hold down the Shift/Control key while selecting the files.

6. Do not save your changes. Leave this project open for the next exercise.

Working with Palettes

Palettes are used to access commands and features that you use less frequently than the tools presented in the Premiere windows. They can be turned on and off as needed. If you were to turn on several palettes at the same time, your screen would soon become so crowded with controls and menus that you would not be able to work efficiently.

When you are selecting clips in the Project window, it is very important that you click on the icon to the left of the clip name. Clicking on the name of the clip only selects the text of the clip name, not the clip itself.

View Palettes

1. Continue working in the open project. To view a palette, click the Window menu on the main Menu bar. A pop-up menu appears, showing all of the available palettes.

2. Select Show Info from the Window menu.

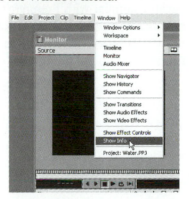

3. The Info palette appears. Click comp 22.mov in Bin 1. In this case, the Info palette repeats the information found at the top of the Project window. It indicates that the clip is a movie.

4. Close the file and exit Premiere.

Hiding Palettes

To hide a palette, double-click anywhere on the bar at the top of the palette. To close a palette completely, click the box in the upper corner of the palette. (Refer to the Getting Started section of this book for the difference between the Macintosh and Windows versions.)

Chapter Summary

In Chapter 1, you explored the key skills of storyboarding and creative visualization. You became familiar with Premiere's main windows, dialog boxes, and palettes. You learned how to set up Premiere to work with the projects and exercises throughout this book. You found out how to create bins for better organization of your footage files. Finally, you learned how to use the Info palette to get more information about the clips included in your movie.

2 Working with Video Clips

Chapter Objectives:

Video, audio, and still image clips are the building blocks of every production. Similar to a puzzle, it's a good idea to gather together all of the production pieces before you begin to assemble them. In this chapter, we explore the steps required to collect, organize, and use video clips in a production. In Chapter 2, you will:

- Learn how, and where, to collect materials for your production.

- Understand why the highest possible audio or video quality is not always the best choice.

- Learn how to create a Premiere project.

- Explore ways to customize a project's settings to meet your exact needs.

- Discover the value of Premiere's Storyboard feature, and how to use it to quickly organize your clips.

- Learn how to render a project so you can view it in real time.

- Find out how to create offline files to reserve space in your film for clips that will be created in the future.

- Become familiar with techniques used to capture and import clips (and entire projects) for use in your final production.

Projects to be Completed:

- The Monkey Movie (A)

- Making Spaghetti (B)

- The Gold Rush (C)

- Central Coast Surfing (D)

Working with Video Clips

Any footage item that you capture or import into Premiere is known as a *clip*. A clip can be a still image, motion video, audio file, or a series of animated stills. Clips are the building blocks of your final movie and, similar to the blocks used to build the ancient pyramids, they must be collected and trimmed to size before they can be used.

Collecting Source Materials

There are several ways to collect source materials for a Premiere project. You can:

- Use existing files.
- Download files from the Web.
- Use audio and video from CD-ROMs/DVDs.
- Create files with your digital camera, audio recorder, or scanner.
- Use other graphics software to draw images from scratch.
- Import video and audio files directly into a Premiere project.

Clip Collection Checklist

While you are deciding what sources to use for your clips, there are several items you must consider. The following tips will be helpful.

If you are going to use your final movie for advertising or trade, or if you plan to post your movie on the Web or distribute it in any way, you must consider copyright violations. You cannot use anyone else's material without permission. Audio and visual images distributed on a CD-ROM are usually copyrighted and not useable unless the license agreement grants you express permission to do so. Often, royalty-free clip art may be imported for your own use, but may not be re-distributed without permission.

You must have permission to use any material found on another person's Web site. If you are browsing the Web and follow a link to another site, any agreement on the original site does not necessarily apply to the new site.

If you plan to distribute your movie, you must have a model or property release for all images of people, pets, buildings, or any other recognizable property. This is very important. You cannot post or use any image of something that can be recognized as a specific person, place, or thing without permission. Of course, if you take a shot of a tree that could be any tree, anywhere, you can use it with no concern. If you take a shot of a cypress tree on the coast of Monterrey, California, and include enough background to identify it as a particular tree, you must obtain a release before you can distribute the image. It's always better to ask than it is to pay penalties and, perhaps, be forced to recall all of your distributed movies.

If you are preparing source files using other software, try to do as much image manipulation as possible using the original software. For instance, if you are creating a file in Adobe Photoshop, adjust the image size and resolution, and make any color balance, sharpness, brightness, and contrast corrections before you save the file. Then, when you import the file into Premiere, it is ready to use with no further adjustments required.

If you are shooting video for use on the Web, try to use large areas of unchanging backgrounds. Be careful not to move the camera while shooting (a tripod is helpful). Compression is based on change. If there are a lot of changes from one frame to the next, you will not be able to compress the frames as efficiently as if they were steady. Of course, there is always a tradeoff between creativity and technology. Don't let this tip lead you to create boring, uninspiring images in order to achieve maximum compression for distribution (quick download) on the Web.

To some extent, output quality predetermines input quality. If your production is going to be displayed on a standard television with a small internal speaker, there is no sense capturing the audio using a high-performance audio system at maximum quality settings. A typical television cannot reproduce such high quality and the effort will only make your files much larger than necessary.

If your final composition is destined to be shown on a computer screen, there is no need to create your images at very high resolution. The average computer monitor is capable of displaying approximately 72 pixels per inch (ppi). Creating a file at 600 ppi does not make the image appear any better on the screen and only results in files that are larger than necessary.

One word of caution: there is always the possibility (albeit unlikely) that someone will see your production on the Web and decide that it has the makings of a theatre production. Keep all of your original materials so you can create a high-resolution version of your work if this opportunity should present itself.

Creating Your First Project

Now that you know a bit about what's required to make a Premiere video, it's time to create and render your first movie. You will be asked to complete some exercise steps that you may not fully understand. We urge you to follow our theory of "learning by doing," and trust that if you complete the exercises as presented, you will soon become a Premiere movie-making master.

The following exercise gives you an idea of how the final project in this book, "Central Coast Surfing," will appear after you have edited it. The exercise results in a "rough cut" of surfers enjoying the waters off the central California coast. The movie you create will have a few glitches in it. You will correct these problems when you complete the Central Coast Surfing project. First, you will establish project settings, and then you will use the automated Storyboard approach to create a Timeline with clips.

Create Your First Project

1. Start Premiere if it is not already running. Select New Project from the File menu. Do not save the previous project.

2. When the Load Project Settings screen appears, click Custom.

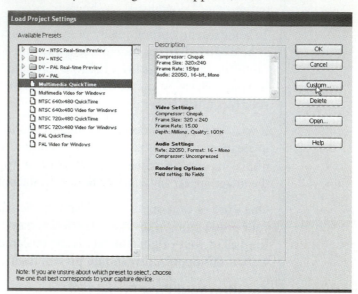

3. Choose settings that deliver a quality video designed for small-screen (computer) display. Select QuickTime from the Editing Mode pop-up menu.

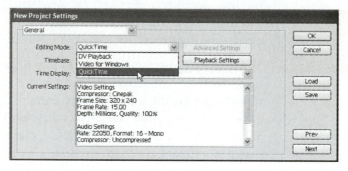

4. Select 30 from the Timebase pop-up menu.

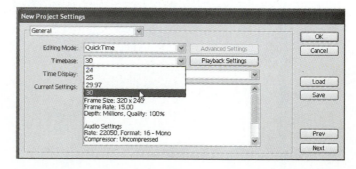

5. Select Video from the Project Settings pop-up menu.

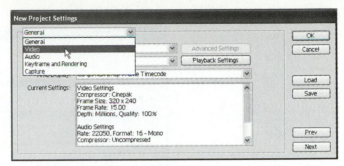

6. Select Sorensen Video from the Compressor pop-up menu.

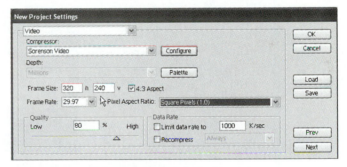

7. Set the Frame Size to 320 h and 240 v. Click the 4:3 Aspect check box. Set the Frame Rate to 29.97, and the Quality to 80% by typing in the value or using the slider in the Quality field.

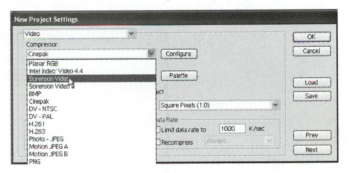

8. Select Audio from the top-left pop-up menu in the Project Settings window.

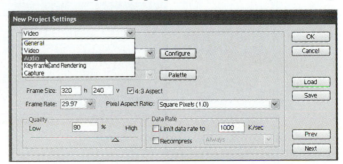

9. Set the Rate to 22050 Hz, then select 8 Bit–Mono for the Format. Leave all of the other values set at their defaults.

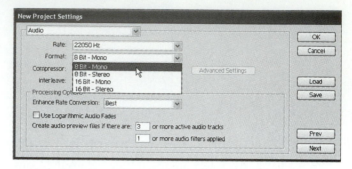

10. Click the Save button.

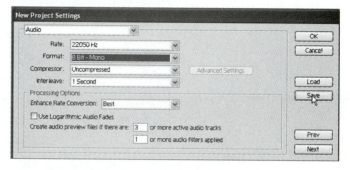

11. Enter a name and description for this Project Setting (use the following example), and then click OK.

12. Click OK in the New Project Settings dialog box. Do not close Premiere.

Premiere opens and incorporates your new settings. The next time you begin a new project, your settings will appear at the bottom of the Available Presets list. To use your custom preset, simply click on it.

Use the Premiere Storyboard

1. From the File menu, select New>Storyboard.

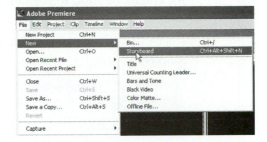

2. A blank Storyboard appears.

3. Be sure the Storyboard window is highlighted (click on it to highlight it), and then select Import>File from the File menu.

4. Find the **surfcut** folder in the **RF_Premiere** folder and open it. Select the files named **surfl1** through and including **surfl9** by holding down the Shift/Control key and clicking on each file name. There are easier ways to select all the items in a continual list, but you must be sure that you do not include any unwanted files; this method ensures that. When all of the files are selected, click Open. All of the selected files appear in the Storyboard window.

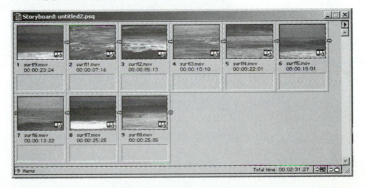

Try dragging the clips around the Storyboard and dropping them on top of other clips. When you are finished, be sure the clips are sequentially organized from surfl1 through surfl9.

In the above image, all clips are shown in sequence with an arrow showing which scene follows. There is a limited amount of information presented about each clip. Notice that the last clip does not have an arrow, but rather an icon that indicates the end of the clips. You can drag any clip to any position and the Storyboard automatically reorganizes the sequence of the clips.

5. Click the arrow at the upper-right side of the Storyboard window to open the Storyboard menu. Click Storyboard Window Options.

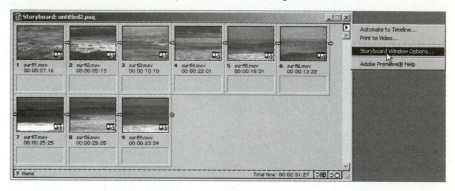

6. The Storyboard Window Options dialog box shows four sizes of icons. The larger the icon selected, the more information is displayed about each clip. The icon size can be changed at any time while the Storyboard window is active. Try each size now, and then decide which one you prefer.

7. Select the second largest icon size (not the largest as shown above), and then click OK.

8. Be sure the clips are in order from 1 to 9. Open the Storyboard window menu and select Automate to Timeline.

Notice that the surfl clips have been added to a new bin labeled "Storyboard: untitled2.psq". Your Storyboard probably has a different name.

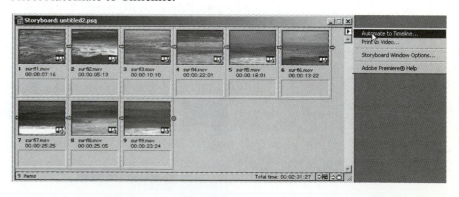

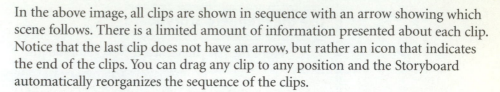

9. Enter the values in the following image: Whole Bin for Contents, Sequentially for Placement, Beginning for Insert At, 0 frames for Clip Overlap. The only change from the default values is to change the value of Clip Overlap to 0 (zero) frames. Click OK.

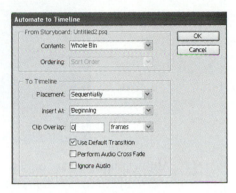

10. All of the clips are assembled on the Timeline in the same order they appear in the Storyboard window. Notice the layout of the entire screen. Drag your windows so they appear in a similar fashion. The Timeline was set to A/B edit mode (see Chapter 1) and the monitor was set to Single View.

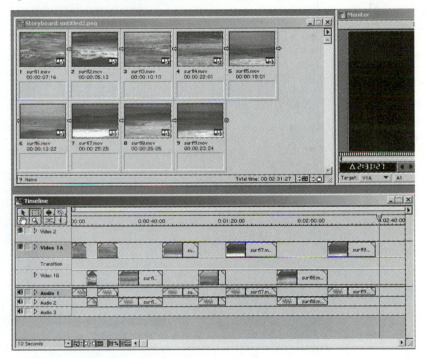

11. To set the Monitor window to Single View, click the arrow on the upper-right side of the Monitor window and select Single View from the pop-up menu.

12. At this point, you are only going to make a rendered video of the Timeline. (There are many features of the Timeline window and they are all covered in Chapter 3.) For now, move the edit line marker to 00:00 and press the Return/Enter key to see a preview of your movie. You will be prompted to save your work before you can preview the movie. Save your work in your **Work_In_Progress** folder. You will not need it again.

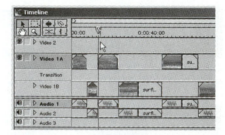

To move the edit line marker to 00:00, click and hold the handle at the top of the marker and then drag it to 00:00, or click on the Timeline ruler at 00:00.

13. To export your movie, select Export Timeline>Movie from the File menu.

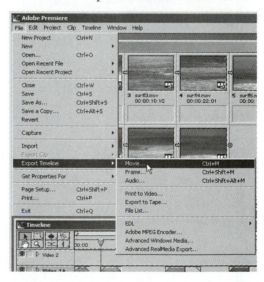

14. You are prompted for a name. Enter "temp" for the file name and save the movie in your **Work_In_Progress** folder. Remember where you save the file so you can locate it later. Notice that all of your custom settings are intact. After Premiere saves the movie, it opens a Clip window for viewing what you just saved. Play the movie, and then close the Clip window.

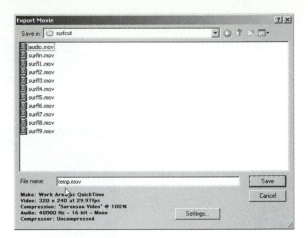

15. Select File>Save As and save the project as "surfers3" in your **Work_In_Progress** folder. Leave this project open for the next exercise.

Offline vs. Online

The words "offline" and "online" have dual meanings in Premiere, depending on whether they are referring to the editing process or the files used in a production.

Offline editing refers to a process of using low-resolution files to create a video that is capable of running in real time on a machine with limited memory and speed. When the final edit is approved, the video is then reproduced as an exact copy using high-cost, high-quality machines that are capable of creating the final video at very high resolution. With today's powerful desktop computers, offline editing is becoming less popular and less necessary.

In reference to files, offline refers to any file that is not currently available to Premiere. The use of a placeholder reserves a clearly defined space for a piece of footage when it is finally made available to the program. Review Chapter 1 of this book to review how to create an offline file (File>New>Offline File). We created one called **temp**, which is the complete movie. When the offline file — referred to by the placeholder — becomes available, you must replace the placeholder with the actual file.

Replace an Offline File

1. Create an offline file (File>New>Offline File) and name it "temp".

2. Double-click the offline file in the Project window. Do not click directly on the name of the file; click on the icon to the left of the name.

3. Click Locate in the File Offline dialog box.

4. Locate the file, click on it to select it, and then click Select/OK.

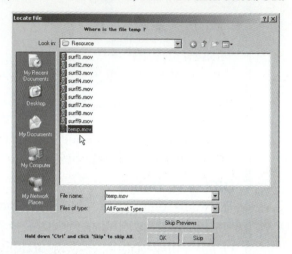

The file is located and replaced. This exercise was designed to demonstrate offline file use, so you can delete the temp file from your list of clips. Highlight the file name (temp) by single-clicking and then pressing the Delete key. In this exercise, you also learned that a movie created in Premiere can be imported back into a project. This technique can be very useful when working on a complex project.

5. Save the project by selecting Save from the File menu. Close the project.

Capturing Video and Audio

Video and audio can be captured from many devices. Cameras, CDs, and tape decks can all provide input. The major difference between input signals is whether the source supplying the signal is analog or digital. When you capture from a digital source, there is very little loss of quality, if any. Analog information suffers a loss of quality every time it is copied or transferred.

Connecting the Analog Video Source

The most common analog connections are S-video and Composite video. *S-video* uses a single connector and generally offers better quality than composite. *Composite video* uses three connectors — one for the video signal and two for the audio signals if your equipment can handle stereo input. Read the documentation that came with your capture card and video camera for proper connection instructions.

Connecting the DV Video Source

Digital video cameras use an IEEE 1394 port that must comply with all Open Host Controller Interface (OHCI) standards. If you are not sure that your equipment meets these standards, check the documentation that came with your interface card. If you are using an older computer, you may need to purchase and install an IEEE 1394 card. You also need the proper connecting cable. Firewire and I-link are common trademarked names for IEEE 1394-compliant connections.

Digital video offers several advantages over analog, including speed and device (the videotape player) control by the computer. If you shot your original footage on analog video, you should convert it to digital before you capture it using Premiere. Several options are available for this conversion, including passing the analog video through a digital camera, taking the analog video to a service bureau for conversion, or re-recording the analog video on a digital deck.

If you re-record the video, be sure there are no breaks in the timecode. The project trimmer requires timecode that runs continually from the beginning to the end of the tape, and timecode is necessary if you are going to search for a particular frame on your tape. Timecode control is not available on analog recorders.

Using the Movie Capture Window

There are two different versions of the Movie Capture window depending on whether or not you have device control. Remember that device control is available if you have a digital camera and the appropriate interface. Your capture screen will resemble one of the following images.

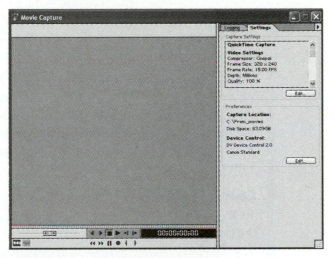

Movie Capture window with device control.

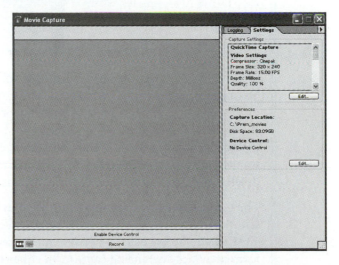

Movie Capture window without device control.

The computer can control some analog tape decks, but digital device control is more common in consumer equipment

If you do not have device control on your computer, you cannot access device control screens or settings.

Device Control

If your system is equipped with device control, you can control your video camera or deck using the controls provided by Premiere. All of the controls are located at the bottom of the Movie Capture window. To access the Movie Capture window, you can select File>Capture>Movie Capture.

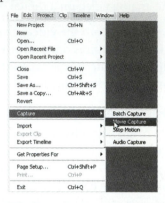

Covering every possibility and setting available in Premiere would require several books, or at least one book that would prove very difficult to carry. The following descriptions cover the major adjustments and set-up items that you need to address while capturing video clips. For further information, visit the Adobe Systems Web site (www.adobe.com).

When you first open the Movie Capture window (with device control active), you are presented with the screen shown above (Movie Capture window with device control). Many of the controls may look familiar if you have used a VCR. Often, you can simply accept the existing values for capture settings and preferences, but you should be familiar with the options used for each value.

Capture Settings

To access the Capture Settings dialog boxes, click the Edit button at the bottom right of the Capture Settings information box.

Clicking the Edit button opens a series of submenus, the first of which is the Capture Settings dialog box. (If you do not see the Capture Settings dialog box, click Prev or Next until you do.) The Capture Settings dialog box allows you to select from various options. If you are using a digital video system, click on DV Settings first; the DV Capture Options dialog box appears (refer to the next screen shot). From here, you can select where you want to see your previews. If your system is taxed to its memory limit, you may want to deselect the Preview During Capture options.

The Capture Format Options dialog box can be seen in the third graphic below. You can select from QuickTime, DV/IEEE 1394, or Video for Windows. If in doubt, use DV/IEEE 1394 when you are using a DV system. We recommend using QuickTime for cross-platform activities and analog capture. In either case, you must have a capture controller card to use these features. There is another way to capture without a controller, which we discuss shortly.

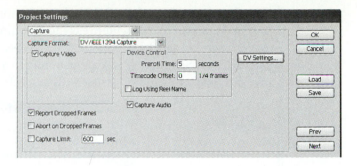

Be certain the Capture Video and Capture Audio options are selected. The Preroll Time setting indicates the number of seconds that will pass before recording actually begins; 5 seconds is an adequate setting. Timecode Offset provides a means to fine-tune your equipment to exactly match a particular frame. Setting a capture limit may be necessary if your operating system is restricted to a maximum capture limit.

Fine-tuning your system can be a very involved process, and is usually done for advanced applications only. For the purposes of this book, you can generally accept the default values provided by Premiere, unless they cause a problem on your particular system.

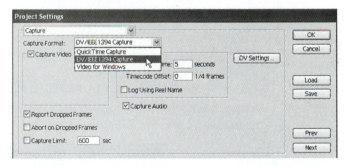

General Project Settings were discussed in Chapter 1. You can select them as needed for your productions.

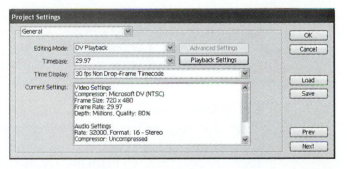

The Output section of the DV Playback Options dialog box determines where your output is displayed. *Scrubbing* refers to scanning back and forth through your movie using a scrubbing tool. A *scrubbing tool* allows you to quickly search your video while you watch it on the screen. If you are planning to add an audio track at a later time, you may decide to turn off Audio Playback while scrubbing.

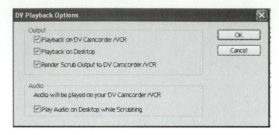

The Video Settings dialog box allows you to enter several parameters to control how you want your video to be compressed for display. A comprehensive discussion of various compressors is available in the Premiere help menu and on the Adobe Web site (www.adobe.com). The following selections are appropriate for small-screen playback on a desktop computer.

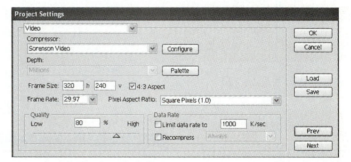

Audio settings can make a significant difference in the size of your finished files. A low rate (22,500) and an 8-Bit–Mono track should be acceptable for a computer speaker system. Reserve 44 Khz and 16-Bit–Stereo for CD-quality recordings. In the following image, if 3 or more audio tracks are used, Premiere combines them into a single preview file to save system resources.

Batch Capturing

Batch capturing can be used only if your system has device control and your tapes contain continual timecode. When you finish an offline edit of your low-resolution files, Premiere can generate a batch list. The batch list is used to re-capture the files used in your final production at a high-quality setting.

The following is an example of a batch list. All the start and stop points for recording are included in the list. The batch capture process takes place automatically.

Still Image Animation

Several programs are capable of exporting a series of still images to create an animated sequence. Premiere can import these images and turn them into an independent video or use them in conjunction with other video or audio clips. Before digital image sequences can be imported into Premiere, they must be properly prepared for import.

All of the images must be contained in a single folder that contains only the images to be used. Each image must have a file name that begins with a name, followed by a number that always has the same amount of digits. When the Windows operating system is used, the file must include the correct three-character extension. For example, Windows supports bitmap images that use .bmp as the extension (Macintosh systems do not require an extension, but it is wise to use one for cross-platform compatibility). Sample file names for a Windows system could be Toon0001.bmp, Toon0002.bmp, Toon0003.bmp, Toon0004.bmp, and so on.

To import the sequenced files into Premiere, you would select File>Import>File, and then choose the first image in the sequence. You would then click on Numbered Stills and the entire sequence would be imported into a selected bin.

Capturing Analog Audio

Analog audio cannot be captured directly into Premiere. You must have an analog audio capture program that works on your system and runs independently of Premiere. Both Windows and Macintosh supply capture programs with their operating systems.

Audio should be captured at the highest quality possible because you may want to make changes at a later time. The audio quality can be reduced when you output your movie, but it cannot be improved beyond the original capture quality.

There are three parameters that determine the quality of an audio capture:

- Sample Rate refers to the number of samples per second. The higher the number of samples per second, the higher the quality of the sound.

- Bit Depth refers to the number of bits used to represent each sample. The higher the bit depth, the higher the quality of the sound.

- The third choice, Mono or Stereo, does not really affect the quality of sound, but it does determine how you can use it. Stereo sound requires twice the storage space of mono.

The first time you select File>Capture>Audio, Premiere asks you what sound capture utility you want to use and asks you to locate the program on your hard drive. From then on, Premiere uses the selected program when you request an audio capture.

Importing Digital Audio

Digital audio is easily imported into Premiere if your setup is entirely digital. The technique is exactly the same as what is used for capturing digital video, except for one additional step. When the Video Capture dialog box appears, remember to deselect the Capture Video option. Then you can select the audio settings (click Next until the Audio Project Settings dialog box appears).

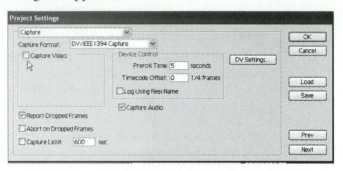

CD audio tracks are written as Compact Disk Audio (CDA) files. To import sound from a CD, you must first use your operating system CD-ROM recorder/player to convert the tracks to files that are compatible with your operating system. Refer to your system documentation to learn how to convert CD audio. Both Windows and Macintosh supply these programs as part of their operating systems.

Pixel Aspect Ratios

Throughout this book (and Premiere menus) you see references to pixel aspect ratios. *Pixel aspect ratios* combine with *screen aspect ratios* to define the shape of your final screen image.

Most video systems use a 4:3 screen aspect ratio. This means that the screen appears as a rectangle that is 4 units wide and 3 units high (some use a 16:9 wide-screen aspect ratio). National Television Standards Committee (NTSC) video typically uses square pixels and displays images in a 640 × 480-pixel window. DV-NTSC uses a rectangular pixel with a 0.9 aspect ratio and displays images in a 720 × 480-pixel window.

If you display rectangular pixels on a square-pixel monitor, the images appear slightly distorted. When the images are displayed on a broadcast monitor, they are correctly presented.

If the pixel aspect ratio of a clip is rectangular, Premiere displays the aspect ratio in an information box that appears when you click on a clip in the Project window (see below). Notice the line that reads 320 × 240 (0.900). More information on pixel aspect ratios is presented in later chapters of this book.

Importing Another Project

You can import another Premiere project into your current project, but you must do so carefully. You would select File>Import>Project to import a project. All of the clips would be imported into a new bin that has the same name as the project being imported.

A project can be imported at the beginning of the project, at the edit line (currently selected time), or at the end of the current project. It is always imported in Insert mode, meaning that if you import the project at the edit line, the current project is split; any remaining footage is pushed to the end of the project. Be sure you have considered all of the implications of this action before you import the project. It is good practice to save your current project before you import another one.

Projects created in earlier versions of Premiere (4.0, 5.0,) must be opened in Premiere 6.0 and then saved as Premiere 6.0 files before they can be imported.

Working with Team Members

Beyond a home movie or a class project, you will soon find that most motion picture work requires a collaborative effort. Several people may be involved in shooting various scenes, collecting audio, and generating stills for use in the final production. Often, there is an editing team involved to accelerate the production process. Adobe thoughtfully designed Premiere to allow more than one person to work on a production. The program includes many useful features that support a group effort. You will learn about these features in future chapters of this book.

Chapter Summary

In Chapter 2, you learned how to set up a Premiere project. You discovered the usefulness of the Premiere Storyboard feature. You learned the difference between online and offline clips. We discussed project settings, analog vs. digital video, and device control. You also learned how to batch capture video. Lastly, you learned how to import an entire project into a new Premiere project, and how to position it on the Timeline.

3 Editing Video

Chapter Objectives:

A Premiere project consists of a series of clips (audio, video, and still images) assembled and precisely placed on a Timeline. Premiere provides numerous tools to make the editing process flow as easily as possible. This chapter presents techniques on how to assemble, trim, and place clips. Detailed descriptions of the editing tools are provided and editing styles are discussed. In Chapter 3, you will:

- Learn how to open an existing project.

- Discover how to effectively use features of the Monitor window.

- Find out how to place markers to speed up production time.

- Learn the difference between Single view and Dual view editing, and when to use each view.

- Understand the difference between a ripple edit and a rolling edit, and how these two edit methods affect the duration of your project.

- Learn how to precisely trim clips so they begin and end exactly where you choose.

- Increase your vocabulary by learning many terms used in the video and motion picture industry.

Projects to be Completed:

- The Monkey Movie (A)

- Making Spaghetti (B)

- The Gold Rush (C)

- Central Coast Surfing (D)

Editing Video

It would be excellent if you could shoot all of your movie clips in the order in which they appear in the final production, but this is not generally possible. Most video is shot out of order. This is done for many reasons. Not every actor is available on any given day, and it is not economically efficient to force an actor to wait around between his first scene that takes place on one day and his next scene that won't take place for four more days. Lighting conditions change during a shoot. Sometimes a new shot has to be added after the fact to enhance or strengthen the story. It is common practice to overshoot a production, sometimes as much as five to one. It is also common practice to shoot video clips with extra footage at the beginning and end to allow for more precise editing.

Nonlinear editing allows video to be shot in any order. The skill of a great editor then brings the story to life. Let's take some time to discuss two forms of editing that are commonly used in video production.

Basic Editing and Run Times

In this chapter, we use the surfers3 project in your Resource folder as the basis for the exercise material. All of the presets have been established and the scenes have been "rough cut." In the following exercises, you will begin to fine-tune the movie and learn how to use the editing techniques that Premiere provides.

Open an Existing Project

1. Launch Premiere and select any preset. It doesn't make a difference at this point because when you open an existing project, all of the project presets are already included.

2. Use the A/B editing mode for this project. Select Workspace>A/B Editing from the Window menu. Several windows and palettes appear. Close each palette by clicking the box in the upper-right corner. Drag the windows on the screen by clicking the top bar of each window and, while holding down the mouse button, drag the window to its proper position. When you are finished, your screen should resemble the following illustration.

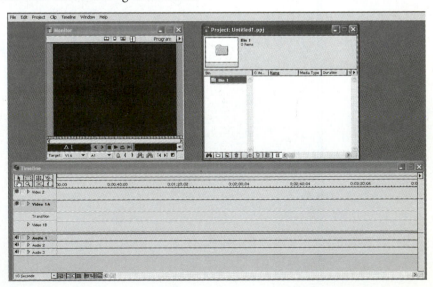

3. If your Monitor window opened in Dual view, you can change it to Single view by clicking the arrow in the upper-right corner and selecting Single View from the pop-up menu.

4. Now that you have some experience setting up the screen, load the **surfers3** project. Select Open from the File menu, and then navigate to your **RF_Premiere** folder. Find the file named **\surfcut\surfers3.ppj**. Highlight it with a mouse click, and then click Open.

5. The appearance of your screen may change slightly because the positions of the windows are included in the project. You may have to locate the required files when this (or any) project is opened the first time, depending on where you store your **RF_Premiere** folder.

6. To view this video in its rough form, press the Return/Enter key.

7. Press the Spacebar to stop playing.

8. Save this project in your **Work_In_Progress** folder. Click on the Project window, then select File>Save As. Locate your **Work_In_Progress** folder.

9. Leave the project open for the next exercise.

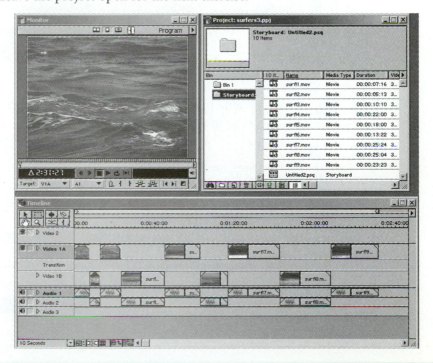

The above screen shows the three major windows in Premiere. The Monitor window is where you view your movie. The Project window contains Bin 1 and another bin named Storyboard. The Storyboard bin contains clips from the Storyboard you created in a previous chapter. The Timeline contains each of the clips from the Storyboard bin, arranged in order and placed end-to-end. At this point, the Timeline is a very rough edit. Several scenes are not yet trimmed to exact length and there are no transitions between the scenes.

Monitor Window Details

There are many controls available in the Monitor window (as there are in the other windows, as well). The buttons that open these controls provide a quick and convenient access method.

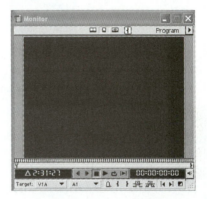

In order to edit your movie, it is important that you understand the functions of the buttons contained in each of the windows. You may want to write notes on the next few pages of your book for easy reference until you commit the meaning of the buttons to memory.

Below is a close-up of the bottom of the Monitor window. Following the graphic are descriptions of the buttons and indicators. Please note that the individual button and indicator images are below their associated descriptions.

- **Frame Jog**. Dragging the mouse pointer on this line moves your movie back and forth in small increments.

- **Set Location**. Dragging the location pointer (edit line marker) to the left or right allows you to quickly change location in your movie. You can also control the In and Out (beginning and end) points of your movie by dragging the { } symbols at the ends of the line.

- **Program Duration**. This indicator shows the length (in time — Hours:Minutes:Frames) of your entire movie.

- **Frame Back**. Clicking this button moves back one frame.

- **Frame Forward**. Click this button to move forward one frame.

- **Stop**. Clicking this button stops the preview.

- **Play**. When you click this button, the preview plays.

- **Loop**. When the movie reaches the end, it loops back to the beginning and starts to play again.

- **Play In to Out**. Click this button to play the movie from the In point to the Out point.

- **Program Location**. This indicator displays the current location in time.

- **Set Volume**. This button is a speaker volume control.

- **Video and Audio Target**. This button designates on which track to place a clip when the clip is dragged into the Monitor window. Selecting None for either Audio or Video inserts an empty space equal to the length of the clip.

- **Marker**. This button opens the Marker Selection menu.

- **Marker Menu**. This menu allows you to select the Mark, Go To, or Clear marker menu.

- **Marker Selection Menu**. This menu is used to set, go to, or clear markers. Setting a marker is very useful for aligning audio and video clips if Toggle Snap to Edges is turned on in the Timeline window.

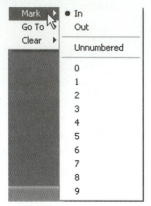

- **Mark In**. This selection option is used to mark the In point of a clip.

- **Mark Out**. This selection option is used to set the Out point of a clip.

- **Lift**. This option allows you to remove footage between the In and Out points, leaving a space equal to the removed section.

- **Extract**. This option allows you to remove footage between the In and Out points and closes the gap created by the removal of the clip. The removal applies to the selected audio and video tracks indicated in the Target button.

- **Previous**. Selecting this option allows you to go to the previous edit point.

- **Next**. Select this option to go to the next edit point.

- **Add Default Transition**. Choosing this button allows you to add a transition (fade, wipe, or others). You must first select a transition as the default.

Let's begin with a scenario where you have collected and imported all of your clips into one bin. There are no clips on the Timeline.

Set Up the Surfers3 Project

1. Continue working in the open **surfers3** project from the previous exercise.

2. Delete all clips on the Timeline. You must click on the Timeline window before you delete clips. Be sure the Timeline window is highlighted, then choose Edit>Select All, and then choose Edit>Clear.

3. Click on the Storyboard bin to display all of the **surfers3** clips.

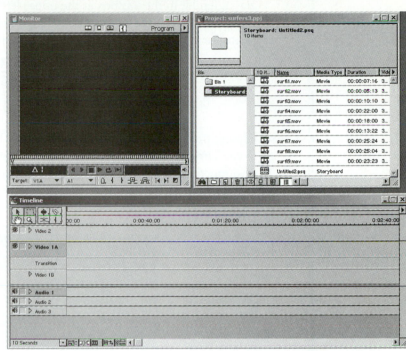

4. At the bottom of the Timeline, click the Toggle Snap to Edges button. You know it is turned on when you see the small lines in the center of the button.

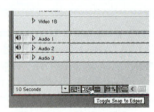

To turn Snap to Edges on or off, open the Timeline menu by clicking the arrow at the upper right of the Timeline window, and then click Snap to Edges.

5. Drag surfl1 and surfl3 to the Timeline. To select a clip, you must click the icon to the left of the clip name. If you click on the name, you cannot drag the clip. Place surfl1 on track Video 1A, and place surfl3 on track Video 1B. (From this point forward, we refer to these tracks as A and B, respectively.) Surfl3 should immediately follow surfl1. If Snap to Edges is turned on, surfl3 snaps into place when you get close to the end of surfl1.

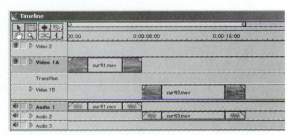

6. Press the Return/Enter key to view the movie. Notice that the surfer seems to jump into the frame when surfl3 begins. You will use surfl2 to smooth the action so it makes more sense.

7. Adjust the size of the Timeline using the Zoom tool (it resembles a magnifying glass). Find it in the toolbox at the upper left of the Timeline window. Clicking on the Timeline with the Zoom tool enlarges it; holding down the Option/Alt key turns the tool into a "minifier" (reduces the image).

8. Choose the Selection tool from the toolbox. Drag surfl2 from the Storyboard bin to the Timeline and drop it exactly at the beginning of surfl3. When it is properly positioned for insertion, surfl3 turns dark. Surfl2 will be inserted between surfl1 and surfl3. Drag surfl3 to the A track and position it at the end of surfl2.

9. Leave this project open for the next exercise.

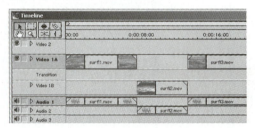

This method may be simple, fast, and effective, but it is not the best way to insert a scene. In the next exercise, you change to Dual Monitor mode so you can see both the source clip and the program (your movie) at the same time.

Set Up Dual View Edit Mode

1. Continue working in the open project from the previous exercise. Repeat Step 2 of the previous exercise to delete all of the clips in the Timeline. Be very careful to follow all instructions exactly. If changes are made in the following exercise, unexpected results may occur. If that happens, simply start over at Step 1.

2. Drag the Project window to the right side of the screen. Click the arrow at the upper-right side of the Monitor window and select Dual View from the pop-up menu.

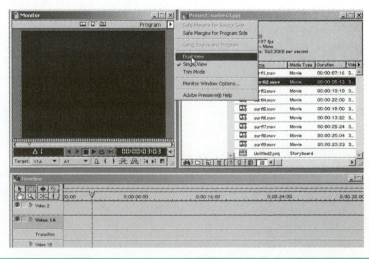

3. The Monitor window appears, showing a Source view on the left and a Program view on the right. Be sure the Storyboard bin is highlighted. If not, click on the Storyboard bin.

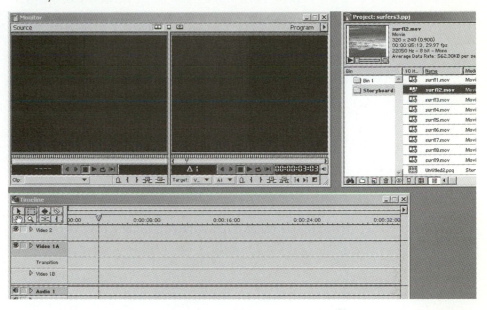

4. Drag surfl1 to the A track. Drag surfl3 to the B track. Position surfl3 so it immediately follows surfl1. Drag surfl2 to the Source screen in the Monitor window.

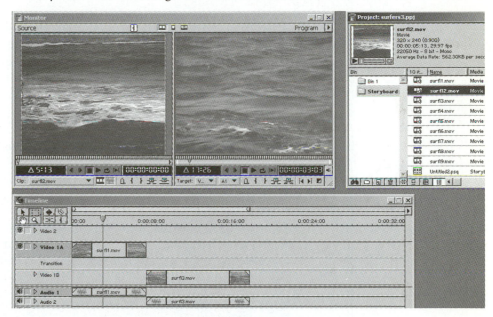

5. Leave the project open for the next exercise.

When you are editing, always check the Target audio and video tracks before you actually commit the edit.

The Source screen shows the clip you are working on; the Program screen shows the entire program. The Source and Program screens are very similar, except the Source screen does not provide a Target button. When you are editing, it is very important to set the Target before you actually make the edit. If you forget to set the Target, you may send the clip to the wrong track.

Dragging the edit line marker (the triangular pointer) to the left and right allows you to scan your clip. This process is called *scrubbing*. When you find the exact In point you want to use, you can click on the In Point button. You can do the same for the Out point.

You have two options when you add the clip to your program. You can insert the clip, which makes the movie longer, or you can overlay the clip, which cuts off the beginning of the clip that follows the edit point.

The Insert button.

The Overlay button.

You can also insert only the video portion or only the audio portion of the clip. You may decide to use only the video portion if you will be adding an audio track later. If you click once on the video symbol at the bottom of the Source window, the video is excluded. A red line appears to indicate this. The same is true for audio. To restore video or audio, click the respective button again.

The Take Video/Audio button.

Perform an Insert Edit

1. Continue working in the open project from the previous exercise. Click the Next (or Previous) button at the bottom of the Program screen until the edit line is between clips surfl1 and surfl3. Click the Insert button at the bottom of the Source screen. Did you remember to set the Target track to Video 1B first?

2. Drag surfl3 to the A track and position it at the end of surfl2. Your screen should appear as follows.

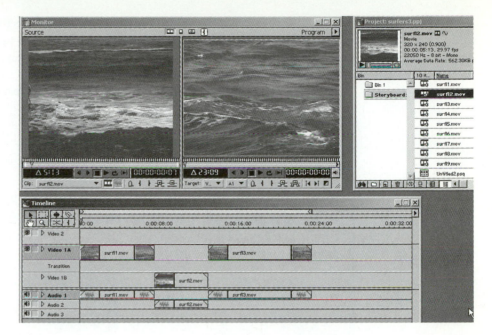

3. Save your project and leave it open for the next exercise.

In the previous exercise, you learned how to insert a clip between two other clips. You also positioned the clips so they alternated between the Video 1A track and the Video 1B track. The main purpose for using A/B edit mode is to allow for transitions between scenes. If you are simply butting one clip against another using straight cuts as transitions, you do not need to use both tracks.

You can also do your editing in Single Track edit mode if you are not concerned with transitions. It is not advisable to switch between Single Track and A/B edit modes while you are working on a project. Doing so can lead to unpredictable results.

We recommend editing in A/B edit mode. You can start by using only the Video 1A track until your clips are trimmed and in the correct order, and then alternate the clips between the A and B tracks so you can add transitions at a later time.

You can insert a clip so it simply pushes the other clips over to make room and lengthens the overall production. This process is a referred to as a *ripple edit*. Alternately, you can insert a clip in such a fashion that the entire production retains the exact same duration. This process is called a *rolling edit*.

The edit tools are found in the upper-left corner of the Timeline. Any time you see a tool with a small arrow in the corner, it means there are variations of the tool. To select a variation, click the tool and hold down the mouse button for a few seconds. The other options appear and you can select the tool you need.

The following image shows the Timeline toolbox. Across the top of the toolbox, you will find icons for the Selection tool, Range Select tools, Edit tools, and Razor tools. The four icons on the bottom are for the Hand tool, Zoom tool, Fade Control tools, and Edit Point tools. These tools and their functions will be introduced in future chapters of this book as needed. All you need to do now is try to remember their names and the appearance of their icons.

Remember, if you do not see a particular tool in the toolbox, you need to click and hold on the appropriate icon to select the correct tool. For example, if you want to use the Ripple Edit tool, click and hold on the Edit tools icon, and then select the Ripple Edit tool from the expanded list.

Ripple Edits

A ripple edit trims the selected clip without changing the duration of the other clips on the Timeline. In other words, a ripple edit lengthens or shortens the overall running time of your production.

The Ripple Edit tool.

The Ripple Edit tool preserves the running times of all other clips by changing the program duration. To do this, you would drag the edit line marker, and the overall program duration would be lengthened or shortened by the number of frames you add to or subtract from the clip you are editing.

To execute a ripple edit, you would select the Ripple Edit tool and position it on the In or Out point of the clip you want to change. You would then drag it to the left or right. The program duration would be extended or shortened to compensate for your edit, but the duration of adjacent clips would remain unchanged.

Rolling Edits

The Rolling Edit tool equally trims both sides of an edit. It does not affect the overall running time of a production. A rolling edit keeps the program duration constant and also preserves the combined duration of the two clips you are editing.

The Rolling Edit tool.

When you adjust the edit line, the frames you add to or subtract from one clip are subtracted from or added to the clip on the other side of the edit line.

To complete a rolling edit, you would select the Rolling Edit tool and position it at the edge of the clip you want to change. You would then drag to the left or right. The same number of frames would be added to the clip and subtracted from the adjacent clip, maintaining the overall duration of the movie.

Complete a Ripple Edit

1. Continue working in the open project from the previous exercise.

2. Delete all clips from the Timeline window.

3. Drag clips surfl1 through and including surfl5 to the Timeline. Place them in sequence on the Video 1A track.

4. Surfl4 is too long. It should be cut at 00:40:00. It retains its meaning when cut at this point.

5. Drag the edit line marker on the Timeline to 00:40:00.

6. Select the Ripple Edit tool from the toolbox. Position it at the end of surfl4 (you see a left-facing bracket appear) and drag it to the left until it snaps to the edit line. Surfl5 slides to the left, shortening the duration of the movie.

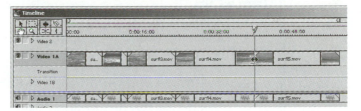

7. Leave this project open for the next exercise.

Complete a Rolling Edit

1. Continue working in the open project from the previous exercise. You decide that surfl4 was fine as it was, and the footage should instead be removed from the beginning of surfl5.

2. Switch to the Rolling Edit tool (click and hold on the Edit tools icon in the toolbox).

3. Select the edit line marker in the Timeline and drag it to the right until the time indicator at the bottom of the Program window reads exactly 00:45:00.

4. Drag the right end of surfl4 to the right until it snaps to the edit line marker.

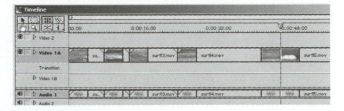

5. Press the Return/Enter key to see the results.

6. Leave this project open for the next exercise.

The rolling edit did not push surfl5 to the right; it cut off the beginning of the clip. Trimming a clip does not shorten the original footage. It remains in your computer, complete and intact.

The edits look a little rough at this point. Soon, you will use transitions to make the action appear smoother.

Ensuring You Have Enough Footage

If you shoot more footage than you need, Premiere makes it simple to trim the excess to fit your exact creative vision. If you shoot too little video, it's more difficult to fit the footage to the production.

Exercise Setup

It is possible to work around the problem of having too little footage. Creative use of stills, adding filters to simulate motion, and tasteful application of dissolves and other transition methods can often help you to fill in the gaps. Be careful not to overuse these techniques — they can distract the audience.

You have already worked with trimming footage (shortening its run length). Now let's look at using trim techniques.

Trim a Clip

1. Continue working in the open project from the previous exercise. Drag surfl6 to the Timeline and place it after surfl5.

2. Double-click surfl6 to open it in a Clip window.

3. Drag the edit line marker to the right to remove the extra footage from the previous scene. Stop dragging at the exact point that the surfer appears at the top of the wave.

4. Click the In point bracket at the lower right of the window, and then click Apply.

5. Close the Clip window (click the box in the upper-right corner). Surfl6 is trimmed, but there is now a space after surfl5. Drag surfl6 to the left to close the gap.

6. Leave this project open for the next exercise.

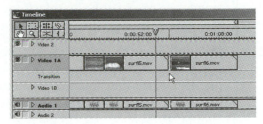

Editing Ranges on the Timeline

There will be many times when you must edit more than one clip at a time — moving the clips on the Timeline, for example, or changing their run times. There are several techniques available that allow you to change or move multiple clips at the same time. Among these techniques is using the Range Select tool.

Use the Range Select Tool

1. In the open project, choose the Range Select tool from the Timeline toolbox.

2. Position your cursor on the lower-right side of the video and audio clips, and hold down the mouse button. Slowly drag diagonally, up and to the left, until all of your clips, except surfl1, are selected. You may need to change the zoom factor to see all of the clips.

3. The cursor turns into a pointer with a plus (+) sign. This is the Range Select tool in action. Drag all of the selected clips to the right. Then drag all of these selected clips back to the left until your video is at the end of surfl1.

4. Deactivate the Range Select tool by selecting the Selection tool from the Timeline toolbox. Save the project, and then press the Return/Enter key to view it. Notice the results of the edit.

5. Leave this project open for the next exercise.

Edits and Production Length

We've discussed rolling and ripple edits and how they impact the length of a movie. Again, if you insert a clip and use a ripple edit, the other clips in the movie aren't affected in any way. The movie becomes longer or shorter, depending on whether you trim an existing clip or insert a new one. If you use a rolling edit, the length of the production stays the same — to accomplish this requires you to make changes to one or more of the remaining clips.

Another way to change the zoom factor is to click the Timeline view factor in the lower-left corner of the Timeline window. Using this method, you can select a view range from a single frame to eight minutes of footage.

Telling a Story

Telling a story requires a great deal more than shooting some footage and assembling the clips. Placing the footage and judging what should be used in precisely what order, trimming individual clips to the correct length, moving and reworking the order and the length to make a finished production — all of these activities and more are essential to the ultimate goal of effectively telling a story.

When all of the footage we used in this chapter is placed in proper combination, a story begins to unfold. It is the story of surfers enjoying some beautiful ocean swells. The only problem is that the clips are not trimmed correctly (yet) and the transitions between scenes are nothing but straight cuts. At this point, the video appears very rough and "jumps" between scenes. (In the next chapter, you will learn how to add transitions to make your feature look much more professional.)

Planning the Types of Shots

Video production is an art form. It uses some of the same rules as painting and drawing. A picture must convey a meaningful message. In painting, this is accomplished with good composition. In video production, the same rule applies.

The video story is told through a series of visual sequences. Each of these sequences is comprised of a group of shots. Often, a variety of shots can help keep a narrative alive and interesting.

So what, exactly, is a shot? A *shot* is an individual unit that is part of a larger classification of camera movements. A shot is the material photographed from the time the camera starts running until the camera stops running. A shot can last a split second or several minutes.

Shot Definitions

Below are definitions of some types of shots. They are usually known as "intershot movements" because they represent the action that occurs during one shot:

- **Cover Shot (CS).** Also called an "establishing shot." The camera sees the entire set. It covers the action or sets the scene. Frequently, the next shot to follow is an interior of the shot just established.
- **Long Shot (LS).** The camera is at the full zoom capacity. This shot usually shows an actor, framed from head to toe.
- **Medium Shot (MS).** This shot shows the actor cropped to include the head, shoulders, and waist. This is the shot most often seen in news broadcasts. It is considered the most neutral shot in television.
- **Close-Up Shot (CU).** The camera shows the actor's face. No background is evident in the shot.
- **Extreme Close-Up Shot (ECU).** The actor's face is cropped so only the chin and the eyes are shown. This is also known as a "reaction shot" as in, "'Mary, the man is dead!' Cut to ECU of Mary's reaction."
- **Down-The-Line Shot (DTL).** The camera is set to pan, or move down a row of subjects. It also makes an interesting reaction shot. Think about a shot of people looking at a bride as she walks down the aisle. The camera shows all of the happy people as they watch the bride approach.
- **Two Shot.** Two actors are framed equally in one shot.

Classes of Camera Movement

To accurately describe the movement of a camera, you must use the correct definitions. Simply saying, "Move in" could mean a Zoom, a Dolly, or a Crane movement:

- **Pan**. Camera movement proceeds from right to left or left to right. It is created in a horizontal format.

- **Tilt**. Camera movement proceeds up or down. It is created in a vertical format.

- **Zoom**. This movement is the in or out movement of the focusing lens. The camera remains stationary.

- **Dolly**. This is the physical movement of the camera and the base, forward or backward, in or out of the shot.

- **Truck**. This is the physical movement of the camera and the base, to the right or left of the object being shot.

- **Pedestal**. This is the raising or lowering of the camera.

- **Crane or Boom**. This movement requires using a crane device that can move in any direction. The camera can often reach substantial height.

Create a Shot List for a TV Show

1. Select a half-hour television show and videotape it (if possible) while you watch it in real time.

2. While watching the show, write down the types of shots that are used as the show progresses. This is called "logging" the shots of the show. It may be difficult at first. You may find yourself wanting to actually watch the show instead of observing the technical aspects. You may find the assignment easier to do if you turn off the sound as you watch and log.

3. If you taped the show:

   - Rewind the tape.

   - Set the counter to zero.

   - Start the tape.

   - Stop at each shot you want to remember and log each of the shots.

4. Use the following format to log your shots. The sample below provides an idea of the range of shots and the notations you will probably want to make for your log.

Video Shot List			
SHOT #	CAMERA	SHOT TYPE	COMMENTS
1	Pine Tree Hospital	Establishing Shot	Sets the scene
2	Interior of hospital	Two Shot of nurses	They look worried
3	Hospital room	Medium Shot	Actress is upset
4	Reverse of door opening	Long Shot	Husband enters
5	Bed	ECU	Actress in tears
6	Door to bed	Long Shot	Husband talks to wife

5. When you are finished, discuss your list with colleagues or friends, especially if any of them have done the same exercise. You may discover that not everyone "sees" television the same way you do. You may also find that you are beginning to look at things in a new and different way.

Chapter Summary

In Chapter 3, you learned about several editing techniques and experimented with many editing tools. You discovered the strengths of the Range Selection tool and the Ripple Edit command.

You learned to trim a clip with In points, Out points, and the edit line marker. You also learned to use a ripple edit to move clips as a group. You became familiar with employing a rolling edit to trim clips and a ripple edit to close gaps.

You learned the definitions for some of the most common types of camera shots and camera movements, and practiced logging shots from existing television footage.

4 Transitions

Chapter Objectives:

Transitions enhance virtually every video production. They smooth the changes that occur between one scene and the next. Without transitions, movies appear choppy and could be considered unprofessional or incomplete. Premiere offers several standard transitions with the program. Many more — hundreds in fact — are available on the Internet. With this wide variety of transitions available to you, you will find the transition type you need for any production situation. In this chapter, you will:

- Learn to recognize many types of transitions and decide which ones are most appropriate for your production.

- Discover how to assign your own (custom) settings to the transitions that Adobe provides.

- Develop skill in placing clips using the Monitor window controls.

- Create a split-screen shot with transitions.

- Learn how to export a single frame as a still image.

- Practice using a still image in a Freeze Frame insert.

Projects to be Completed:

- **The Monkey Movie (A)**
- Making Spaghetti (B)
- The Gold Rush (C)
- Central Coast Surfing (D)

Transitions

A transition occurs when one clip replaces another — the scene changes from the fireside to the ski slopes, for example, or from the fisherman drinking a cup of coffee to the shark lurking beneath the hull of his boat. Transitions are at the heart of all video production and editing.

Premiere ships with more than 75 built-in transitions that can be found in the Transitions palette. Each can be customized in a variety of ways, providing an almost unlimited array of choices.

Transitions can be overused; in most cases, subtle transitions are best. If you place too much emphasis on your transitions, the importance of the clips can be diminished. Remember that it's the footage that contains the content of your production, not the transitions.

It is advisable to leave a substantial amount of extra footage at the beginning and end of your clips until you decide what transition you are going to use. Most transitions require the end of the previous scene to overlap the beginning of the next. A/B editing mode is the best mode to use when adding and experimenting with transitions. It enables you to see the required overlap in the Timeline.

Transitions Palette

Transitions are accessed from the Transitions palette. They're organized within folders, arranged in categories, with an icon and/or description representing each.

To access the Transitions palette, you can select Window>Show Transitions. The Transitions palette would then appear, showing all of the major transition categories.

Under the black triangle in the top-right corner of the palette is the Transitions palette Options menu. One very useful function available from the Transitions palette Options menu is Animate. If you select Animate, the icons show a preview of that transition to the extent that you can actually see the transition in a 12-pixel square.

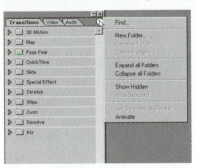

Customizing the Transitions Palette

The Transitions palette offers a number of special features that enhance your workflow. Let's examine several of the special properties in the Options menu.

To add a folder to the palette, you can select New Folder from the Options menu. Once you create a new folder, you can populate it by dragging transitions into it from other folders.

Clicking the triangle to the left of a folder reveals its content, and clicking the triangle again collapses the folder. To view all the content of every folder, you can choose Expand All Folders from the Options menu.

You might want to hide your transitions to reduce on-screen clutter and make it easier to move around in the palette. If you're using a Macintosh, you can Shift-click to select non-contiguous transitions; Control-click is the Windows equivalent of this command. You can use this method to select transitions in separate folders.

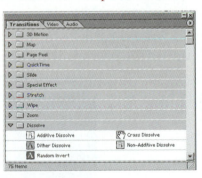

Types of Transitions

Before computer editing, transitions were made by splicing scenes into an A roll and a B roll. The two rolls of film were then printed on a third roll with an overlap equal to the duration of the transition. Premiere's digital techniques mirror conventional methods, as well as provide transitions that are very difficult — or impossible — to achieve using manual techniques.

Premiere provides an extensive assortment of transitions and many more are available both free of charge and commercially. Frequently used transitions include:

Cross Dissolve is the default transition when Premiere is first installed. You can select any transition in the Transitions palette and use the Set Selected as Default command to make a new transition the default.

- **Cut.** This is the simplest form of transition. One clip is replaced with another in a single frame.

- **Dissolve.** With this transition, the clip that's playing dissolves from the scene, and the new clip dissolves into the scene, replacing the first one.

- **Blur.** This transition is similar to a dissolve, except that one clip loses focus while the next clip sharpens.

- **Blend.** With this transition, the incoming clip is seen on top of the current clip, increasing in intensity until the previous clip disappears.

- **Wipe.** This transition enables the incoming clip to "wipe" or erase across the screen, displacing the previous clip. You can control where the wipe begins — at the top, bottom, sides, or corners.

Editing Transitions

You can customize any transition. The exact adjustment settings depend on several factors, including the type of transition. There are two ways to edit a transition. Understanding the difference between the two is quite important, and can have a major (and, at times, unexpected) impact on your productions:

- **Editing a single instance.** If you double-click a transition that's already in place on the Timeline, you're making changes to that instance only. The original transition (the one in the Transitions palette) remains untouched, as are other uses of the same transition elsewhere on the Timeline.

- **Editing an original transition.** If you double-click a transition in the Transitions palette, the changes you make affect every instance of the transition on the Timeline — the change is global. Once it is edited, any time you drop that transition onto the Timeline from that point forward, the use of that transition also reflects the change.

If you want to revert to the original default settings for your transitions, you can delete the Preferences file. (If you need to do this, refer back to the Getting Started section of this book to review how to discard your Preferences file.)

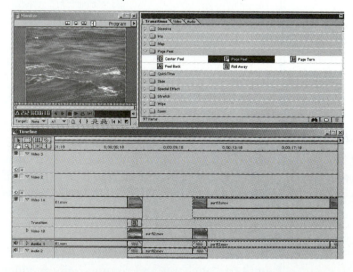

This graphic illustrates editing a single instance of a transition. We first dropped two clips on the Timeline, trimmed them to the desired size, and then dragged one of the Page Peel transitions onto the Timeline between the two clips.

Once the transition is in place on the Timeline (in the Transitions track), you're able to double-click it and access that transition's Settings dialog box. Take a moment to familiarize yourself with the controls.

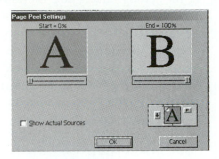

In the lower-right corner of the Settings dialog box is a small rectangular icon. The arrow on the left determines the A/B order of the transition, and the "F" or "R" on the right side of the transition determines its direction — forward or backward, respectively. Some transitions also include an anti-aliasing selection and a direction selection.

Customizable transition box

Click to choose A>B or B>A

Click to choose Forward or Reverse Effect

Click to turn Anti-aliasing (smoothing of edges) on and off.

Click to select the side, or corner, where the transition will appear.

At the top of the Settings dialog box are controls for the start and end percentages of the transition. If you experiment with these settings, you'll find you can't start one transition at a point beyond the end of another.

Although we've shown the use of the generic A/B graphic up to this point, you can click the Show Actual Sources check box to replace the graphic with the actual footage from the Timeline. Checking this is particularly helpful for visualizing the exact effect of the changes to the start and end percentages. You can get a good idea of how the transition looks by dragging the slider at the bottom of either Source view from full left to full right.

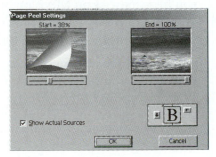

Custom Settings

Some transitions can be customized, as indicated by the Custom button in the lower left of the Settings dialog box. All transitions can be customized with the general controls, including the start and end percentages of the transition, their stacking order, and whether or not Show Actual Sources is activated. In the case of the Barn Door Wipe, for example, you can also control the thickness of bars used for the transition. You can look at the various transitions available to you by either dropping them on the Timeline or double-clicking them in the Transitions palette. Make sure you are careful when you use the latter option to make changes.

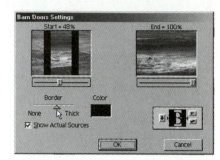

Transitions — particularly custom transitions — can create some dramatic effects. An example of one you may have seen is the ability to freeze a transition so you can create picture-in-picture effects. This effect is frequently used in news broadcasts.

Picture-In-Picture

Imagine this: It's time for the six o'clock news and there's a massive traffic jam on the turnpike. The tense newscaster opens with the special news report that all traffic heading west will be delayed until the problem — a protest rally — has ended. As the newscaster speaks, a graphic pops up to enhance the broadcast.

Almost every event that is broadcast on television is shown with a graphic insert of some kind, typically a still or a video. In television studios, this effect is generated using a professional video mixer called a "switcher." Premiere can also generate this effect. Known as a "split screen" or an "inset," the effect is created by freezing a transition at its midpoint.

Exercise Setup

In the following set of exercises, you have the opportunity to create some of the effects you frequently see on television broadcasts. You'll create a picture-in-picture (inset) effect. With this transition in place, you'll observe two pieces of video playing at once. A sound track is included to provide a professional touch.

Preview the Finished Piece

1. Launch Premiere if it is not already running. Create a new project using the standard settings we've been using throughout the book. Save it as "broadcastnews.ppj" to your **Work_In_Progress** folder.

2. Select File>Import>Folder. In the ensuing dialog box, select **RF_Premiere>the_news**, and then click Choose. The folder, along with its content, transfers to the Project window.

3. Double-click **the_news** folder to reveal the three clips you will work with in this chapter. Double-click **newsfin.mov** to view it in the Clip window. Click the Play button to preview your final project. Close the separate Clip window.

4. Leave the project open for the next exercise.

Place the Clips

There are other ways to mark the timecode. You can enter the number directly in the Timeline window. On a Macintosh, it turns green when you select it. You can also use the Navigator palette and the Arrow keys to exactly mark the time.

1. Continue working in the open project. Drag **news1.mov** from the Project window to the Timeline window, and position it at the beginning of Video 1A.

2. Drag **flamingo1.mov** from the Project window to the Timeline window, and position it on Video 1B at 00:00:10:22. You can easily accomplish this by first dragging the edit line to 00:00:10:22. Look at the bottom of the Program view in the Monitor window. As you move the edit line, the numbers at the bottom change to 00:00:10:22. As an alternative, you could select the Program Location at the bottom right of the Monitor window (click at the right-most edge, directly to the right of the numbers), enter "10:22", and then press the Return/Enter key. You could then drag **flamingo1.mov** from the Project window to the Timeline window where it would snap to the edit line.

Monitor method.

Edit line method.

3. Use the Scrub tool to view the production. All you see is the footage on Video 1A. You need to create the split screen that inserts one video clip into another. Save the file and leave it open for the next exercise.

Add Transitions and Create the Split Screen

1. Continue working in the open file. Drag the Wipe transition from the Wipe folder in the Transitions palette to the Transition track at 00:00:10:22. It should snap into position in the space where the two movies overlap. (If you do not see your transitions, select Window>Show Transitions. You may also need to scroll down to the Wipe transition.)

2. The transition needs to be stretched to the same width as **flamingo1.mov**. Position the cursor at the end of the Wipe transition. The cursor turns into a two-sided arrow with a red bracket. Drag the two-sided arrow until the transition is the same length as **flamingo1.mov**.

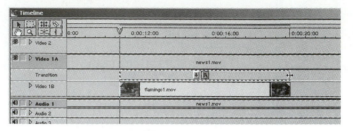

You should notice that there's an audio track at the bottom of the Timeline. Although we won't be working with audio to any major extent until Chapter 7, there are certain situations where we chose to include an audio clip to enhance an exercise.

3. Let's create the inset for the newscast. On the Timeline, double-click the Wipe transition. A dialog box appears.

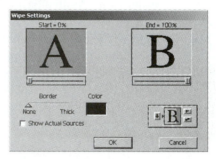

4. Click the Show Actual Sources check box. You see a preview of your video clips. Set the left slider (Start=) to 50% and the right slider (End=) to 50%. You see a preview of the final result. (Notice that the small blue Wipe preview stops moving.)

5. We want our newscaster to appear on the left of the screen and the flamingos on the right. Notice that your images may be backward. Look to the lower-right side of the screen. The arrow to the left of the A/B (in the same box as the reversing switch) should be pointing up. This puts the newscaster on the left and the flamingos on the right.

When you are working on the Timeline, you may need to change the zoom factor to enhance your view.

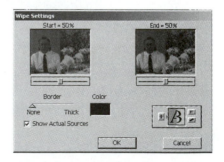

The Start (0%) and the End (100%) that you see in the transition's dialog box represents the beginning and end of your wipe. By altering these numbers to 20% and 70%, for example, you can create a partial wipe that slowly brings a transition onto the screen so the action can be seen.

6. Move the Border triangle from None to the right, just a little. A thin border appears.

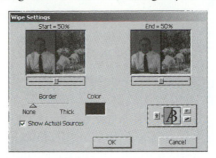

7. At the moment, the border is black (the default). A border color would help to define the individual sections. Click the black rectangle. The Color Picker appears. Set Red to 255, Green to 0, Blue to 31.

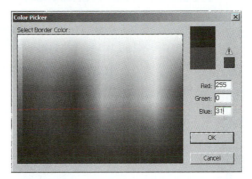

When you choose this color, a warning flag appears, indicating that this color will not be faithfully reproduced on an NTSC monitor. Clicking the warning flag causes Premiere to select the nearest color that is safe to use, and will be reproduced accurately. Click OK twice.

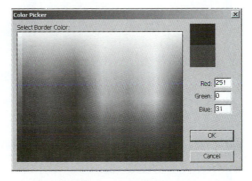

8. Check to see if the work area bar (the yellow line at the top of the Timeline) has extended to the end of the production. Extending the bar all the way to the end allows you to view the entire production.

9. Press Return/Enter. It takes several moments for Premiere to render these new changes. This time, the entire production plays from start to finish. Now as our newscaster discusses a news event, a split screen appears halfway into the production.

10. Save the file and leave it open for the next exercise.

Exporting Video Clips as Single Frames

In most newscasts, the announcer delivers a news story while a single still image is placed in the upper-right corner of the frame. As we discussed earlier, this is usually referred to as a "camera insert."

In the previous exercise, you created an insert with a moving picture-in-picture effect. If you decide that a single-frame insert would be a better choice for your story, it would be quite easy to do.

As with any video, the flamingo movie is just a series of frames that are linked together to form a continual video clip running at 15 frames per second (fps). To make this freeze-frame insert, all we have to do is select a single frame of the movie and transform it.

Create a Freeze-Frame Insert

If you want to experiment with editing settings for a specific transition, it's probably safer to drag an instance onto the Timeline between two short clips and edit it there. That way, you'll avoid making changes to the original transition in the Transitions palette.

1. Continue working in the open file. Click and delete **flamingo1.mov** and the Wipe transition from the Timeline window. Leave everything else on the Timeline.

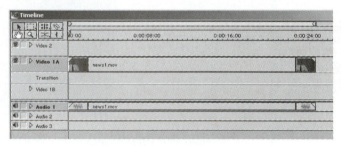

2. Drag **flamingo1.mov** from the Project window to the Source view. The movie appears in the Source view window.

3. Move the Scrub tool in the Monitor window until the clock reads 00:00:05:08. This is the section of the video clip that will turn into a freeze-frame insert.

4. With the Monitor window active (highlighted), choose File>Export Timeline>Frame.

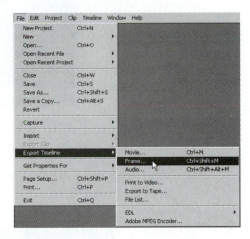

5. You need to select the correct options for the frame you are about to create. Click the Settings check box. From the File Type pop-up menu, select TIFF. Check the Open When Finished box. Click the Next button at the bottom of the dialog box. Set the Frame Size H to 240 and V to 180 for the Export Size of the frame. Click OK.

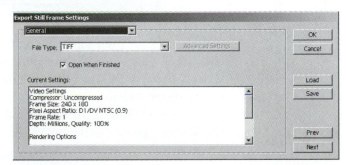

If you have used older versions of Premiere, you may have noticed that a number of special effects are missing in this version of the program. Many of Premiere's older effects have been replaced by After Effects video filters. If you are working on a project created in earlier versions of Premiere, and your project uses an obsolete effect, you can still use it in Premiere 6.0. All obsolete video effects can be found in the Obsolete folder in the Video Effects palette.

6. Name the file "newbird.tif". Save it to your **Work_In_Progress** folder. A new single frame of the clip appears as an independent window on your desktop.

7. Click the Duration button at the bottom left of the Clip window. Change the Duration to 00:00:09:00. Drag **newbird.tif** to the Project window, and then close the Clip window.

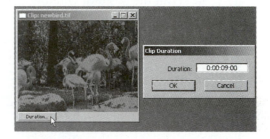

8. Now drag **newbird.tif** to Video 1B at 00:00:10:22. Use the edit line to mark the starting point for the new clip before dragging the file.

9. Select the Inset transition from the Wipe folder in the Transitions palette. Drag it to the Timeline, and place it on the Transition track between **news1.mov** and **newbird.tif**. Stretch it to the length of **newbird.tif**.

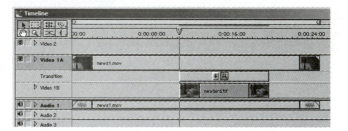

10. Double-click the Inset transition on the Timeline. In the dialog box that appears, click Show Actual Sources. You see a preview of your video clips. Drag the left slider (Start=) to 56% and the right slider (End=) to 56%. Click the small triangle on the upper-right corner of the transition control box (see the arrow in the illustration below). Selecting this corner changes the inset to show the newscaster with the flamingo picture in the upper-right corner of the screen.

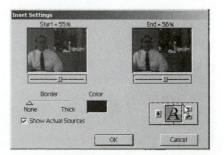

11. At the moment, there is no border to separate the video clips. A border color would help to define the individual sections. Click the black rectangle. The Color Picker appears. Set Red to 0, Green to 159, Blue to 160, and then click OK.

12. Move the Border triangle from None to the right, just a little. When a thin, light-blue border color appears, click OK.

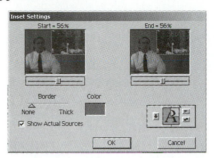

13. Render the production by pressing Return/Enter. You should see the newscaster talking while an inset screen appears halfway into the production. Close the production when you're done viewing. We're going to pick it up again in Chapter 7 when we add background music to the piece.

Chapter Summary

In Chapter 4, you learned more about transitions and how to control the way one clip replaces another. You learned to split a picture and create freeze-frame inserts from a video clip. You also learned about the options in the transitions dialog boxes and found out how to adjust transitions. Finally, you discovered how to create picture-in-picture transitions.

Complete Project A: The Monkey Movie

5 Audio

Chapter Objectives:

Silent movies can certainly tell a story. Movies with sound, however, tell a story and set the mood for the viewer. Sound effects dramatically enhance the entertainment value of the movie. You should be well versed in how to add sound effects, edit special effects, and modify audio tracks to meet the needs of your productions. Mastering these skills allow you to make exciting and unique audio enhancements to your video presentations. In this chapter, you will:

- Learn how to "view" audio clips and their associated waveforms.

- Investigate techniques for editing audio clips and recognize the similarity to editing video clips.

- Learn about rubberbands and how to use them.

- Discover how background music can be added and extended.

- Develop your ability to properly mix audio.

- Learn how to use cross-fades and special effects.

- Find out how to create your own special effects.

Projects to be Completed:

- The Monkey Movie (A)

- Making Spaghetti (B)

- The Gold Rush (C)

- Central Coast Surfing (D)

This version of Premiere adds considerable horse-power to its built-in audio-editing functions. It offers a real-time Audio Mixer window, and a broad selection of After Effects filters and special effects. Pan and Fade controls are easy to select, and you can turn on a waveform display when you need to apply fine edits or more accurately synchronize your soundtracks to the footage in the Timeline.

Audio

Sound creates atmosphere. It establishes reality, sets mood, and supports all visual footage. Without sound and music, there would be no scary scenes in horror movies, no tears as the hero embraces the woman of his dreams. Even in the days of silent movies, sound effects and background music (often played in the theatre) were used to embellish the video production.

Although many beginning videographers wait until the end of the production to add music, it's arguably among the most critical components of any professional production and should be considered from the start. Many of the most memorable movies derive their power as much from the subtle impact of the soundtrack as from the visuals.

Do you remember the girl who was going for a swim at the beginning of *Jaws*? The scene contained a very simple soundtrack — the splashing of the swimmer, the gentle lapping of the waves on a warm summer night, distant laughter, subdued conversations, and guitar music from the people on the beach. In the meantime, below the surface, a silent and brutal killer was approaching. No sounds were emitted by the beast, but the sound-track for that scene contained strong, deep horns — duundunn, duundunn. Dundun dundun dundun. It successfully instilled such a sense of impending terror that it remained imprinted on the consciousness of millions of viewers for quite some time after the release of the movie. If you heard that sound, you knew it was time to get out of the water — and fast!

The star of Jaws was a beast of few words; but add deep horns and underwater footage, and his message of fear and doom was easily established.

Another excellent example of a powerful soundtrack is Spielberg's *Close Encounters of the Third Kind*. The method of communication chosen by our extraterrestrial visitors was musical notes — no words, just sounds.

The Audio Workspace

Premiere offers a predefined audio workspace. When you're working with the background music, sound effects, or dialog boxes, selecting this option positions the Audio Mixer in the center of the working area. To select this option, you can choose Window>Workspace>Audio.

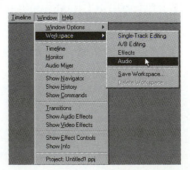

By default, new Premiere projects contain 3 audio tracks. You can, however, add up to 96 more for a total of 99 possible audio tracks. You can also delete any audio track except Audio 1, Audio 2, and Audio 3. Add to that the ability to render multiple tracks, transitions, fades, and other effects into a single track, and you are offered virtually limitless potential in what you can accomplish with the program's audio-editing features.

Viewing Clips and Waveforms

A *waveform* is a visual representation of an audio track. Using vertical bars, the waveform displays volume and tonal ranges on a horizontal graph. As you work through this chapter, you'll have an opportunity to use waveforms and see how they translate what you're hearing into a visual-editing aid.

Audio clips are imported into Premiere in the same fashion as video footage, and appear in the Project window. When you select an audio clip, a small version of its waveform appears in the upper-left corner of the Project window, complete with a Play button. Clicking the Play button plays the audio in the Project window.

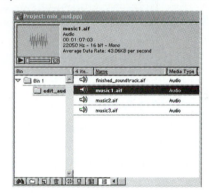

Audio Clip Windows

Double-clicking the clip in the Project window opens an audio Clip window, similar in appearance and function to a video Clip window. The difference is that instead of seeing the footage play, you see the audio clip's waveform.

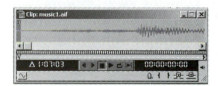

You can use the zoom icon in the lower-left corner of the audio Clip window to move in and out of a waveform. This helps you position In and Out points more accurately. As you gain more experience with audio, you'll come to understand the relationship between the waveform and the sound, and be able to instantly focus on a specific piece of audio.

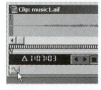

Audio Channels

To place audio tracks into your movies, you can simply drag them from the Project window to one of the audio tracks. As we said earlier, Premiere provides 3 audio tracks by default, you can add up to 96 more — which should be plenty to meet the demands of any project.

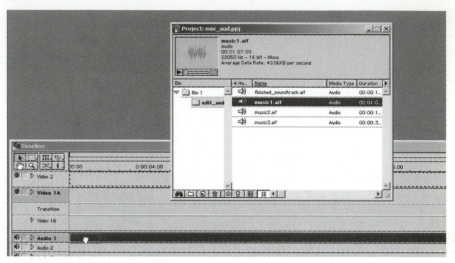

Editing Audio

Editing audio clips is essentially the same process as editing video footage. You can create In and Out points, adjust volume, control *panning* (the movement of sound from the left to right channel and back again), and fade one audio track into another.

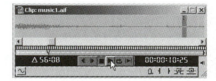

Timeline View Options

As with video tracks, audio tracks can be expanded to display additional information for a particular clip. Clicking the small triangle to the left of the track's name expands that track. You can keep any or all tracks expanded or collapsed; either way, there is no effect on the clip itself.

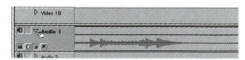

If you expand an audio track and look in the lower-left corner underneath the Mute and Lock check boxes, you'll see four small buttons.

You'll find yourself frequently using these buttons. Starting on the left, these buttons are:

- **Show/Hide Waveform**. The Waveform button toggles the display on and off in the Timeline. We find that it's usually easier to work with the waveform in an audio Clip window instead of on the Timeline itself, but it's a matter of personal preference.

- **Display Keyframes**. Since you can apply effects to sound clips in much the same way as to video footage, keyframes are equally important in your audio tracks. This button toggles their display on and off.

- **Display Volume Rubberbands**. This rubberband controls the overall volume of a clip on the Timeline. Note that if you're using the Audio Mixer to adjust a track's *gain* (volume), the rubberband settings take affect first, and then the Audio Mixer's adjustments are applied.

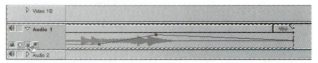

- **Display Pan Rubberbands**. Panning refers to sound moving from the right speaker to the left, or vice versa. Click this rubberband to display a change point, and then drag the marker up to shift the sound to the left speaker or drag it down to shift the sound to the right speaker. Set in the middle, the sound balances between the two speakers, based on the original recording. Panning is also critical to keeping sound environmentally accurate. For example, as a car moves from right to left, the sound should not move from left to right, nor should it stay in the middle.

Exercise Setup

It's time to apply some of these concepts to a real-world assignment. In Chapter 4, we developed a news broadcast using footage of a newscaster, a number of very angry flamingos, and several split-screen effects.

The footage of the newscaster came complete with its own audio track. In the following exercise, we're going to fine-tune the audio of that production — specifically, we're going to add background music. To do so, we must use several of Premiere's audio functions.

Add Background Music

1. Open the project named **broadcast_news.ppj** from your **Work_In_Progress** folder.

2. Drag **music1.aif** to the Audio 2 track, and position it at 00:00. The music expands to its finale. Click the triangle on the left side of the Audio 2 track to expand the track. When the triangle points down, you should be able to see the rubberband (flexible volume control) for music.

3. Render the production by pressing Return/Enter. Now the newscaster discusses a news event while music plays.

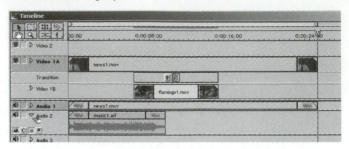

4. Press Return/Enter to play the movie again. Notice that the music does not play long enough to cover the entire newscast. There is a dead spot at the end of the broadcast. Let's solve this problem by duplicating the music. In the next step, you will place the extra music clip at the end of the video clip to complete the production.

5. Drag another copy of **music1.aif** to the Audio 2 track. Place it at the conclusion of the first piece of music. Drag a third copy of **music1.aif** to the Audio 2 track. The music now expands beyond the end of the video.

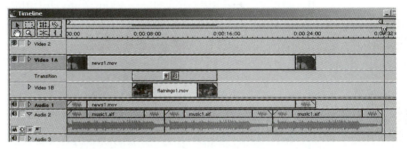

6. Render the production by pressing the Return/Enter key. You should see the newscaster discussing an item while the music plays. Save your project in your **Work_In_Progress** folder.

7. On the Timeline, move the edit line so it is located near the end of the first piece of music on the Audio 2 track. The Target clock (on the right in the Monitor window) should read 00:00:09:20.

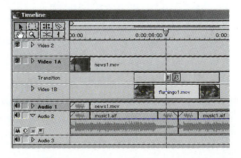

8. Position the cursor at the end of **music1.aif**. The pointer changes to a two-sided arrow with a red bracket. Drag the music to the left until it snaps to the edit line.

9. Now that the music has been shortened, we have a hole in the music track. We need to fix the hole.

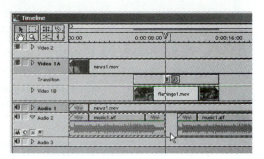

Select the second **music1.aif** clip. Move it to the left so it bumps up against the first music clip.

10. Let's trim this copy of **music1.aif**. Position the edit line at 00:00:19:10. Drag the right corner until it snaps into position. Drag the third (farthest right) copy of **music1.aif** to the left to cover the newly created gap.

11. Render the production by pressing the Return/Enter key. The newscaster discusses a news item while the music plays continually. Save the file.

12. The music ends abruptly at the finish of the newscast. A fade would be more effective. Move the edit line to 00:00:24:24 and click on the red rubberband. At this position, a second red square appears. Click again at 00:27:00, and drag that handle (red square) to the bottom of the audio area. This creates a fade-out between the two marks.

13. One more frame must be altered. Position the edit line at the end of the production and click on the red rubberband. Drag that last handle to the bottom of the audio area. This keeps the music from fading back in.

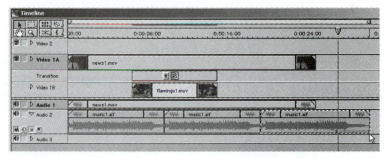

14. Render the production. As the newscast plays, the background music plays and then fades out.

15. Save the project and then close it.

General Audio Settings

The higher the rate you specify, the better the sound quality — with an associated cost. Stereo sound requires much more disk space than mono sound. It is important to decide what the final use of the project will be before selecting a sample rate for your sound. Projects destined for the Web do not need the same sound quality as a production played on television or a CD-ROM. Sound can always be resampled or changed to a different rate. Resampling is usually done at the end of a production.

When you begin a project, you are presented with a number of options for processing audio. These options include Compressor, Interleave, Enhanced Rate Conversion, and Use Logarithmic Audio Fades. Each option provides a way for Premiere to create the best possible sound for your production. Let's explore these settings.

The first option is the Compressor setting. Notice that its default is set to Uncompressed. In general, most productions are created in this basic format. When a project is ready to be exported, you can select another Compressor option or choose to use no compression. The selected setting depends on how the sound will be used by the particular output equipment.

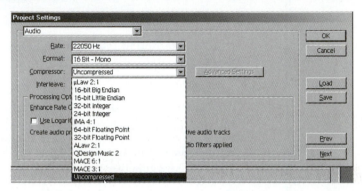

The Interleave option specifies how often audio information is inserted among the video frames in a preview file. The default for this option is 1 Second. This number indicates that when Premiere plays back a frame, the audio for that frame is loaded into RAM. It then stays in RAM and plays until the next frame appears. The smaller the number, the more smoothly your production plays, and the more RAM you need — very possibly a lot more RAM than available on your computer.

The Enhanced Rate Conversion option allows you to select the level of quality for your sound as it is imported. The options are Off, Good, and Best. Each option resamples the audio:

- Off is the fastest, but generates only average sound.
- The Good option tries to balance both quality and overall processing speed.
- The Best option resamples audio at the highest level but requires huge amounts of RAM.
- Most videographers select Off while editing.

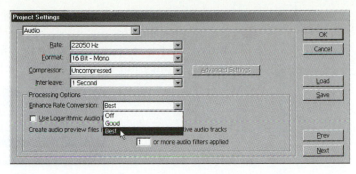

The Use Logarithmic Audio Fades check box controls how audio gain increases or decreases are perceived during playback in Premiere. Selecting this option creates a more natural overall sound; the downside is that it also increases the time it takes to render a file.

You can tell Premiere how to display your audio tracks on the Timeline using the Create Audio Preview Files If There Are setting. This function specifies when Premiere will create an audio preview instead of real-time playback, based on how many audio tracks are active. This setting directly affects the time you must wait for a preview to generate. You will know when you have overloaded your RAM — you will hear pops and clicks while playing back the audio in Premiere.

Option/Alt-click on the work area bar to quickly extend the bar to the end of the production.

Mixing Audio Clips

Commercials are frequently created with a musical effect called a bridge. A *bridge* is a section of music that is repeated several times until the end of the commercial, when the final main chorus is played. Bridges are usually created to provide time for the announcer to speak about the product. A bridge is easily created using a longer piece of music that is precisely trimmed so the overlap offers no evidence that two clips have been connected.

Edit Music

1. From the **RF_Premiere** folder, open **Audio>mix_aud.ppj**. Once the file is open, select Window>Workspace>Audio.

2. There are four audio clips inside the project's bin: **music1.aif**, **music2.aif**, **music3.aif**, and **finished_soundtrack.aif**. Double-click the **finished_soundtrack.aif** clip. Click the Play button, and listen to the finished track. When you're done listening, close the Clip window.

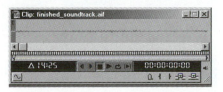

3. Drag **music1.aif** to Audio 1. The music extends to 1:07:02 on the Timeline. This is much too long for our music bridge. Let's tighten it up a bit. Double-click **music1.aif** so it opens in a separate Clip window. Slowly drag the left edit line marker to the right until it reads 00:00:15:01. Click the In point bracket.

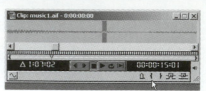

4. Next, drag the edit line marker to the right until it reads 00:00:29:25. Click the Out point bracket. You see a blue rectangle marking the file's new boundaries.

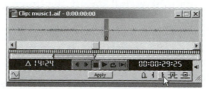

5. Click the Apply button. This shortens **music1.aif** from the Timeline. Drag **music1.aif** to the left to the beginning of the Timeline.

6. From the open **music1.aif** Clip window, drag a copy of **music1.aif** to the Audio 1 track. The two copies should be aligned, side-by-side. Close the Clip window.

7. Save this file to your **Work_In_Progress** folder as "bridge.ppj". Render the file and listen to the result. Listen carefully and note that the two files seamlessly blend together. Delete all the audio clips from the Timeline. Leave the project open for the next exercise.

Using the Audio Mixer Window

Premiere provides an Audio Mixer window that offers a high level of control over the audio tracks in your productions. Changes made in the Audio Mixer are also visible in the Timeline.

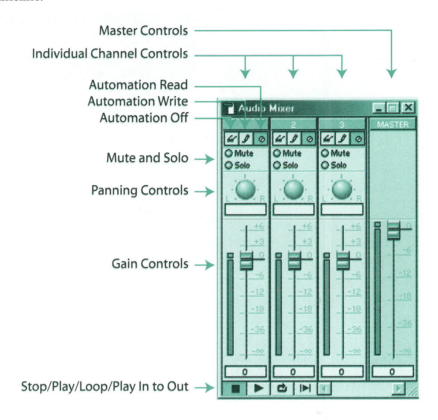

Master Controls

Individual Channel Controls

Automation Read
Automation Write
Automation Off

Mute and Solo →

Panning Controls →

Gain Controls →

Stop/Play/Loop/Play In to Out →

The sliders control the gain (volume) of each clip.

By default, the Audio Mixer displays a set of individual controls for each track you create in the Timeline. In addition, it provides a Master control that affects all of the channels at one time.

Each track of the Audio Mixer includes a pan/balance control. You may have monophonic sound, but you can simulate stereo by applying panning controls. You can change the setting of this control by dragging clockwise or counterclockwise, or by entering a value from -100 to +100 in the box below the control and pressing the Return/Enter key.

Automation States

One of the easiest and most interactive ways to control sound levels in Premiere is with the Automation state buttons. For each audio track, three buttons determine the sound state during the mixing process. These buttons are Automation Read, Automation Write, and Automation Off:

- Automation Read translates the audio information for an audio track and records any adjustments you make in the Audio Mixer window. In other words, Automation Read starts with the initial changes you made to the audio on the Timeline, and then visually displays the adjustments as the music plays.

These adjustments are stored as a set of handles under the audio on the Timeline track. You can simply click the triangle to the left of the track name to expand the audio track you want to modify, and then you can fine-tune your adjustments using your mouse.

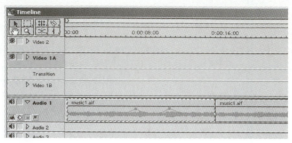

- Automation Write works in the opposite way to Automation Read. In Automation Write mode, you start the music and make the changes in the Audio Mixer as the music is playing. The changes are immediately available on the Timeline.

- Automation Off is the default mode for Premiere, allowing use of the Audio Mixer without the limitation of the rubberbands on the Timeline.

Mute and Solo

Mute and Solo are two of the channel-specific settings available on the Audio Mixer window. Mute does exactly what it suggests — it turns off the sound for that channel. This is particularly useful if you're working on a project that has a lot of audio tracks. Solo is the opposite of Mute — it mutes all other tracks in the production, leaving only the selected channel playing.

Ganging Tracks

Besides using the Master gain control, you can *gang* (or connect) two or more channels so you can simultaneously adjust their gains.

Adjusting Audio Levels on the Timeline

If the change you wish to make is a simple one, you might want to work directly on the Timeline. You may have noticed that all audio clips include two handles that you can't remove — one at the beginning of the clip and another at the end. You can also *cross-fade* two audio clips so one fades out as another fades in. The rubberband in the Timeline corresponds to the volume fader in the Audio Mixer window.

Here are additional methods you can use to adjust sound:

- To adjust volume in 1% increments, position the pointer over the volume handle, hold down the Shift key, and drag the volume handle up or down. A numeric display appears over the audio track to indicate the current volume level as you drag.

- To adjust two handles simultaneously, select the Fade Adjustment tool from the Timeline toolbox and position it between the two handles you want to adjust. Drag that segment up or down. The sound adjusts for the entire clip.

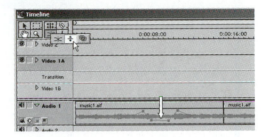

Naming Audio Tracks

Premiere provides the ability to incorporate up to 99 video tracks and 99 audio tracks on the Timeline. Working with so many tracks can make a production confusing. In order to reduce confusion, Premiere enables you to name both your audio and video clips. By default, your tracks are named Audio 1, Audio 2, Audio 3, and so on. To rename an audio track, you can choose Track Options (in the Timeline), or access the Track Options Dialog box. To rename a track, you would select it, click Name, enter a new name, and then click OK.

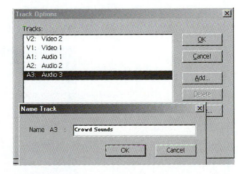

New audio tracks appear on the Timeline below existing tracks. Deleting a track removes all clip instances on the track, but does not affect the source clips stored in the Project window.

Cross-Fades

There will be times when your music does not play long enough for a production. One of the easiest solutions to this problem is to extend the music by cross-fading two pieces. As we discussed earlier, cross-fading causes the sound of one audio to fade out as another fades in. If cross-fading is cleverly done, the viewer never notices that two pieces are spliced together.

Cross-Fade Audio Clips

1. Continue working in the open project from the previous exercise. Play **music2.aif** to get a feel for the music. Drag **music2.aif** to Audio 1. The music extends to 00:00:10:22 on the Timeline. This is very short and ends too abruptly for the production. If necessary, click the triangle to the left of each track name to expand the audio tracks you want to cross-fade. Drag a second copy of **music2.aif** to Audio 2. Position the music to start at 00:00:08:13 on the Timeline.

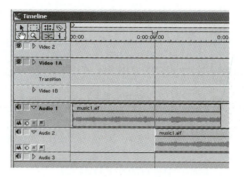

2. Select the Cross-Fade tool. Click **music2.aif** in Audio 1. This is the fade-out. Click **music2.aif** in Audio 2. This is the fade-in. Premiere automatically creates and adjusts volume handles on both clips.

3. Save this file in your **Work_In_Progress** folder as "bridge2.ppj". Render the file and listen to the result. The two files cross-fade and blend together nicely.

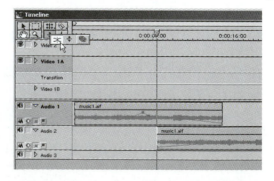

4. Delete all the audio from the Timeline. Leave the project open for the next exercise.

Audio Special Effects

As you know, music definitely adds to your production, but sometimes the music you select doesn't have the sound quality you need. Adobe Premiere includes a variety of audio effects (located in the Audio palette) designed to alter or enhance audio clip properties.

Here are some of the most useful audio enhancement effects:

- **Auto Pan**. This effect (located in the Channel folder) makes audio sound much richer by automatically panning or moving an audio track in a cyclical manner between the left and right audio channels. Several options are available in this area. Depth specifies how much of the audio clip is moved back and forth. Rate specifies how quickly the pan occurs.

- **Bass & Treble**. If your sound is a little too tinny, you can make basic adjustments to audio tone with this option. Bass (located in the EQ folder) specifies the amount of sound that is applied to the low frequencies of the audio clip, while Treble specifies the amount of sound that is applied to the high frequencies of the audio clip. Flat restores the clip to its original state without any adjustment.

- **Boost**. This option (located in the Dynamics folder) compensates for weaker sounds. It accomplishes this while leaving the loud sounds unchanged.

- **Chorus**. If your audio sounds a little flat, Chorus (located in the Effect folder) can add depth to your audio clip. This effect applies a copy of the sound and plays it at a sound level slightly higher than the original. Mix specifies the overall balance. A value of 50 is the default. Depth specifies the amount of delay. If you want a deeper chorus sound, try increasing this number. Regeneration applies an echo effect.

- **Compressor/Expander**. This option attempts to compensate for the differences between sounds. It is sometimes referred to as "dynamic range" and is located in the Dynamics folder. Use this effect to raise the level of a soft sound without affecting a louder sound in the same clip.

  This option is sometimes used to reduce noise. Ratio affects how quickly the change occurs. Threshold specifies where the compression begins or expansion ends. Adjusting the Gain setting affects the overall output level.

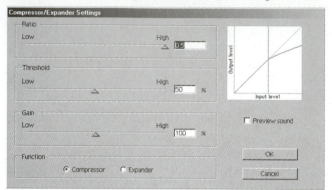

- **Echo**. This option (located in the Reverb & Delay folder) repeatedly plays the same sound during a defined period of time. This effect might create the effect of a ball bouncing up and down in a room with a lot of echo. Moving the Delay slider from Short to Long lengthens the delay between the original sound and its new echo effect.

- **Equalize**. This effect polishes the overall tonal quality of your audio. It is located in the EQ folder. It attempts to attune the highs and lows of the audio clip using presets that measure the frequency settings.

- **Fill Left and Fill Right**. These effects play the entire audio clip in the left or right stereo channel. They are located in the Channel folder.

- **Flanger**. This option can add interest to your audio by reversing audio signals. It accomplishes this effect in a similar manner to the Chorus effect. It sometimes adds an underwater effect to the audio. Additional options in this effect include Mix, Depth Change, and Rate. It is located in the Effect folder.

- **High Pass and Low Pass**. The High Pass effect (located in the Bandpass folder) removes low frequencies from an audio clip, and the Low Pass effect removes high frequencies. These effects are used to correct recording situations for which you might not otherwise be able to compensate. One such situation might be nearby power lines that generate a sound that affects the quality of the audio.

- **Multi-Effect**. This option can generate novel echo and chorus effects by allowing you to change audio rhythm and emphasis. The controls include Delay, Feedback, Mix, Modulation, Rate, and Waveform. It is located in the Effect folder.

- **Multitap Delay**. This effect (located in the Reverb & Delay folder) actually contains a number of different controls for managing delay effects in the sound-track. It can be useful for adding an extra touch to scary-sounding music. These controls are called taps. *Taps* apply a delay to an audio effect. Each tap can include a unique combination of delay, feedback, and stereo-channel balancing. Combine multiple taps to create elaborate new sound effects.

- **Noise Gate.** This option (located in the Dynamics folder) removes faint background noise during the quiet moments of an audio clip. Threshold is the control point at which the unwanted effect is triggered and removed. It is especially useful if important audio is cut off at the end of the track.

- **Notch/Hum Filter.** *Hum* is the sound created when you are shooting too close to audio cables or equipment that is improperly shielded or grounded. Use the Notch/Hum Filter effect to remove any annoying sound from an audio clip. It can be found in the Bandpass folder.

- **Pan.** This effect allows you to control how much of the music plays from either the left or right speaker. Use the slider to control how far to the left or right the sound plays. It is located in the Channel folder.

- **Parametric Equalization.** If you have a good ear for music, this is the effect for you. The Parametric Equalization effect (located in the EQ folder) allows precise isolation of frequency ranges. It enhances up to three different bands of the audio clip. Other controls in this effect area include Enable, Frequency, Bandwidth, and Boost/cut.

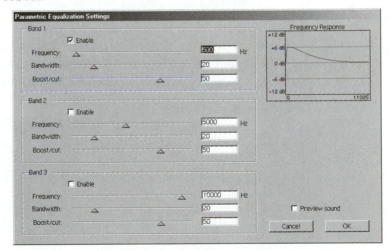

- **Reverb.** If you want to simulate the sound of a big auditorium, the Reverb effect can accomplish this for you. It can effectively simulate sound that is being produced in a large room. You can input the room size and then adjust the other settings accordingly. Reverb can be found in the Reverb & Delay folder.

- **Swap Left & Right**. This effect (located in the Channel folder) swaps the left and right channels of a clip imported as stereo. This effect can be useful during special effect sequences such as when a train moves through a tunnel.

Applying Effects

Unless you have access to an orchestra, chances are you will have to compromise with your musical selections. Music that you can use for free (or a very small fee) is referred to as "royalty-free" music. Royalty-free music is available from many sources. There are many excellent companies offering literally thousands of music clips. You can find these companies in the yellow pages or on the Internet.

Let's take a moment to mention copyright law and how it applies to music. No matter what type of project you work on, you must pay for the music you use (unless it is royalty-free music). This is mandated by law, which is designed to protect musicians. An artist writes music as a source of income, so using that music without the express permission of the artist is the equivalent of stealing. Most of the royalty-free music companies offer very attractive rates for smaller projects. Special promotions are often made available. Don't be afraid to ask about them.

Sweetening Music

There is a fine art to working with voice, sound effects, and music. In fact, entire books have been devoted to the subject. The process of enhancing or *sweetening* music involves the method of modifying bad music to make it better, and improving good music to make it excellent. Something you should keep in mind: if you can clearly hear the improvement, you've improved the music too much. Sweetening is a subtle process.

Adjust Audio Gain

1. Continue working in the open project from the previous exercise. Double-click **music3.aif** in the Project window. Play it to get a feel for the music, and then close the Clip window. Drag **music3.aif** to the Audio 1 track.

2. Select Window>Show Audio Effects, and then expand the Dynamics effect (click the triangle to the left of the word Dynamics). Drag the Compresssor/Expander filter onto **music3.aif**. The Effect Controls palette pops up (if it is not already open).

3. Click Setup in the Effect Controls palette. A dialog box appears. Set Ratio to .39, Threshold to 87%, Gain to 138%, and click the Preview Sound check box to hear your changes. When you are satisfied with the result, click OK.

4. Render the file and listen to the result.

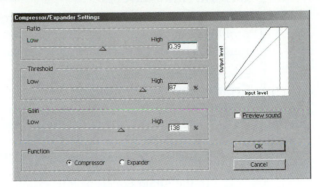

5. Take a moment to listen to the music as it sounded before and after the effect was applied. Select Edit>Undo Filter to return to the original sound. Render the file again, and listen to the result.

6. Let's adjust the gain another way — using the Audio Mixer. With the Timeline and clip active, click the trash can icon in the Effect Controls palette to clear the effects placed on **music3.aif**. When you are asked to confirm the delete, click Yes.

7. Select Audio Mixer from the Window menu. Click Automation Write in the first section, and then click the Play button.

8. Music begins to play. Raise and lower the audio fader bar to increase and decrease the volume of the music.

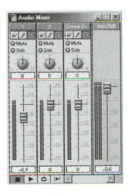

9. When you are finished, click the Stop button. Expand the Timeline and look at the audio. Zoom in to 2 seconds to closely view the result. Fine-tune the newest changes by moving the Audio 1 handles up (or down) until the music sounds just the way you want it.

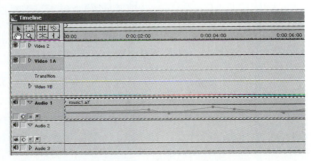

10. Delete the audio from the Timeline. Leave the project open for the next exercise.

Custom Audio Effects

Sometimes, no matter how hard you try, you can't find the right music. A solution to this problem is at hand. Premiere provides controls that allow you to completely alter existing music to create a new set of customized sounds.

Create New Audio Effects

1. Continue working in the open project from the previous exercise. Double-click **music1.aif** in the Project window, and then play it to get a feel for the music. Close the clip preview of **music1.aif**, and then drag **music1.aif** to Audio 1.

2. In the Audio Effects palette, expand the Effect folder, and drag Multi-Effect onto **music1.aif**. The Effect Controls palette pops up (if it is not already open).

3. Click Setup in the Effect Controls palette. A dialog box appears. Set Delay Time to 44.00, Delay Feedback to 60.00, Delay Mix to 70.00, Modulation Rate to 2.07, and Modulation Intensity to 100.00.

4. Click the Preview Sound check box to hear your changes. Click OK. Render the file and listen to all of the modifications.

5. With the Timeline active, click the trash can icon in the Effect Controls palette to clear the effects placed on **music1.aif**. Click Yes to confirm the delete.

6. In the Audio Effects palette, expand the Reverb & Delay folder. Drag Multitap Delay onto **music1.aif**.

7. Click Setup in the Effect Controls palette for Multitap Delay. A dialog box appears. Place a checkmark in Taps 1, 2, 3, and 4. Place a checkmark in the Cross boxes for Taps 1, 2, 3, and 4. Set Mix to 100% Effect, Time Signature to 4/2, and then click the Preview check box. Click OK. Render the file and listen to all of the modifications.

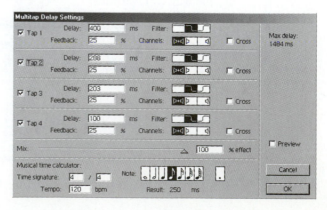

An equalizer, combined with careful selection of frequencies, can often remove unwanted sounds, such as the hum caused by power lines, or the sound of wind from an unprotected microphone used outdoors.

8. If you are using the Windows version of Premiere, select the TC EQ effect. Click the ON button to the left of the word JOYSTICK. Select Channels 2 and 3. Click Preview, and then click and hold on the joystick ball. Moving vertically adjusts the GAIN (volume) and moving horizontally selects the FREQ (frequency).

9. Save and close this file.

The possibilities for modification of audio tracks are virtually limitless. There are times when you will modify your audio tracks to make them sound like an exact reproduction of the original sound, and times when you will create a special effect. If you spend enough time testing different effects, you will eventually be recognized for your own personal style.

Audio track reminders:

- You can add or remove tracks at any time, except for the Video 1, Video 2, Transition, Audio 1, Audio 2, and Audio 3 tracks, which cannot be deleted.
- Two audio clips cannot overlap on the same track, so you must place each audio clip on a different audio track.
- When creating a cross-fade, the order in which you select the clips is not important.

Chapter Summary

In Chapter 5, you explored Premiere's audio controls. You learned about the importance of music and its ability to enhance a production. You produced an audio bridge and created a cross-fade.

You practiced ways to create new and unique sounds. You discovered many of Premiere's audio options and used these options to sweeten music. You then used the Audio Effects palette to create a set of new sounds.

Free-Form Project #1

Assignment

A local multimedia company is creating an educational product that showcases their ability to construct complex, DVD-based projects. The project will feature 24 lessons, each on a different subject.

To make it more compelling and interesting to potential clients, and to garner some community support, the creative team is gathering work from many content experts in the area. You were selected as one of those content experts.

Your assignment is to create a one-minute video that teaches the viewer how to do something. The subject can be anything that you know well enough to teach: gardening, fishing, riding a bike, repairing a screen door, teaching a trick to your pet dog, preparing homemade bread, or climbing a ladder. As long as you can fit the content in the allotted time, the choice is yours.

Applying Your Skills

Create the training video by applying the following skills:

- Create a storyboard.
- Develop a shot list.
- Decide upon or prepare a location.
- Shoot the video.
- Capture the video.
- Assemble the video clips.
- Use the Title Designer window to superimpose instructions over the scenes.
- Add a split-screen sequence with content relative to the lesson.
- Create a QuickTime movie.

Specifications

Complete your project as follows:

- Finished length: 1 minute.
- At least 12 video shots.
- Easy-to-read instructions appearing where necessary.
- Transitions placed on all clips.
- Color added to transitions as needed.
- One split-screen sequence.

Included Files

No files are included with this assignment. It's up to you to collect and capture the video. Caution: any information collected from the World Wide Web, CDs, or DVDs may be copyrighted information. Be certain to properly reference all of your sources.

Publisher's Comments

Educational video is widely used — videographers experienced in this specialty area are in high demand. In this assignment, you'll get a feel for what's important and what's not — there's no room for extraneous video, special effects, or drawn-out transitions. Everything must be compact, concise, and to the point. Furthermore, since you will not be using audio, you must use the Title Designer window to create succinct, easy-to-read instructions for each scene.

One minute is not much time for an instructional video. Be sure to choose a topic that can be fully covered in that short amount of time.

Review #1

Chapters 1 through 5

In the first five chapters of the book, you learned the importance of up-front planning when making movies with Premiere, and how visualization and story-boarding are critical factors in the planning process. You discovered how to gather together the building blocks of a movie — video, audio, and still image clips — and how to place them on the Timeline. You experimented with many of the tools you can use to assemble, trim, and place clips on the Timeline, and discovered many ways to view your clips in the Monitor, Source, and Program windows. You explored the use of transitions, and found they add a professional quality to your movies that is impossible to achieve with simple straight cuts. And finally, you learned the value of audio in a movie, and found how audio clips are used to set the mood of the movie and add depth that would not otherwise be possible. Through this series of discussions, exercises, and projects you should:

- Be familiar with making storyboards and using visualization to plan and outline your production.

- Be able to locate and use the various palettes, windows, screens, and dialog boxes used during movie development.

- Know how to collect the footage required for your movie and how to place that footage in a new Premiere project.

- Understand how to edit your movie clips after they have been placed on the Timeline using Single View and Dual View editing modes, and rolling and ripple edits.

- Be capable of applying any number of transitions to a movie, and know how to create your own custom transitions.

- Be comfortable analyzing and editing audio clips and applying audio to a movie.

- Know how to apply special effects to a movie and how to create your own custom effects.

6 Creating Titles

Chapter Objectives:

Titles provide a powerful addition to your visual toolbox. They can be used to identify, entertain, and inform. Learning to create and apply animated titles is the next step in making a professional presentation. The Title Designer is a powerful Premiere feature that provides control over type objects, font selection, rolling titles, and more. In this chapter, you will:

- Learn the components of the Title Designer window.

- Discover how to add titles directly into the Project window.

- Become familiar with the difference between static and rolling/crawling titles, and how to use each.

- Learn the basic shapes available in the Title Designer window.

- Learn how to select color for your titles.

- Explore and become familiar with the many attributes of a title such as font, kerning, leading, baseline, positioning, and fill.

- Find out about type styles and families and which ones are most effective for titles.

Projects to be Completed:

- The Monkey Movie (A)

- **Making Spaghetti (B)**

- The Gold Rush (C)

- Central Coast Surfing (D)

Creating Titles

Titles are critical components in video productions. Almost all of today's movies start with titles — the names of the actors, producer, and director. When the movie ends, we see the credits. Besides repeating the names of the actors and director, credits often offer us insight into the people and logistics behind the scenes — special effects artists, costume designers, set locations, musicians, stunt people, and wardrobe personnel, to name a few.

Titles and Graphics

In addition to titles, simple graphics — rectangles, ovals, lines, and polygons — are often used to isolate titles and draw the viewer's attention to specific elements. A good example might be placing a newscaster's name in a rectangle that fades into the scene. Using superimposition techniques with Premiere's graphic and text tools make it easy to achieve very professional results when creating titles.

Creating Titles and Graphics

In Premiere, titles (and graphics) are created in the Title Designer window. To create a new title or graphic, you can select File>New>Title. Alternatively, you can click the Create Item icon at the bottom of the Project window and select Title from the pop-up menu.

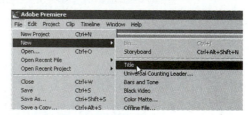

Text and graphic objects created in the Title Designer window are vector graphics — the same as those created with Macromedia Flash, Adobe Illustrator, Macromedia FreeHand, and other illustration programs. You can also create graphics and text elements in those applications and import them directly into your Premiere productions.

Titles are production components, the same as any other clip or still, so you must save them, preferably in the same folder as the rest of the project's assets. In the following example, we named the title surfcc.prtl.

Once you create a title, you can use it in your project as you would any source clip, by editing it into your video program using cuts and transitions, or by superimposing it over clips. You can also use the Title Designer window Options menu to specify the size of the title area and the background color.

Title Designer Window

Let's take a brief tour of the Title Designer window, beginning with the toolbox found in the upper-left corner. In it, you will find all the tools needed to position elements, create textual content, and draw basic shapes.

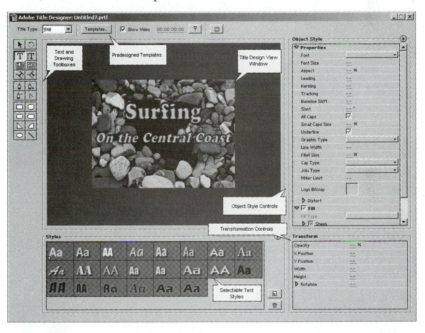

The Title Designer window provides a workspace for creating titles, credits, and graphics.

Positioning Tools

You can use these tools to move the elements in a title:

- **Selection Tool.** The default tool (the straight black arrow) is the Selection tool. It is used to select and move text and graphic objects.

- **Rotation Tool.** Use this tool (the circular arrow) to rotate a block of text to any angle.

Text Tools

Six of the tools on the Title Designer window are used to create text elements:

- **Text Tools.** These tools (the top four) are used to create static (non-rolling) text elements. Type can be vertically or horizontally oriented. Once text is on the drawing area, you have full control over its attributes, including color, font, size, and a host of others.
- **Path Text Tools.** These are pen-type tools (the bottom two), used to draw a path for text. When the path is complete, the title that you type follows the path.

Pen Tools

Pen tools are used for drawing and modifying free-form shapes.

You can use these tools to create fairly complex shapes. Realize, however, that Premiere isn't meant to be a drawing program. If you need to develop a background or a very complex graphic, consider using Adobe Illustrator or Macromedia FreeHand to create the object and then import it into your Premiere project.

Shape Tools

The shape tools are used to draw primitive shapes. The basic shape tools allow you to draw ovals and rectangles by clicking and dragging the tools.

The shape tools.

Each of the tool icons has two parts: select the right side of the icon when you want the tool to create solid or filled shapes; select the left side of the icon when you want the shapes to be hollow, displaying a line, but no fill. If you want to draw a perfect circle or square, hold down the Shift key while drawing the shape.

Selecting the Rectangle shape tool from the Shape menu created this shape.

If you're working on a Windows system with file extensions enabled (visible), the .prtl suffix appears automatically. Windows uses these suffixes to connect data files with their native applications. If you're working on a Macintosh, you don't need to use extensions, but we recommend that you do so. Most of today's editing environments are cross-platform, and the extensions ensure compatibility between the Macintosh and Windows computer workstations.

Next, the Object Style dialog box was used to create a filled linear gradient. The Object Style dialog box is located on the right side of the Title Designer window.

The Object Style dialog box is used to modify the characteristics of the objects (including text) that you place in your title. Several modifications are available as can be seen above. The Object Style selections change, depending on what type of object you are modifying.

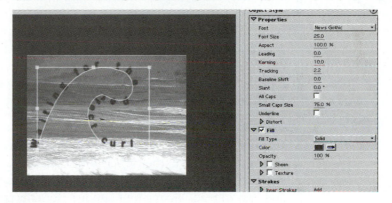

Title Attributes

Premiere enables you to control many attributes of your titles. You can change typefaces, control the size and color of text, add gradients and drop shadows, and use the object as you would any other clip.

Font Selection and Type Size

You can use any font on your system for titles. To set the font, you can simply select the copy you want to change, and select Font from the Object Style dialog box.

Using a slider or entering a value directly into a value box controls type size and many other attributes. To use a slider, click and hold on a value, then slide the mouse pointer back and forth to change the value. Try to avoid using very small type because it's difficult to read.

Safe Areas

Safe areas are zones defined by dotted rectangles displayed in the drawing area. The outside rectangle is the *Safe Action margin*, where objects are still visible to the viewer. The inside, or *Safe Title margin*, defines the maximum region where type can be displayed in the final production. To access the Safe Title and Safe Action margins, Control/right-click on the Title Designer window. Keeping your text and graphics within the indicated areas ensures that no part of the image is cut off when viewed on a television screen.

Using Text Effectively

As an exercise, watch television for a few minutes and record your observations regarding the fonts and spacing used for titles and credits.

Your first consideration when working with text is the choice of font, also known as the typeface. A font is a complete set of all uppercase and lowercase characters, numerals, and symbols that share a common style, weight, and width. A family of fonts consists of characters that share common elements and styles. Arial, for example, has several variations ranging from boldface to narrow, but all fonts in the Arial family can be used together. A type style is a variation of an individual font in a font family. Common styles are bold, italic, and regular (the actual name of a style may vary from family to family).

Legibility

The font you choose can have a major impact on how successfully your titles communicate your message to the viewer. Your titles and credits are only visible for a short period, and they are often moving across the screen. It is important to choose fonts that are clear and easy to read. Mixing font families (for effect) is not recommended unless, for one reason or another, you are intentionally trying to make your titles look confusing.

Kerning

Kerning is the process of removing (or sometimes adding) small bits of space between letters. For example, consider the abbreviation for Washington (Wa., or WA). Without kerning, the "W" appears to be spaced too far from the "A" and the "a". Other combinations that can require adjustment are To, Ty, Ta, Tu, and We, among others.

Tracking is the process of distributing an equal amount of space across an entire group of characters. Kerning and tracking are often used in combination.

Leading

While kerning represents the spacing between letters, *leading* (rhymes with sledding) refers to the spacing between lines of text. Leading is measured between the invisible baseline of a line and the baseline of the following line. Leading is typically set to approximately 120%. For example, 20-pt. text would use 24-pt. leading.

Text Attributes

Unless you are trying to create a special effect, highly embellished or "old world" fonts should not be used in titles. They are not clear enough to be read quickly (particularly when titles are moving). Sans serif fonts (fonts without the little lines and curls) are good choices for clear communication.

Letter spacing is controlled with the Tracking tool, which appears in the Object Style dialog box under Properties.

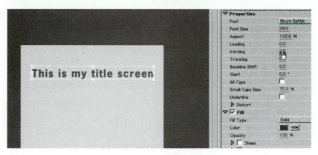

To track a title, click the Text tool inside the word or phrase to select it. Once it's selected, simply click the appropriate icon to increase or decrease the letter spacing. Two examples of identical titles using different tracking values are shown below.

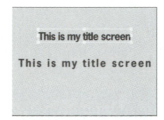

To adjust spacing between two letters (kerning), click the Text tool between the letters you want to kern, and then adjust the kerning value to produce the desired effect.

Alignment and Orientation

Text can be centered vertically, horizontally, or both horizontally and vertically using the Title>Position pop-up menu. Selecting Lower Third from the menu centers the text over the bottom third of the Title Designer window.

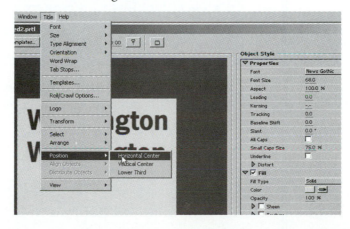

Examine a Title

1. Launch Premiere. The New Project dialog box appears. (If Premiere is already running, select File>New Project.) Select Multimedia QuickTime Video as the Default, and then click the Custom button. Click Next in the Settings dialog box to open the Video Settings. Set the Frame Size to H: 240 and V: 180. Set the Frame Rate to 15 frames per second, and then click OK. The program finishes loading. A set of new Project windows is created. Save the file as "pelbay.ppj" in your **Work_In_Progress** folder.

2. From the File menu, select Import>File. When the dialog box appears, select **Pelbay>pelbay.mov** from the **RF_Premiere** folder, and then click Choose/Open.

3. Drag **pelbay.mov** to Video 1A in the Timeline. Press Return/Enter to preview the movie.

4. From the File menu, select Import>File. When the dialog box appears, select **Pelbay>bayt.prtl** from the **RF_Premiere** folder. Drag **bayt.prtl** to the Video 2 track, and position it at 00:00.

All titles must be placed on track Video 2 or a higher numbered track. Placing a title on Video 1A or Video 1B causes incorrect results.

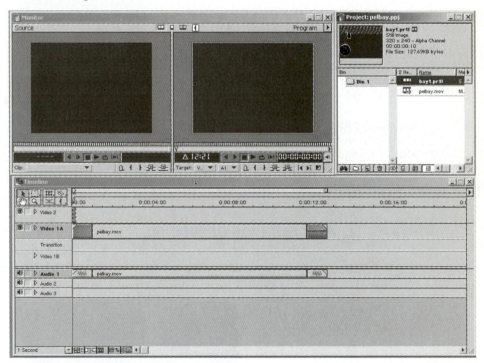

5. Make sure the work area bar is extended to the end of the production so you can view the entire production as you create it.

6. Notice that the title track is too short. Using the Selection tool, drag the right end of the title clip to the right until it is the same length as the movie. Press Return/Enter to render the production and see how it looks. Save the file when the rendering is complete.

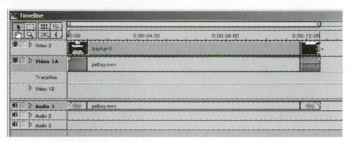

7. Double-click **bayt.ptrl** in the Timeline window. There may be a change in the predefined title page size, so Premiere may ask you to convert the title's settings. Click Yes when prompted. The Title Designer window appears. Be sure the Selection tool is active. Click the Show Video button until a checkmark appears. Set the Title Type to Roll.

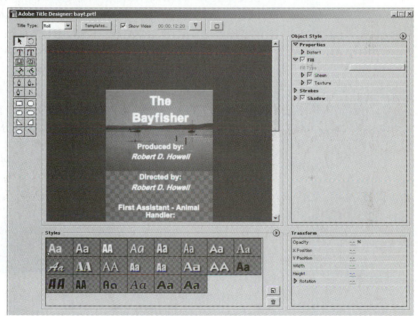

8. The video image in the background is the same frame as the edit line marker when you opened the Title Designer window. Drag the time (or enter the value) to set the frame at 00:12:20.

9. By dragging the scroll bar at the right side of the Title view window, you can see the position of the title as the movie progresses. Drag the scroll bar to the bottom. This view shows how the title looks at the last frame of the movie.

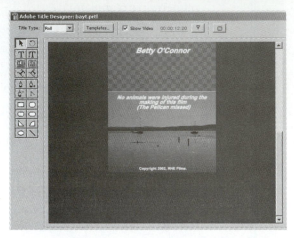

10. Select Title>View>Safe Title Margin (if it is not already visible). A box appears, indicating that the text is outside the Safe Title margin. There is a good chance that the title would be partially cut off when viewed on a television screen (even though it looks fine on a computer monitor).

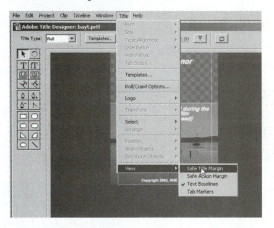

11. Move the scroll bar up and down to see the entire rolling title. Notice the spacing between lines. Leading adjustments affect the entire text block, so each line must be adjusted individually. Scroll to the top third of the title. Select the Text tool. Click on the first occurrence of Robert Howell. There are several attributes of this text that appear in the Object Style dialog box.

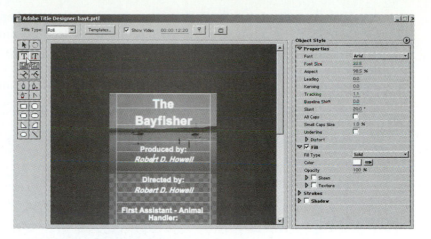

The selected Font is Arial, the Font Size is 22.5 (22.0 on a Macintosh), the Tracking is set to 1.1 (1.0 on a Macintosh), the Slant is set to 20.0 degrees, and the Fill is turned on (checked) using Solid/White as the Fill Color with an Opacity of 100%.

12. Adjust each of the controls in the Object Properties menu to see their effects on the lettering. When you are finished, reset the values to match the image above. Do not save the title at any time. If you do, you will overwrite the original title and lose the current values.

13. Let's look at two more important settings and then you can create your own rolling title. Select Title>Roll/Crawl Options. A dialog box appears.

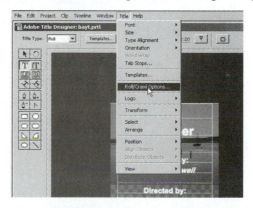

14. Enter the following in the Roll/Crawl Options dialog box: Pre-Roll set to 30, Ease-In set to 0, Ease-Out set to 0, Post-Roll set to 115, and then click OK (do not check the Start Off Screen or End Off Screen boxes).

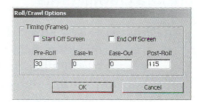

15. From the Title menu, select Position, and then select the positioning option you want to use. Selecting a position affects the entire title block. If you select Vertical Center, the entire block of text is centered over the video image. Doing this at the end of the clip would not make any sense. Try all three options and immediately undo each by selecting Edit>Undo Title Change before testing the next option.

16. Close the entire project when you are finished experimenting.

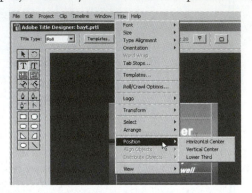

This project was designed for viewing on a computer screen; if it were destined for television, all text would have to be within the Safe Title margin.

Roll/Crawl Options

The Roll/Crawl Options menu offers several possibilities on a frame-by-frame basis:

- **Start/End Off Screen**. When this option is selected, the titles begin or end off screen.
- **Pre-Roll**. This setting determines how many frames are displayed before the title begins rolling.
- **Ease-In.** This option controls how many frames are used to accelerate the rolling title to maximum speed.
- **Ease-Out.** This setting controls how many frames are used to decelerate the rolling effect at the end of the title sequence.
- **Post-Roll.** This option determines the frame where the title completes its rolling effect.

Adjusting any of these values has an effect on how fast the title scrolls up the screen. If Pre-Roll and Post-Roll are set to high values, the entire title roll must happen between the selected Pre-Roll and Post-Roll frames.

Create a Crawling Title

1. Select File>New Project. If prompted, do not save the current project. Accept the default settings for the new project. Select File>Import>File. When the dialog box appears, select **Pelbay>pelbay.mov** from the **RF_Premiere** folder, and then click Open. Drag **pelbay.mov** to the Video 1A track, and position it at 00:00. Be sure the yellow work area end pointer is positioned at the end of **pelbay.mov**.

You should remember that all television sets have slightly different Safe Action margins (often because of the age of the television). It's wise to stay well within the safe area display lines.

2. Select File>New>Title. When the Title Designer window appears, select Crawl from the Title Type pop-up menu, and make sure the Show Video check box is selected.

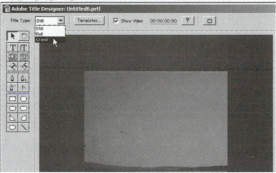

3. Select the Text tool from the toolbox. Click-hold and drag a text box across the image about 2/3 of the way down. Make sure the box is wider than the image. In the Object Style dialog box, set the Font to News Gothic, Size to 30.0, check the Fill box.

4. Click the small square to the left of the eyedropper to open the Color Picker. In the Color Picker, set the Color to Red 255, Green 255, and Blue 255. Click OK in the Color Picker dialog box.

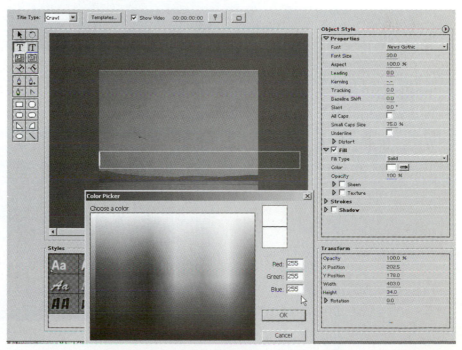

5. Select Title>Roll/Crawl Options. Click Start Off Screen and End Off Screen, and then click OK.

6. With the Text tool selected, click inside the text box you created and enter the following (without the quotes): "— Flash! Fish Health News has just been informed that the Pelicans are hungry again. Use caution when swimming near the surface! —"

   Don't be concerned if the text does not fit in the box; we will fix that shortly.

7. Choose the Pointer tool and stretch the right side of the text box to the right until all of the text fits on a single line. If you drag the box too far, simply drag the edge of the box back to the left (this may take a little practice).

8. Drag the horizontal scroll bar, found under the image, all the way to the left. Use the Pointer tool to position the beginning of the text just inside the lower-left corner of the video image.

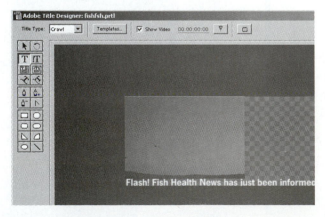

9. Select File>Save As and save the file as "fishfsh.prtl" in your **Work_In_Progress** folder.

10. Close the Title Designer window. The **fishfsh.prtl** file appears in the Project window. Drag it to the Video 2 track. Drag the right end of the clip until it aligns exactly with the right end of **pelbay.mov**. Press the Return/Enter key to render the movie preview. Save the project as "fishfsh.ppj" in your **Work_In_Progress** folder.

11. Leave this project open for the next exercise.

Importing Titles from External Applications

Many videographers use external applications to create titles, feeling that programs such as Adobe Illustrator, Macromedia FreeHand, and Macromedia Flash are better suited to producing high-end textual and graphical effects.

Some programs, such as Adobe After Effects and Adobe Dimensions, can generate a series of numbered sequences of still images. These files start as individually saved files. Once they are imported to Premiere, they are converted into a numbered sequence. You can choose to import individual still images or convert a numbered sequence of still images into a single animation as you import. If you create 30 still images, you will have 1 second of video because video runs at 30 frames per second. It's a lot of work to create this sort of special effect, but well worth the effort.

When you import an individual still image, it is assigned the duration specified in the Edit>Preferences>General and Still Image dialog box. You can change the duration of a still image after you import it. In the Still Image section of the dialog box, you can specify the number of frames you want as the default duration for a still image. The projects in this book were set at 15 frames per second. The default of 15 frames per second at 150 frames equals 10 seconds of footage.

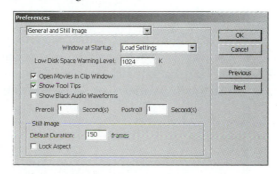

You can also change the speed or duration of an animated sequence once it is on the Timeline. To change the duration of a still image you have already imported and placed, you can select the clip and choose Clip>Duration. Then you can enter the new duration and click OK. You can see the extended time of the clip on the Timeline.

By default, Premiere attempts to change the size and proportions of your still image to match the current project. This can cause some very unexpected results. If you know the final project will be 240 × 180 pixels, create the numbered stills at the same size. This is particularly important if there is type involved.

To lock the size or aspect ratios of still images before you import them, you can choose Edit>Preferences>General and Still Image. You would select Lock Aspect to preserve the proportions of a still image in Premiere. When you import a still image that has a different size than the project, Premiere resizes the image to fit, whether you want it to or not. Lock Aspect Ratio will still retain the proportions. Remember to be careful. Don't resize images unless it is absolutely necessary to do so.

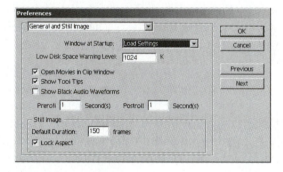

Importing Images to Create a Sequence

Let's take a moment to discuss animation. An animation is different from live-action video because it is "synthetically generated." Let us explain that term: suppose you want to create a battle sequence with the good guys and the bad guys fighting with light sabers. You can't exactly go to the local mall and buy "real" light sabers, but you can create their appearance. You would start by slowly creating and saving a series of still images. These stills would then be imported into Premiere where they would be reassembled into one complete sequence — an animation.

As mentioned earlier, some programs, such as Adobe After Effects and Adobe Dimensions, can generate a series of numbered sequences of still images. A still-image sequence cannot include layers, so you must flatten images (in Photoshop, for example) that are included as part of the new animation.

When importing numbered stills, there are different rules for Macintosh and Windows users. In Windows, begin the process by creating a unique directory to hold each of your numbered sequences. As you create your numbered files, make sure each still-image file name has the correct file extension, and ensure all file names in the sequence show the same number of characters at the end of the file name — for example, file000.bmp, file001.bmp, and so on. To create the animation, you would choose File>Import>File. You would then locate and select the first numbered file in the sequence, select Numbered Stills, and then click Open. Premiere would then create the sequence with the information provided.

The rules are similar for Macintosh users. You would create a unique folder for each of your numbered sequences, making sure all file names in the sequence have the same name. Then you would add the same number of digits — for example, File000.tif, File001.tif. If your software does not add an extension, you should do so; it makes file identification easier. Then you would choose File>Import>File, locate and select the first numbered file in the sequence, select Numbered Stills, and click Open. Premiere would then assemble the animation based on your numbered stills.

Title Opacity and Fade Controls

Being able to control the opacity of titles is an important technique and commonly used in contemporary video production. Some excellent examples of transparent titles and graphics can be seen in professional sports footage — names, statistics, colored boxes, rules, and other graphics are often defined as slightly transparent. This transparency enables the viewer to see the information while at the same time being able to view the action and images in the background.

Exercise Setup

As you will see in the following exercise, the title graphic of the video starts and ends rather abruptly. What we want to achieve is a smoother, more professional start. We will accomplish this by having the graphic ease in and ease out. This is referred to as a "fade-in" and "fade-out" effect. Premiere has built-in controls for managing the opacity of the graphic during fades.

Set the Opacity for Titles

1. Continue working in the open project from the previous exercise. Expand Video 2 by clicking the triangle at the left of the track name. It expands to show the opacity levels for **fishfsh.ptrl.**

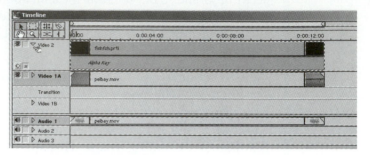

2. You should see a thin red line at the top of this window (the rubberband). This shows the title at 100% opacity. At the far left of the red line, notice a red handle.

3. Move the cursor slightly to the right of this handle (00:01:00), and then click on the red line. A second handle appears.

4. Position the cursor over the far-left handle, and drag the handle to the bottom of the window. This becomes the fade-in for the title.

5. Slightly move the cursor in from the right (00:11:00) and click again on the red line. A fourth handle appears.

6. Position the cursor over the far-right handle, and drag this handle to the bottom of the window. This becomes the fade-out for the title.

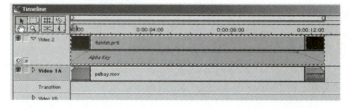

7. Save your project and render this production. You should see your title fade in and fade out on top of the video background. Save this project in your **Work_In_Progress** folder, and then close Premiere.

Chapter Summary

In Chapter 6, you learned how to create and save movie titles. You became familiar with how to add and merge titles with video clips. You learned about text spacing and how to adjust it. You discovered how to create rolling and crawling titles and the difference between them. Finally, you learned how to soften the effect of a title using fade in and fade out, and the transparency rubberband.

Complete Project B: Making Spaghetti

7 *Superimposing Clips and Stills*

Chapter Objectives:

Superimposition offers a special-effects editor a virtually unlimited variety of effects that can be applied to movies. This chapter presents two frequently used methods for creating superimposition in Premiere. You will also learn about Chroma key and Alpha matte techniques that create the appearance of animation in still images, and allow you to develop scenes that could not possibly be shot "in camera." In this chapter, you will:

- Discover how tracks Video 2 through Video 97 work the same as layers in other programs.

- Learn how to use blue screening to put background footage behind other objects after the live footage has been shot.

- Become familiar with Chroma keys to replace one background with another.

- Learn how to work with transparency and the opacity of clips created in other programs.

- Study many different key types, including non-red, luminance, and RGB difference.

- Become familiar with mattes, where one clip hides or exposes clips on Tracks 1A and 1B.

- Review how to change editing modes from A/B to Single-Track and how to eliminate the Preferences file on startup.

- Learn to use and manipulate alpha channels.

- Gain experience using several different types of transitions.

Projects to be Completed:

- The Monkey Movie (A)

- Making Spaghetti (B)

- The Gold Rush (C)

- Central Coast Surfing (D)

Superimposing Clips and Stills

While it would be nice to have unlimited budget and be able to shoot every scene on location — no matter how exotic or logistically difficult the locale might be — there are certain scenes that are impossible to shoot. Scenes involving great danger to the actors or scenes that don't reflect reality are two such situations. Regardless of how much money you have to spend, there are times when you must create the illusion you require in a particular scene.

The technique of *superimposition* allows you to stack multiple clips, stills, and graphics. The process works much the same as layers in Adobe Photoshop, Adobe Illustrator, Macromedia FreeHand, and Macromedia Flash. The difference is that instead of using layers, you combine footage and stills on tracks that exist above Tracks 1A and 1B (both numerically and physically).

Among the techniques used to create these illusions of reality is blue screening. Many people have heard about this technique, including many who are not involved in the film industry. *Blue (or green) screening* is a technique that places an actor, car, plane, house, or action figure in front of a blue (or green) screen. Once the footage with the actor (or object) is shot, the director can drop out the blue background and replace it with the background footage of his choice. When the two are rendered together, it looks as if the two clips were shot at the same time.

The blue (or green) background is used for a good reason — it's a solid color that's easy to select and isolate. This time-honored technique is known as "using a Chroma key." You can achieve the effect fairly easily in Premiere by superimposing clips or imposing specific portions of one clip onto another.

The Greek word *chroma* means color, and a *Chroma key* is actually another term for color substitution. A Chroma key is the process that substitutes one color, such as the blue (or green) of a background, and replaces it with something else — such as another clip. It's a great way to place someone in a room that's halfway around the world without sending the entire crew. One person could shoot the footage in India, for example, and then others could use it as a backdrop for a scene they're shooting in Los Angeles, Tampa, or Chicago. For all intents and purposes, the final footage shows the stateside actor sitting in the palace of a Pasha in 18th Century India.

Star Wars serves as an excellent example of high-powered chroma-key effects. At an intellectual level, we all know those scenes weren't really filmed in space, but it certainly looked as though they were. Using models, actors, interior sets, and Chroma keys, the director, George Lucas, took us into the void and provided us with a nice, cozy seat from which to view the action. Watch old movies, car chase scenes, war movies, or an Alfred Hitchcock classic. Look closely, and you'll see the effects used to create virtual reality where the "real" scene doesn't actually exist.

Before 1970, blue screening wasn't nearly as sophisticated as it is today. Watch a few old movies or television programs and you'll probably be able to see discrepancies between foreground action and background footage. Watch the "Long, Long Trailer," directed by Vincente Minelli, starring Lucille Ball and Desi Arnez, to see the cast chatting in the car as the California countryside whizzes by at a breathtaking speed of 25 miles per hour.

Transparency

Transparency is a term that describes the ability to see through one object to another below it. The transparency of an object (footage or still) is defined as *opacity*.

The easiest way to describe transparency is to imagine a photograph and a piece of black cardboard. If you cover part of the photograph with the cardboard, it would naturally hide that portion of the photo. The cardboard would have an opacity value of 100% (completely opaque). Nothing behind it could show through. Place clear glass (with an opacity of 0%) on top of the photograph, and it wouldn't be hidden at all.

Premiere's transparency commands allow you to define a clip's transparency values. The top clip's opacity determines how much of the underlying video shows through. At 0% opacity, the top image is completely transparent; at 100% opacity, the top image is completely opaque, having no transparency at all.

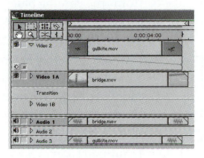

Transparency Keys

You can make clips transparent by using keys. A *key* is a tool that locates pixels of a specific brightness or color and then transforms those pixels. The pixels become transparent or semitransparent, depending on the type of key you select. This process of applying a key to change certain pixels' transparency is called "keying" or "keying out" the color. The most popular type of key is the Chroma key. Chroma keys generally use ranges of blue or green to create the transparency effect. (You'll learn more about this in the Key Types section of this chapter.) Keys can also use the clip's alpha channel to create the transparency effect.

Once a clip has been placed on Video 2, the Transparency Settings dialog box becomes available for use. When Transparency is first selected, the default Key type is set to None. At this point, no part of the superimposed image is keyed out.

Clip transparency is activated after the clip is placed in a superimposition track. Each new project, by default, includes one superimposition track — Video 2. You can, however, add as many as 97 superimposition tracks.

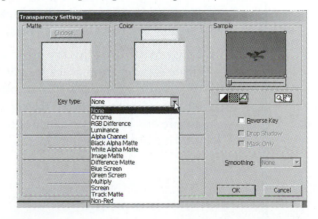

The different types of keys available in the Key type menu are shown below:

- **Chroma Key.** This key is used to replace a color of your choice with an image or video clip. Chroma keys are difficult to set up properly, so Premiere provides a number of controllable settings that can be used to create the best possible key effect. These include Similarity, Blend, Threshold, Cutoff, and Smoothing. Chroma keys work because they blend similar colors. You will learn more about this topic in Chapter 8.

- **RGB Difference Key.** This key is very similar to the Chroma key — one color is selected and keyed or replaced with an image. You select a range of color, but you do not blend or adjust transparency in grays. It is best used with day shots because it requires bright conditions to work correctly.

- **Blue Screen and Green Screen Keys.** These keys are used to create transparencies from true chroma blue or green. (True chroma blue is a blue color that was specially created for this purpose.) Television studios frequently use this type of screen for weather segments. The weather forecaster is placed in front of a green wall and weather maps are superimposed on the wall while the information is read.

- **Non-Red Key.** This key is similar to the Blue and Green Screen keys, but it fine-tunes images to a greater degree. Images can be softened so they blend better into the background. This key also allows you to superimpose two video clips on top of the base image.

- **Luminance Key.** This key creates transparency for darker values in an image while leaving the brighter areas opaque. This key only works on images that have extremely dark or light colors.

- **Multiply and Screen Keys.** These keys create effects by using the underlying image as a map to determine what part(s) of the keyed image to make transparent. The Multiply key creates such an effect based on the lightest areas of the underlying image. The Screen key bases its effect on the darkest areas of the underlying image.

- **Alpha Channel Key.** This key is the fourth channel in an RGB image or video clip. The key defines the parts of the image that are transparent or semi-transparent. It partially or completely masks portions of the image. When it is electronically removed, another image is revealed, replacing the wholly or partially masked portions.

- **Black Alpha Matte and White Alpha Matte Keys.** Similar in process to an Alpha Channel key, these keys use a black or white channel to create the mask effect.

- **Image Matte Key.** This key uses a still image or matte to define the area and create the transparency for the portions of the clip that you want to remove. White areas remain intact while black areas become fully transparent to allow the second image to appear as the superimposition. For example, we could create a picture of a keyhole, and then allow you to look through it to see the action that is taking place inside the room.

- **Difference Matte Key.** This key creates an effect by combining two images with similar-looking color pixels. The matching areas are then eliminated. When the Reverse button is selected, a static background can be keyed out to add the effect to the foreground picture.

- **Track Matte Key.** This matte is used to create a vignette effect on a video clip. A *vignette* is a frame around a picture. It can be soft-edged, like an old-time picture, or hard-edged for a more modern look. The clip is surrounded by an opaque frame while it plays. This effect is frequently used because it can move or travel with the video shot. Think of the spy movies in the 1960s where the black background shot (usually a gun or another spy) travels with the secret agent.

Additional Transparency Options

These tools, which provide additional options for controlling transparency, are found under the Sample image on the right side of the Transparency Settings dialog box. The first group is represented by icons rather than a name on a menu. The last four are found as check boxes or sliders, all in the right column of the same dialog box.

- **Color Key-Out Tool.** This tool places a black or white background behind the keyed-out image. Click on the button to toggle between black and white.

- **Transparency Tool.** This tool displays a checkerboard transparency pattern to help you view transparency in areas that may be difficult to see against a solid background or against the actual underlying image. If necessary, you can click to reverse the checkerboard pattern.

- **Underlying Image Tool.** This useful tool displays the actual underlying image in your project. It slows down the render when you set the Transparency slider under the Sample box.

- **Zoom and Hand Tools.** These tools are used to zoom in to or zoom out of the image in the Sample area. To zoom in, you would select the Zoom tool, and then click an area of the image. If you click again, you increase the zoom. To zoom out, you would select the Zoom tool, hold down the Option/Alt key, and click the image. To view other areas of the image at the same zoom level, you would select the Hand tool and drag the image.

- **Collapse Tool.** This tool — available only in the Macintosh version of Premiere — moves the image to the Program view in the Monitor window.

- **Reverse Key Check Box.** This check box allows certain transparent and opaque areas to be reversed. (It is only available for some keys.)

- **Drop Shadow Check Box.** This check box allows you to add a 50% gray/50% opaque shadow to opaque areas. (It, too, is available only for certain keys.) The new shadow is inserted four pixels below and to the right of any adjoining opaque region. Drop Shadow is most effective with titles or simple graphics.

- **Mask Only Check Box.** This check box is used to produce a special effect that displays only the alpha channel matte view of the clip. It becomes available only when certain keys are selected.

- **Transparency Slider.** When you drag this slider beneath the Sample box, you can sample or preview transparency settings for the clip.

Keying

We know that Premiere provides 14 keys for creating various transparency effects. You can use:

- Color-based keys for superimposing.

- Brightness keys for adding texture or special effects.

- Alpha channel keys for clips or images already containing their own alpha channel.

- Matte keys for adding traveling mattes and other creative superimpositions.

Your selection depends on the kind of lighting conditions you encounter during a production, or the special effect you are attempting to create.

Chroma Keys

Chroma keys are used to replace a color that you choose for an image or video clip. Chroma keys are best used when you shoot a scene against a screen that contains a range of one color, such as a shadowy blue or green. As we briefly discussed, a popular use of the Chroma key is the nightly weather report. The weather reporter looks as if she is standing in front of a large weather map. In reality, the background is a large blue or green backdrop. This color is electronically removed and another image, such as a map, is substituted. The most important aspect of lighting the Chroma key set is even background illumination. The background must be carefully lighted to create soft shadows. A key that has not been properly set creates a distracting halo effect around the weather reporter.

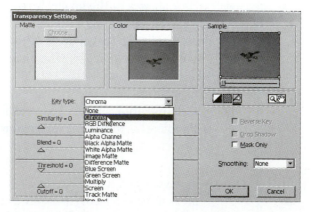

As noted above, Chroma keys blend similar colors. Premiere has a number of different settings that can be altered to create the best possible key effect:

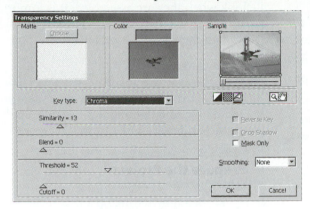

- **Similarity.** The Similarity setting looks for similar color values. For instance, Similarity looks for a range of blues that can be made transparent.

- **Blend.** The Blend setting mixes two clips that are superimposed on top of each other. The higher the value, the more the underlying clip shows through.

- **Threshold.** This setting controls the shadows in the clip. A higher value allows some clips to seamlessly slip into the background image.

- **Cutoff.** The Cutoff setting controls the shadow areas. Dragging to the right darkens the shadows of your clip. Don't drag beyond the level that is set for Threshold, since doing so turns the pixels gray.

- **Smoothing.** The area between the transparent and opaque regions can be smoothed with this setting. Smoothing finds the similarities in the pixels to produce softer edges. Choose None to produce sharp edges with no anti-aliasing. This setting can be used for type that has sharp lines. Low to High settings produce different effects, depending on the graphic or clip.

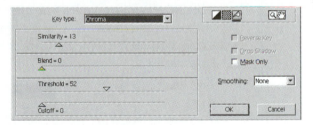

Using the Blue Screen and Green Screen Keys

As you might imagine, Blue Screen and Green Screen keys create transparency using true chroma blue and true chroma green. A video that is created in a studio environment uses these keys to superimpose the actor in front of a different setting. You can adjust the following Blue Screen and Green Screen key settings:

- **Threshold.** This setting controls the overall transparency of the effect. Drag to the left until the background begins to show through.

- **Cutoff.** This setting helps to fill in any stray pixels. Drag this slider in small increments to create subtle effects.

You can quickly access the transparency settings for a clip by clicking Setup next to Transparency in the Effect Controls palette.

Using Chroma Keys to Combine Footage

The trick in producing Chroma key effects is to decide, in advance, how the two shots will look when they are assembled. It is important to shoot the actor at the correct angle and at the correct distance. This ensures that when the shots are merged, they will look as though they belong together.

Exercise Setup

The video you are about to create was taped in two parts. The first taping involved our actress, Lorna. She was taped in a video-production studio. A blue screen was placed behind her and lighting was carefully applied. The second shot was taken while on a trip to the San Francisco Bay area.

Prepare the Project

1. Begin by setting up a new project. Select File>New Project. The New Project dialog box appears. Select Multimedia (QuickTime for Windows) as the Default. Click the Custom button. Click the Next button. In the Project Settings dialog box that appears, set Frame Size to 240 h and 180 v, Compressor to Cinepak, Frame Rate to 15, and then click OK. The program finishes loading. A new Project window is created. Save the file as "using_keys.ppj" in your **Work_In_Progress** folder.

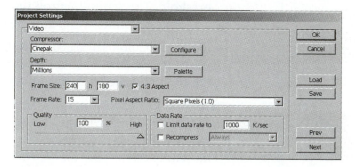

2. Select File>Import>Folder. A dialog box appears. Select the **keying** folder from the **RF_Premiere** folder. The folder and its content transfer to the Project window. You should now have a bin named keying in the Project window. Double-click it to see the content. (Click the Thumbnail View icon if your clips show as a simple list.)

3. Double click **chroma.mov** to view it in the Clip window. When it has transferred, click the Play button to preview your final project.

4. Close the Clip window and save the file.

5. Drag **bridge.mov** to the Timeline window at the beginning of Video 1A.

6. **Bridge.mov** comes to the Timeline with an audio track that appears on Audio 1. This clip contains a lot of background noise. You must delete the audio track to make room for new music. Control/right-click **bridge.mov** on Audio 1. When the pop-up menu appears, select Unlink Audio and Video. Make sure only the audio track is selected. Press the Delete key. The audio disappears.

7. Drag **gullkite.mov** to the Timeline window at the beginning of Video 2. Unlink and delete the audio track.

8. Drag **music8.aif** to the Timeline window on Audio 1 so it falls at the beginning of the production, directly under **bridge.mov**.

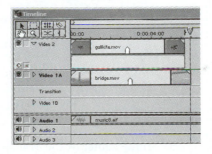

9. At the top of the Timeline window, locate the work area bar. If it has not automatically extended to the end of the project, extend the bar all the way to the end of the video, or about 10 seconds. This allows you to view the entire production as you create it.

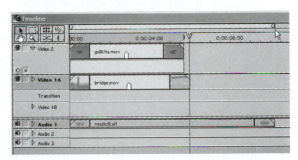

10. Render this production and save it. You should see the bird kite fly (against a blue sky), but you do not yet see the Golden Gate Bridge. Some up-tempo music plays in the background. **Bridge.mov** extends slightly beyond **gullkite.mov**. Pull the right end of **bridge.mov** slightly to the left to shorten the clip so it ends with **gullkite.mov**.

11. Leave the file open for the next exercise.

Exercise Setup

In the next exercise, the main shot of our actor was created in a video studio. It's a rather ordinary shot. The actor simply smiles at you — but we're going to change that. We'll take an excellent shot of the Golden Gate Bridge and superimpose it behind our actor.

Superimpose with the Chroma Key

1. Continue working in the open project. Highlight **gullkite.mov** in the Video 2 track. Select Clip>Video Options>Transparency to display the Transparency Settings dialog box.

2. At the moment, the Key type is set to None. Click on the arrow to the right of None. A new list of choices appears. Select Chroma as the Key type.

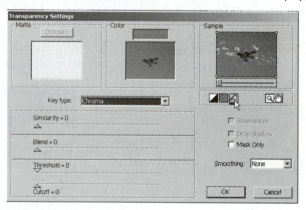

3. In the center of the Transparency Settings window, directly above the bird, you see the Color box. At the moment, it is set to White. This is the color that is keyed out so a new color can be substituted. Click the Underlying Image button (the third from the left, under the Sample image).

4. Drag the cursor over the blue background that surrounds the bird. It changes to an eyedropper. Click and hold on the blue background. That blue color now appears in the previously white Color box.

5. The blue-sky background is not a perfect blue, as it would be in a studio with controlled lighting. Move the eyedropper around in the bird image until you get a wide selection of colors (including some brown values) showing through. Do not place the eyedropper on the bird.

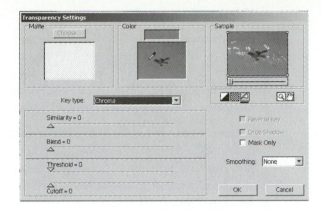

6. Now click on the Color box. The Select Transparent Color dialog box appears. Notice the numbers in the RGB mode boxes. Set Red to 116, Green to 137, Blue to 162, and then click OK. Note how close you came to those colors with the eyedropper. That new color now appears in the Color box.

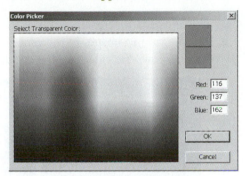

7. Now let's complete the blending process. Set Similarity to 13, Blend to 0, Threshold to 52, Cutoff to 0, and then click OK.

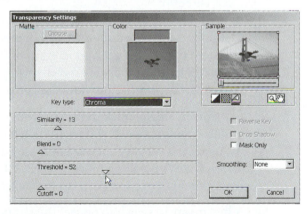

8. Save and render this production so you can see the effect in action. After several moments, you should see our actor and the Golden Gate Bridge. It looks as though she is actually at the California location.

9. Close the file and exit Premiere.

Alpha Channels

Every television commercial and program you see starts with a ten-second countdown. The producer (or the engineer running the video computer) uses it to cue productions before they air. Since it takes roughly three to five seconds for a videocassette device to come up to speed, this provides just enough time to get the next footage ready. Done correctly, it results in the commercial starting immediately after the show fades to black.

All images composed for television or the Web are created using the RGB color model. RGB images consist of three separate images called "channels" that contain the red, green, and blue components of the image. An *alpha channel* is a fourth channel that is used to determine what portions of the underlying (RGB) channels can be seen, and at what opacity.

Many third-party applications, such as Adobe Photoshop, use alpha channels to mask or make specific portions of the image appear transparent. Premiere can read alpha channels created in Photoshop and import them directly onto the alpha channel of the Premiere Timeline.

This illustration, created in Photoshop, shows a background image on the left and one of ten foreground images in the center. An alpha channel in the shape of the old television screen allows the videographer to superimpose the numbers onto the set's screen.

Exercise Setup

In the following exercise, we're going to create a ten-second-countdown clip. Feel free to customize the finished product with filters or transitions, but be sure to follow the specified steps first so you get a good grasp of the concepts involved. Until now, you have been using A/B editing mode. In an earlier chapter of this book, Single-Track editing mode was discussed; this exercise provides the perfect opportunity to use it.

Remember, Single-Track mode is easy to use, but does not provide all of the possibilities of A/B editing mode. If you try to switch from A/B to Single-Track with Premiere open, you will get a warning message because Single–Track mode may not be able to interpret some of the A/B editing mode settings. (If there is nothing on the Timeline, you can ignore the message and perform the switch.)

A better way to switch to Single-Track mode is to re-start Premiere without the Preferences file from a previous project. All preferences will be removed, and it will appear as if you are starting Premiere for the first time after initial installation.

Preview and Begin the Project

1. Be sure Premiere is not running. Hold down the Control and Shift keys, and then start Premiere while continuing to hold down the keys. When Premiere appears to stop loading, release the keys (you may have to try this a few times to get the timing right). Choose Single-Track Editing from the Initial Workspace dialog box.

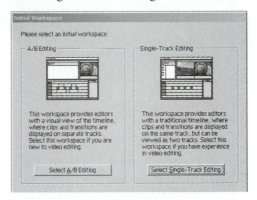

2. Begin by setting up a new project. Select Multimedia QuickTime (Macintosh) - Video for Windows (Windows) as the Default, and click the Custom button. Set Frame Size h to 240 and v to 180, Frame Rate to 15 frames per second, and then click OK.

3. The program finishes loading and a set of new Project windows appears. Save the file as "countdown.ppj" to your **Work_In_Progress** folder.

4. Close the Navigator/Info/History palette group if it gets in your way. Leave the Transitions palette open (if it is not open, select Window>Show Transitions).

5. Switch to Single view by clicking the button at the top of the Monitor window, and then drag the right side of the Monitor window to the left to resize it.

6. You know that most of your still images will be displayed on the screen for one second (30 frames). To avoid having to reset the duration of each frame, set the Still Image Duration to 30 frames before importing any footage. Select Edit>Preferences>General and Still Image. Set the default Duration to 30 frames in the General and Still Image dialog box (the setting is near the bottom of the dialog box), then click OK.

7. Select File>Import>Folder. A dialog box appears. Select **RF_Premiere>television**, and then click Choose. The **television** folder and its content are brought into the Project window. Double-click the imported folder to see the clips we're going to use in this exercise.

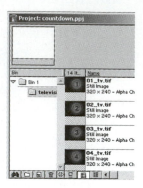

8. Select **countdown.mov**, and double-click it. When it has been transferred to the Clip window, click the Play button to preview your final project. After you've seen the movie, close the Clip window.

9. Leave the project open for the next exercise.

Using Still Images

By default, all still images imported into Premiere are automatically assigned a duration of five seconds. Once the clip is placed on the Timeline, the duration can be adjusted to any length of time you choose.

Set the Duration Options for Still Images

1. In the Project window of the open file, double-click **tv.tif**. The still image **tv.tif** displays in the Clip tv.tif window.

2. Click the Duration button at the bottom left of the image. In the Clip Duration dialog box, change the number from 0:00:01:00 to 0:00:13:00, and then click OK.

Special effects such as transparency should always be created in the Video 2 or 3 tracks.

3. Position your cursor inside the TV screen. Drag the picture to the Video 2 track on the Timeline. It should stretch to the 13-second mark. Close the Clip tv.tif window.

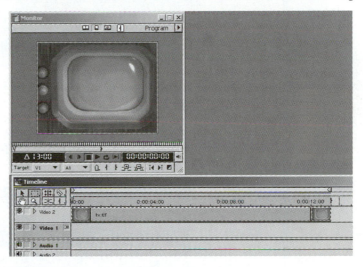

4. Double-check that the work area bar extends all the way to the end of the production, allowing you to view the entire production as you create it.

5. In the Project window, double-click **tv-blank.tif**. The still image clip **tv-blank.tif** displays.

6. Click on the Duration button at the bottom left of the image. In the Clip Duration dialog box, change the number to 00:00:02:00, and then click OK. This lengthens the clip to 2 seconds.

7. Position your cursor inside **tv-blank.tif** and drag the picture to the beginning of the Video 1 track on the Timeline. It should stretch to fill 2 seconds. Close the Clip tv-blank.tif window.

8. Return to the Project window, drag **10_tv.tif** to the Video 1 track. Place it immediately after the **tv-blank.tif** image.

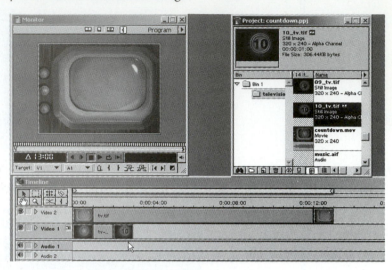

9. In the Project window, drag **09_tv.tif** to the Timeline and place it immediately after **10_tv.tif**.

10. Repeat Step 9 for each of the remaining countdown numbers. Continue to place them on the Timeline, counting down from left to right. Place **tv-blank.tif** as the last picture at the end of the Timeline.

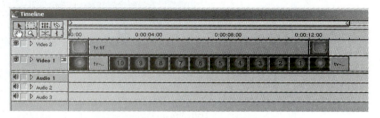

Option/Alt-click on the work area bar to quickly extend it to the end of the production.

11. **Tv-blank.tif** has a duration of 02:00 (you changed it in a previous step). Control/right-click on **tv-blank.tif** and set the Duration to 00:30.

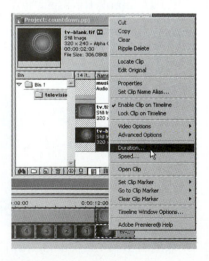

12. Leave the file open for the next exercise.

Use Alpha Channels to Generate Special Effects

1. In the Project window of the open file, click the Alpha button at the bottom of the window. Look at the black mask. This black area is where you can place new (substitute) image data. Anytime an image with an embedded alpha channel comes into Premiere, that image's black or white channel can be altered. Click the RGB button to return to the TV picture. Close **tv.tif**.

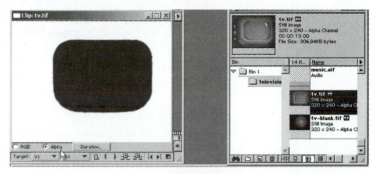

2. On the Timeline, click to select **tv.tif**. Select Clip>Video Options>Transparency.

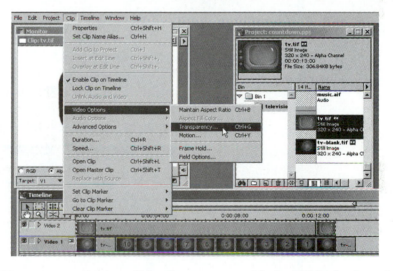

3. The Transparency Settings dialog box appears with the TV in the Sample box.

4. Notice that the Key type is set to None. Change the Key type to Alpha Channel. Click the Underlying Image icon (a small button that resembles a page curl, found under the Sample box). Your first picture, **tv-blank.tif**, suddenly appears inside the television screen. Click OK to close the Transparency Settings dialog box.

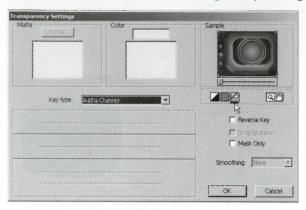

5. Save your work. Render this production by pressing Return/Enter. After your project renders, you should see your countdown playing inside a television screen without transitions.

6. Open the Slide folder in the Transitions palette (select Window>Show Transitions if you can't see the Transitions palette). The default Duration should already be 30 frames. A quick way to reset the default is to choose any transition (we chose Slide>Band Slide), and then click the arrow at the upper-right side of the Transitions palette. In the pop-up menu that appears, choose Set Selected as Default. In the dialog box that appears, enter 15 Frames for the Effect Duration and choose Center at Cut for the Effect Alignment.

7. Drag the Band Slide effect to the Timeline and drop it between **tv-blank.tif** and **10_tv.tif**.

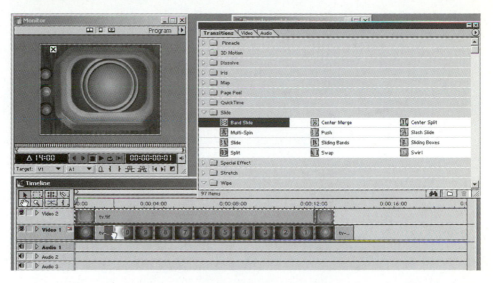

8. Continue to select and drag transitions onto the Timeline between each successive clip pair. This production requires 11 transitions. You may choose any transitions from the Transitions palette for your production.

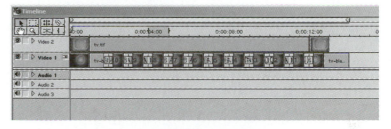

9. Save your project by pressing Return/Enter to render these additional changes. After building the preview, you should see your countdown playing inside a television screen with all of the new transitions.

10. Take a moment to change any of the transitions that are not satisfactory. As a final touch, drag **music1.aif** to the Audio 1 track in the Timeline. When you are satisfied with the result, save the final production and close the file.

Chapter Summary

In Chapter 7, you learned how to superimpose clips using a number of techniques. You became familiar with transparency, and now know how to control the transparency of a clip or still image over time. You learned about Chroma keys, and how they're used to combine footage when using the blue-screening technique. You learned to use alpha channels, and to combine them with still images and assorted transitions to create special effects. You also learned how to control the duration of still images on the Timeline.

8 Using Filters and Special Effects

Chapter Objectives:

Premiere filters are used for everything from major graphic changes to subtle corrections of video footage. Proper use of filters can easily enhance a scene and create effects that are not possible when you are taping original footage. The trick is to use filters only when they enhance a scene; overuse of filters can actually detract from your movie. In this chapter, you will:

- Learn the basics of Premiere filters.

- Explore filter applications.

- Practice using the Video Effects palette.

- Observe the difference between native effects and effects from other applications, and how to recognize each type in the Video Effects palette.

- Discover how to work with the Effect Controls palette, which controls the attributes and variables for each specific filter.

- Learn to use keyframes.

- Learn to combine filters to achieve custom effects.

- Learn the difference between correction and distortion of your video footage.

- Discover how to use the Razor tool to edit clips.

Projects to be Completed:

- The Monkey Movie (A)

- Making Spaghetti (B)

- **The Gold Rush (C)**

- Central Coast Surfing (D)

Using Filters and Special Effects

Special effects provide the foundation for many of today's hit movies — it almost seems as though a movie without special effects is somehow lacking. While that conclusion may be questionable, there's no doubt that you must include special effects in your arsenal of video development skills. Premiere helps you acquire this skill by providing an extensive collection of filters that can be dragged from the Video Effects palette onto any clip on the Timeline.

Suppose you want to create the effect of an old black-and-white silent movie. Premiere accomplishes this for you with a filter called Black & White; it strips the video clip of its color. You can then apply Film Noise, another filter that can give the clip an old-time appearance by adding some graininess. The best part of using filters such as these is that they do not in any way alter the original video footage. This means you can experiment until you find the proper filter for your production without harming your original footage.

Once a production is underway, you can begin to add special effects to any or all of your clips. You do this by using the Video Effects palette in conjunction with the Effect Controls palette. The Video Effects palette contains the different types of effects, and the Effect Controls palette controls the adjustment or appearance of the effect over time. If you don't like an effect, you can easily delete it. You can even apply the same effect multiple times to the same clip with different settings.

Video Effects Palette

The process of selecting filters begins in the Video Effects palette, which offers a selection of 74 different filters or effects. These effects may be added to any clips that are placed on the Timeline. Effects are grouped in folders, which can be expanded or contracted as you make your selections. Unused filters remain out of the way until you need them. Two types of filters appear in the Video Effects palette. The first type is native filters, which are built into Premiere. They can be identified by the "V" in the icon placed next to the filter's name. The second type is plug-ins — After Effects plug-ins from the Adobe application of the same name. The plug-ins icon is a small electrical plug.

Be aware that rendering special effects filters can add considerable time to the rendering process — which, by itself, can be a lengthy process. Some filters require significant processing power and can consume considerable system resources during rendering.

Using filters does not alter your original video footage. You can add as many special effects as you wish to the same clip. You can even apply different filters to the same clip and use it at different times in the same production.

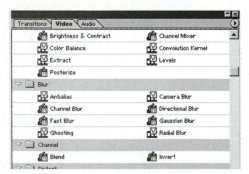

We resized our Video Effects palette so we could show two columns of icons — yours probably shows only one column.

The Video Effects palette provides a number of productivity enhancements. One such enhancement is the Find feature, represented by a small set of binoculars at the bottom of the palette. Clicking this icon allows you to search the effects for the one you need. In this example, we clicked the icon and entered the name of the Crystallize filter in the Find value field.

Pressing the Find button at the bottom of the Video Effects palette can locate any effect. Click the folder icon and enter the name of the filter. When finished, click Done.

Effect Controls Palette

When you apply an effect to a clip, the effect is listed in the Effect Controls palette. You can use this palette to manage your effects. The palette contains information about every effect applied to clips in your video production. If you have applied multiple effects to a clip, the Effect Controls palette lists all of them in order from top to bottom. You can reorder the effects in this list to change the effects that are rendered first.

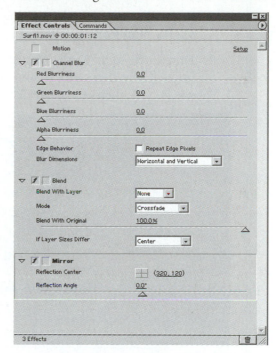

Each effect also shows on the Timeline, along with a set of triangles that represent the keyframes for the effect.

A *keyframe* is a marker that tells Premiere when to begin applying an effect and at what intensity. Filters have different settings, which you can control and change at specific points on the Timeline through the use of keyframes. There are no limits to the number of keyframes you can apply to a clip.

Let's say, for example, that you're dissolving or crystallizing a clip. You want the process to start slowly, then increase in speed; your clip begins free of the effect, but the effect speeds up and intensifies toward the end. Keyframes enable you to control an effect over time; they are used to delay the start of effects, speed them up, and adjust other effect-specific values on the Timeline.

Similarly, if you want the full effect of the filter to show at the beginning of the clip, slowly resolving to the finished unfiltered footage, you would use keyframes to accomplish your goal. You would need to set two keyframes — the first with heavy crystallization, and the second with light crystallization. The second keyframe would be placed partway into the clip. Premiere automatically updates the distortion (impact of the effect) between keyframes, so the crystallization would gradually decrease between the first and second keyframes, and would end after the second keyframe.

Import Video Clips in a Folder

1. If it is not already running, launch Premiere. This exercise uses a large amount of RAM and disk space. Close all other programs except Premiere.

2. When the Project Settings dialog box appears, select Multimedia QuickTime, then set A/B Editing mode (use the arrow in the upper right of the Timeline to access the selection menu). You will get a warning message regarding editing mode changes. Ignore the message, and click OK to continue.

3. Select File>Import>File. A dialog box appears. Select **surfl1.mov** through **surfl5.mov** from the **surfcut** folder in the **RF_Premiere** folder.

4. Drag surfl1 to the Video 1A track. Drag surfl2 to the Video 1B track, and place it immediately after surfl1. Continue with the next three clips, alternating tracks as you go (1A, then 1B, then back to 1A, and so on).

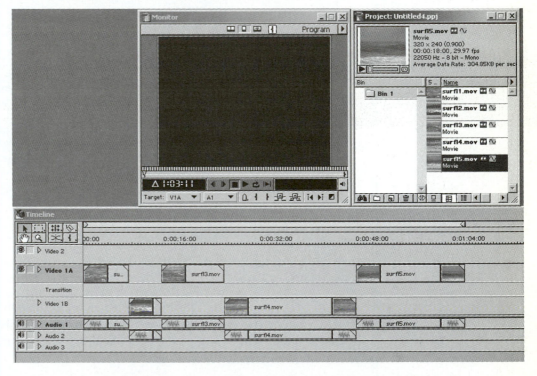

5. Save this project as "surftest.ppj" in your **Work_In_Progress** folder. Leave this file open for the next exercise.

Apply a Special Effect for Correction

1. In the open file, press Return/Enter to view the movie. The first problem you see is that the brightness and color balance of surfl1 do not match the brightness and color balance of surfl2.

2. Select surfl1, then choose Window>Show Video Effects if you have not yet opened the Video Effects palette. Open the Adjust effects by clicking the triangle to the left of the word Adjust.

3. Single-click the surfl1 clip to be sure it is selected. Drag the Color Balance icon and drop it on surfl1. Next, drag the Brightness and Contrast icon to surfl1.

4. The two effects appear in the Effect Controls box (Motion is there by default). Set the Color Balance to the following values: Red to 102, Green to 97, and Blue to 99. Set the Brightness & Contrast to Brightness -35.0, Contrast to 10.0 (note that there is a minus (-) sign before the Brightness value). You can use the triangle sliders to set the values or double-click a numeric value and enter a new value.

5. Drag the In point of surfl1 to the right to shorten it to a few seconds. Press Return/Enter to render the movie and view the changes. The Color Balance and Brightness might not be perfect on your monitor. Adjust the values as necessary.

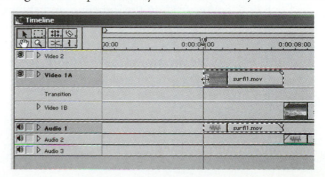

If you know the value you want to use for a setting, it is faster to manually enter it. The sliders are very sensitive and cover a wide range.

Every time you add an effect, the entire clip must be rendered to see the full effect. You can save a lot of time by shortening the clip (drag the left side of the clip to create a new In point) until the effect is perfect. Then you can drag the In point back to its original location and render the full effect.

6. Drag the In point of surfl1 back to full length, go to the Effect Controls palette, and turn off both effects.

7. Move the edit line marker to surfl3. The buoy in the background is distracting. Crop it out.

8. You need to retain a full-screen image, so use the Image Pan effect. Open the Transform effects and drag Image Pan to surfl3. Click Setup (to the right of the Image Pan effect name in the Effect Controls palette), and enter a Top value of 24 in the dialog box. This effect causes slight distortion in the image, but in this case, it is not significant.

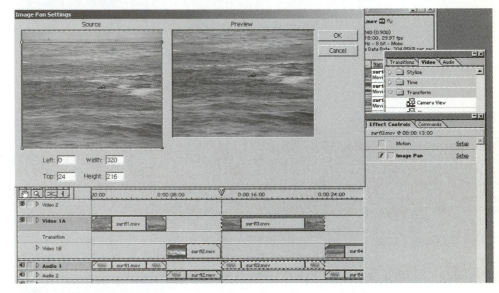

9. Leave the files open for the next exercise.

The previous effects were applied to correct problems in the video footage. Changes such as these are often used to correct unavoidable differences in your source footage. A color shift or contrast difference can appear if you shoot with two cameras or collect footage on different days.

Premiere also supplies effects that cause intentional (and obvious) distortion of a scene. Try not to over use these effects. They often look good the first time you see them, but they soon make your film seem boring and appear overworked.

Apply a Special Effect for Distortion

1. Continue working in the open project. Drag the Emboss effect (Stylize>Emboss) to surfl4 on the Timeline, and enter the following values: Direction of 45.0 degrees, Relief of 6.00, Contrast of 150, Blend With Original of 12%. (Be patient. This effect will take a long time to render.) Press Return/Enter, select File>Save to save the project in your **Work_In_Progress** folder, and take a break while the effect is rendered.

The more transitions and filters you use, the more time it takes to render the production. Moral of the story — you need patience and a lot of RAM.

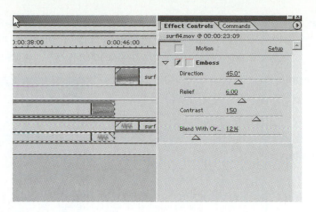

2. This next effect uses keyframes to avoid having the effect occur across the entire clip. Select surfl5. Drag Mosaic from the Stylize menu to surfl5 and drop it. To expand the Video 1A track, click the triangle to the left of the track name.

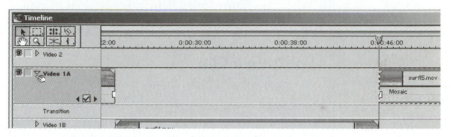

3. The Mosaic filter divides your image into a mosaic of squares. The clip appears normal until it gets near the middle. It returns to normal by the end. Move the edit line marker to 50:00. Turn on keyframes by clicking the box to the left of the word Mosaic in the Effect Controls palette. Clicking this box sets the first keyframe. From this point forward, entering a new value for Mosaic sets a new keyframe. Enter a value of 400 for Horizontal Blocks and a value of 400 for Vertical Blocks.

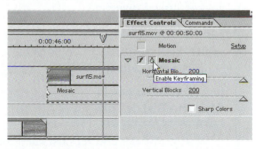

4. Move the edit line marker to 54:00, enter a value of 20 for Horizontal Blocks and a value of 20 for Vertical Blocks (the keyframe is set when you enter the value). Move the edit line marker to 58:00 and enter a value of 400 for Horizontal Blocks and a value of 400 for Vertical Blocks.

5. When Step 4 is complete, you see 5 keyframes in the surfl5 clip. The first and last keyframes determine the value of the effect at the beginning and end of the clip. The middle 3 keyframes cause the Mosaic effect to appear and disappear as the clip plays.

The peach-colored line that shows above your newly placed transition in the Timeline window tells you a transition is in place but not yet rendered. Once rendered, the line changes to an aqua blue color.

The green line that shows above your newly placed effect in the Timeline window tells you an effect is in use.

6. To quickly move to another keyframe, click the Next Keyframe or Previous Keyframe arrow to the left or right of the check box located on the Video 1A effect line. Set the first and last keyframes to Horizontal and Vertical values of 400.

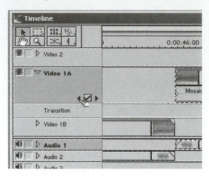

7. Press Return/Enter, and take a well-deserved break while the file renders. When you return, press Return/Enter again to view all of the effects you added.

8. Save the project, and leave Premiere open for the next exercise.

Splitting a Clip

You can split a clip in the Timeline with the Razor tool found in the Timeline toolbox. Splitting a clip creates new and separate parts of the original clip. This process can be useful when you want to use different effects at the same time. For example, you might want a jogger to run at two different speeds. It is also useful if you want to quickly add transitions to a series of captured clips.

When you split a clip, Premiere creates a new slice or section of the clip and any clips to which it is linked. Premiere allows you to split any clip into two or more parts. Each part becomes independent and can have unique filters applied to it. Premiere splits only the audio or video portion of unlinked clips (clips where the audio and video are not locked/linked together).

One important tip: always be sure to return to the Selection tool when you are finished using the Razor tool. If you don't click back to the Selection tool, you will continue to cut your clip into smaller and smaller pieces.

Use the Razor Tool

1. In this exercise, let's use the Razor tool so we can see the zebras, first from a distance, and then from a much closer vantage point. Start a new Premiere project using Multimedia QuickTime as the preset. Import **surfl9.mov** from the **surfcut** folder in the **RF_Premiere** folder. Move surfl9.mov to the Video 1A track.

2. Position your cursor on the Timeline at 00:14:00, and then click. Select the Razor tool from the Timeline toolbox.

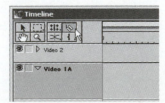

3. Position the Razor tool on the surfl9.mov clip so it lines up with the edit line, and then click. The clip splits in two. You see two portions (or segments) of surfl9.mov on the Timeline, positioned side by side.

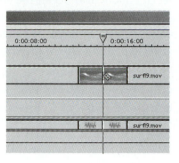

4. Position the edit line at 00:16:00, and use the Razor tool to make another cut. Choose the Selection tool (or press the "V" key). Remember: if you don't first click back to the Selection tool, you will continue to chop your clip into ever-smaller pieces with the Razor tool. Select the center portion of surfl9. Press the Delete key to delete the center section.

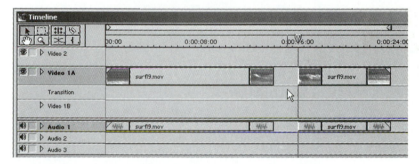

5. Now that you have two distinct sections of surfl9.mov, you can apply a transition.

6. Drag the right-side clip of surfl9.mov to track Video 1B and place it so it overlaps surfl9.mov on Track 1A by about two seconds. Open the Transitions palette, and then select Page Peel>Center Peel. Drag the transition to the Transition track and place it so it fits the overlap at the end of surfl9.mov on the Video 1A track.

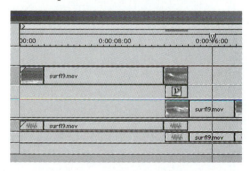

7. Press Return/Enter to render it. Observe your latest changes. You do not need to save this file.

Chapter Summary

In Chapter 8, you learned to use multiple filters on a single clip to create a variety of special effects. You began the chapter by becoming familiar with how to view the Video Effects palette and find the effects you want to use. You learned how to apply special effect filters to a clip, and remove effects from a clip through the use of keyframes. You also learned to split a clip in order to add special effects to parts of the clip, or add a transition to a previously uncut clip.

Complete Project C: The Gold Rush

9 Producing Final Video

Chapter Objectives:

When you are ready to output your final video productions, you must be ready to distribute them to a variety of media. In this chapter, we will explain the difference between high-resolution output for television distribution and low-resolution/high-speed output to the Web. It is also important to learn about platform-specific output options and the plug-ins that support them so you will be ready for any output situation. As there are so many different video programs available to the artist, it is necessary to understand how to create graphic output for other programs, not only Premiere. In this chapter, you will:

- Learn the four basic categories of Premiere output.

- Learn about export file types and when they are used.

- Discover how to export directly to videotape.

- Understand the difference between a machine that has device control and one that does not.

- Learn about the QuickTime Exporter for use on a Macintosh system.

- Become familiar with non-video output and learn how you can use it to produce files for other programs.

- Learn to produce GIF animations for Web pages.

Projects to be Completed:

- The Monkey Movie (A)

- Making Spaghetti (B)

- The Gold Rush (C)

- Central Coast Surfing (D)

Producing Final Video

At the beginning of this book, you learned that much of what you do in Premiere depends on how the end product is going to be used and/or distributed. Is it for use on the Web? Will you deliver it on videotape or a CD-ROM? If you decide to play it directly from your hard drive, which viewer will you use?

There are literally hundreds of possible output methods you can use to present your project (you have already used several as you completed the exercises in this book). Fortunately, you don't have to learn all of them. There are relatively few export options that must be memorized in order to successfully create a final presentation. Once you decide what you want to do with your video, Premiere can do most of the work for you.

Exporting Video

There are four major presentation areas where you will use your video productions: videotape, CD-ROM, the Web, and other programs into which you will import your video to build another type of project. The choices you make while creating your Premiere project directly affect how easily — and effectively — you can accomplish your final goal. Each production goal has its own specific requirements and limitations.

Videotape

Exporting to videotape places the greatest demand on your system and requires the most powerful (fastest) equipment. A project destined for videotape is relatively easy for a project designer because the settings remain the same throughout the entire project.

If you are working in Digital Video (DV) format, you can simply select the DV settings you want to use, import the video, edit it, and record it back to tape. To accomplish this, your system must be able to sustain the data rate required for high-quality digital input and output. Fast hard drives, a powerful capture card, a capable video display card (if you want to see what you are doing), and a high-speed interface between the video deck and computer (Firewire or iLink) are required.

In addition, it is wise to review suggestions provided throughout this book. For example, you do not want to capture video to the same hard disk that is running Premiere. For more information on this subject, review the sections on scratch disks and capture settings.

CD-ROM

When you produce a movie for playback on CD-ROM, you must be sure the person receiving the disk is able to play it. Typical CD-ROMs can hold about 650 MB of data; DVD-ROMs can hold much more. Disk space, however, is not the issue here; compatibility is the concern. If you are working on a Windows-based system and your recipient has a Macintosh, you must be sure the movie is cross-platform compatible. If you record on a DVD, you must ensure that the same DVD standard is found on the player used for your presentation. If the movie is copied from the CD-ROM to the viewer's hard drive, is the drive fast enough to play without distracting pops and pauses? (Was this the case on your system while you were completing the projects in this book?)

Web Display

File size and data rate are the two major considerations when you are outputting your movie for display on the Web. There are many video players available for Web display, but not all are compatible with every platform. You also cannot be sure how fast the viewer can receive data. If you design your movie for streaming over a DSL or cable line, a viewer with a 28K modem will see little more than skips and jumps between random still frames. If you recommend that viewers with slower systems download the movie for viewing, they may have to wait over an hour for the video to arrive in entirety. Some viewing programs allow a movie to start playing before it is fully loaded, but these often display the downloaded portion of the video and then stop while the video stream continues to fill the video buffer. This "progressive download" method is helpful, but it often does not completely solve the speed problem.

Building Blocks

Many Adobe programs (After Effects, Photoshop, and Illustrator) can incorporate output from Premiere. Other vendors' programs can also use output from Premiere if it is in a compatible format. File name extensions, alpha channel information, and compression type must be the same in each program.

File Types Available for Export

Premiere provides several export formats. To save yourself time and aggravation, be certain your destination platform and software are Premiere-compatible before you export. The following list shows several options that are available in Premiere 6.5 on a Windows platform (Macintosh includes other choices):

Video/audio output formats.

Audio output formats (audio also includes the AIFF format).

Premiere also exports directly in several specialized formats including the following:

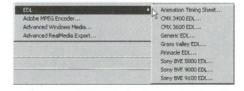

The output of a video still image is at a screen resolution of 72 dots per inch, which is not very useful if you output your images to a printer.

- **EDL.** EDL stands for Edit Decision List. This list contains information regarding every edit and the In and Out points of every clip in the program. High-end editing machines (see the list above) use this information to reproduce an exact copy of the edited program.

- **MPEG Encoder**. This option offers an excellent solution for creating MPEG files to produce DVD-ROM disks. These files are especially compatible with DVDit!® LE, a DVD-editing program supplied on the Premiere disk. Unfortunately, MPEG Encoder for DVDit! is only available on the Windows platform.

- **Advanced Windows Media** and **Advanced RealMedia Export**. Similar to MPEG Encoder, Advanced Windows and RealMedia formats are only available for the Windows operating system.

Exporting to Videotape

When you started your project at the beginning of this book, you made several decisions regarding the size and appearance of your final movie. You selected the image size, the amount of compression, and the codec used for the compression. You also determined the audio quality of your final presentation. The following image shows the default settings for Multimedia (Multimedia QuickTime on a Windows platform) — the format you used for most of the exercises in this book.

Multimedia QuickTime offers 16-bit–Monophonic audio with no compression. The image size is 320 pixels wide and 240 pixels high, and will play back at 15 fps. The selected codec is Cinepak. Cinepak is an excellent choice for output displayed on multiple platforms.

You are not committed to these settings simply because you chose them at the start of your project. The settings can be changed at any time by selecting Project>Project Settings, and then choosing Video or Audio settings.

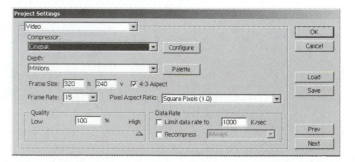

To move through the various Project Settings input boxes, click the Previous (Prev) or Next button.

To produce your final movie, you can choose to output from the Timeline or from a clip. If you choose the Timeline, you can output the entire production or a portion of it by dragging the ends of the work area indicator to selected Start and Stop points. If you are outputting from a clip, you can choose to output the entire clip, or only the footage between the In and Out points.

The method you use to output to video depends on the type of equipment you are using. If you are fortunate enough to be using a DV (Digital Video) deck, you can use device control to operate all of the camera controls directly from your computer. The quality of digital video is usually better than an analog system (such as VHS).

If you do not have device control, you must manually operate the camera controls. Manual operation without device control is not a problem; DV adds convenience and ease of use, but you can certainly manage without DV.

After your recording equipment is set up, you can select File>Export Timeline>Print to Video. If you have device control, you would select File>Export Timeline>Export to Tape.

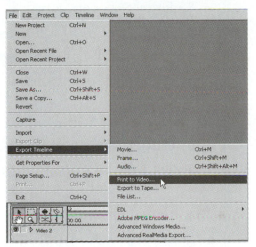

When you are capturing video, a Mini-DV or DV camera in VCR mode performs the same functions as a dedicated DV deck.

The next screen that appears (the Print to Video dialog box) asks for information regarding the start-up and appearance of your movie. Color bars are used for calibrating the viewing monitor. Adjust the color controls on your monitor until these standard color bars look correct; this ensures optimal color viewing. The Play Black for Seconds option determines how many seconds of black screen appear before the movie starts playing. The remaining options determine the size of your image and whether or not the movie continually repeats on the screen.

Keep in mind that selecting Full Screen or Zoom by 2 degrades the quality of your image. We recommend using these options only if your original footage was captured at a high-quality setting. If you choose Loop Playback, the movie continually repeats. This can make it easier to time the manual control of the camera to start recording, but the color bars and black screen only appear at the beginning of the first loop.

Output to Video

You do not need to be connected to a video recorder to complete this exercise.

1. Start Premiere.

2. Import **surf19.mov** from the **RF_Premiere** folder.

3. Drag the Surfer clip to the beginning of the Timeline.

4. Select File>Export Timeline>Print to Video. When asked to save your project, save it as "colbar.ppj" in your **Work_In_Progress** folder.

5. Enter a setting of 5 seconds for Color Bars, and a setting of 5 seconds for Play Black.

6. Remove all checkmarks from the boxes.

7. If you are recording on a deck, start the recorder now, and then click OK.

8. Repeat Steps 4 and 5.

9. Check the boxes for Full Screen and Loop Playback.

10. Click OK. Notice how the quality degrades when you go to full screen.

11. When you are finished viewing the looped movie, press the Escape key to return to Premiere.

12. Leave the project open for the next exercise.

It can take a tape deck a few seconds to get rolling at full speed, so leave plenty of Color Bar time and a few seconds of Play Black to ensure you successfully get the beginning of your film on tape.

Creating Internet Media

When you post or send video to users on the Web, you usually do not know what kind of equipment they are using. There is a significant difference between a 28.8K modem and a high-speed T1, DSL, cable modem, or ISDN line. The best you can do is guess, and make your compression choices accordingly. Some advanced Web presenters actually render several versions of a movie and ask the user to identify the connection speed of the receiving equipment. You also need to know which platform the viewer is using. A movie made for the Windows Media Player will fail if the recipient does not have that player installed on his system.

Movies created for a 56K modem will play (with some problems) through a 28.8K modem. They also have reasonable quality when received through a DSL or cable modem if the screen size is not too large (do not use full-screen mode).

Once you make a decision regarding output format, Premiere makes it simple to render the movie. As we briefly discussed earlier in this chapter, there are three options (provided as plug-ins) in the latest version of Premiere: the Adobe MPEG Encoder, Advanced Windows Media, and Advanced RealMedia Export.

Adobe MPEG Encoder

The Adobe MPEG Encoder (Windows only) is specifically designed to output files that will be transferred to DVD or VCD (video disks that can be played through a Set Top Video Disk through your television). These files are custom designed to work with DVDit! — the DVD-production program supplied with the Windows version of Premiere.

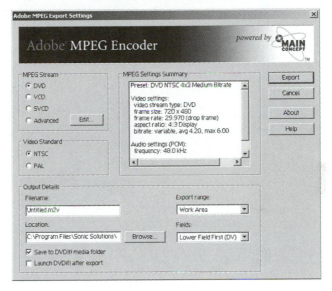

Media 8 Export

The Media 8 Export plug-in offers output options for numerous situations ranging from Color Pocket PCs (very high compression and significant loss of data) to Best Quality Broadband (better than CD quality) images. Remember that the end user of your video must have a player available.

The Media 8 Export option includes a Properties window that allows you to enter information regarding the Author, Title, Copyright, Description, and Rating of your film.

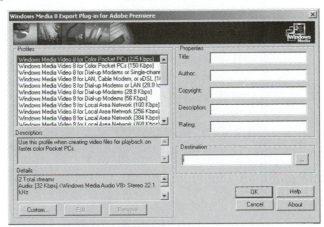

Advanced RealMedia Export

The Advanced RealMedia Export option allows multiple simultaneous choices for rendering your movie. All you need to do is check the boxes for the most likely combination of your viewer's compression and playback equipment. The user of your video must, of course, have the latest RealMedia player installed on the viewing machine. The most recent (limited) player is available for downloading from the Web at no charge.

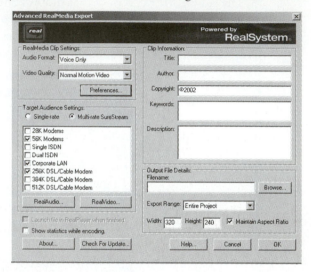

RealMedia also offers several choices regarding the quality of audio and video you are delivering. Voice Only audio format offers the lowest quality and highest speed; Stereo Music offers the highest quality and lowest speed.

Video quality settings range from Slide Show quality (fast) to Smoothest Motion Video (high quality, but requires more processing power).

When you are using the RealMedia Encoder for export, be sure to check the other available options. *Streaming* refers to the process of sending real-time video to another machine. The video begins playing before it is completely transferred to the viewer. Streaming is also used to broadcast live events across the net. A group of input boxes provides many choices regarding final quality, special features, filters, and streaming options. Review the filtering options in the following image.

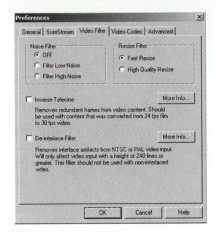

In addition to selectable modem rates, Advanced RealMedia allows for specific control over individual bitrates. By clicking the RealVideo button (found below the Modem selection box), you can select the actual bitrate that will be used. *Bitrate* determines the speed at which information is transferred across the Web. Included in the selection menus are comments describing the best selection options.

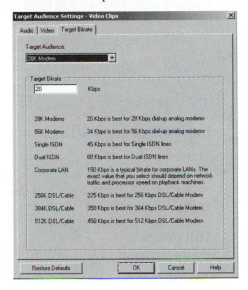

The previous three output methods are available only with the Windows version of Premiere. If you are using a Macintosh platform, there is one option that offers many of the same choices.

Premiere 6.5 for Mac OS includes the QuickTime File Exporter option in the Export Movie Settings dialog box. This option uses QuickTime-supplied exporters to convert Premiere clips or the Timeline to a variety of other file formats.

If you have Apple DVD Studio Pro installed on your system, you can also export your footage to the Apple MPEG Encoder.

To use the QuickTime File Exporter, you can:

- Choose File>Export Timeline>Movie.
- Select a clip in the Source display of the Monitor window, or activate a Clip window and choose File>Export Clip>Movie.

In the Export Movie dialog box, you would click Settings. You would choose QuickTime File Exporter from the File Type menu, and then click Advanced Settings. You would click Options to specify settings to create a custom preset, and then click OK.

You can set either of the following options:

- **Export**. This setting specifies the file type of the exported movie.
- **Using**. This option specifies the preset used for exporting the file. Choose Default Settings to export a particular file type using the default settings for that file type, or choose Current Settings to export using a custom preset you created. You can set options in the Movie Settings dialog box as desired and then click OK.

Premiere DV movies can be used with Apple iDVD. You can export a DV movie using the DV presets, and then open that movie in iDVD. iDVD converts the file into MPEG2 format for use in a DVD project.

Creating a Video File for CD-ROM Playback

Most CD-ROM drives available today play back at 50 (or more) times the speed of the initial hardware releases. That's (certainly) fast enough for 30-fps video with excellent sound quality. Even so, you must remember that not all machines are new. Some of the older, slower CD-ROM drives are not fast enough to play back high-quality footage without skipping or jumping — sometimes the video will simply stop.

Do your best to determine the destination of your films. If it is likely that your film will be played on a slow CD-ROM drive, cut the sound rate to 22 KHz–Mono, and reduce the frame rate to 15 fps.

Exporting Non-Video

Video and audio are not the only types of footage you can export from Premiere. Occasionally, you may want to export a single frame to your printer. You may also want to export a series of frames as still images, retouch them in Photoshop, and import them back into Premiere.

Still Images

To export a still image, you would move the edit line marker to the frame you want to export, and then select File>Export Timeline>Frame.

Next, you would select a name and location for the file, and then click the Settings button at the bottom of the Export Still Frame window.

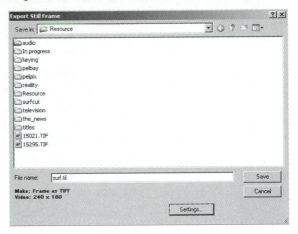

You would select the video preferences by clicking the Prev (Previous) or Next button, and then enter the required dimensions of the exported image.

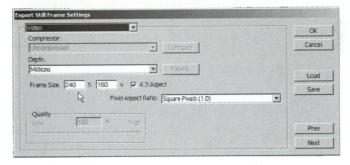

Sequences

You can export a clip or program as a sequence of still images, with each frame in a separate still-image file. This technique is often used to create an animated series for inclusion in 3-D rendering and animation programs. When you export a still-image sequence, Premiere automatically numbers the files.

To export a sequence, you would choose File>Export Timeline>Movie. If you click the Settings button, you would see the File Type menu, where you could choose a still-image sequence format (any file type ending in the word "sequence"). You would choose the frames to export from the Range menu (Entire Project or Work Area). After ensuring that Export Video is selected, you would click Next to confirm your video settings.

You can specify any required options in the Keyframe and Rendering Options panel. From there, you can specify an export location for all of the still-image files. It would be best to create a new folder for the sequence files so they stay separate from all other files.

To name the files in the sequence, you must determine how many digits are required to number the frames, and then add additional zeros if you prefer. For example, if you want to export 20 frames and you want the file name to have 5 digits, you would enter Surf000 for the first file name, and Premiere would automatically name the remaining files as Surf00001, Surf00002, and so forth, until Surf00020. You would then click OK to export the still-image sequence.

Animated GIFs

Animated GIF files are often used to provide animations for Web pages. Generally, they are small in size and composed of solid colors and simple graphics. You can export an animated GIF the same way as you would any other format, but be sure to choose Animated GIF as the File Type in the Export Movie Settings dialog box.

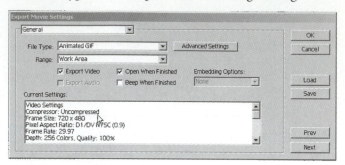

Adobe Photoshop Filmstrips

Exporting the Timeline (or a clip) as an Adobe Photoshop filmstrip allows you to import the filmstrip into Photoshop, retouch it, or animate part of each frame, and then import the modified filmstrip back into Premiere for output as a movie. This technique (known as "rotoscoping") can produce very unusual effects on a frame-by-frame basis.

Chapter Summary

In Chapter 9, you learned several Premiere output options. You learned how to create video for television, CD-ROMs, the Web, and for use with other software programs. You learned about MPEG compression and found out which specialized plug-ins the Windows and Macintosh platforms support. You learned how to produce highly compressed video for distribution on DVD, and know which programs support it. Finally, you learned how to export multiple still images for rotoscoping, animated GIF files, and filmstrip editing.

10 *Final Considerations*

Chapter Objectives:

In this final chapter of the book, we will further prepare you for outputting your Premiere movies. You will increase your understanding of the specific settings required for creating the best quality productions using this software. You will find out about video interlacing and learn when it is needed and why. We will provide many tips and techniques that help a new moviemaker avoid many common mistakes and pitfalls that can cause distracting defects in final exported movies. In this chapter, you will:

- Learn about timebase and how the Timeline is divided.

- Learn the difference between timebase and timecode.

- Learn how to avoid gaps in your recordings.

- Investigate non-NTSC colors and learn how to fix the problems they cause.

- Explore the interlacing theory and learn how to avoid problems with slow and freeze-frame playback.

- Review and extend your knowledge of video codecs.

Projects to be Completed:

- The Monkey Movie (A)

- Making Spaghetti (B)

- The Gold Rush (C)

- **Central Coast Surfing (D)**

Final Considerations

When you import a clip into Premiere and move it to the Timeline, a lot of computer processing occurs in the background. Premiere calculates and applies changes in frame rate, bit depth, frame size, and a number of other properties — all in what appears to be real time. Many of these changes are controlled by the settings you choose at various stages in your project (for example, the capture and output stages).

To make intelligent decisions regarding the settings you use, you must acquire a thorough understanding of what functions the settings perform and why they are important. This final chapter provides a review of information you learned earlier in the book, and presents new information as well. There are no exercises, just useful knowledge you can apply as you learn more about digital video production.

Project Settings

Many of the settings you choose depend on the content of the film, its final purpose, and your distribution method:

- If the film includes a close up of a person talking, and you can see the person's lips moving with the words (lip synch), you cannot easily change the speed of the audio portion of a clip and hope to keep the synchronization intact.
- If the film is destined for Web streaming over a modem, you must be prepared to forfeit some level of quality in exchange for download speed.
- If your work will be shown in a theatre, you will be working with large files and slow render times.

The following parameters must be considered in every case.

Timebase

The *timebase* of a video determines how many divisions are included in a single second of film. Each division is referred to as a *frame*; the timebase is expressed in frames per second (fps). NTSC (the standard for video in North America) specifies 29.97 fps. Other common standards are 24 fps for film, 25 fps for PAL and SECAM (standards used in other countries), and 30 fps for non-NTSC video.

If you record a clip using one timebase and select another for your project Timeline, Premiere must recalculate each frame to make it fit correctly. Precise editing of a video depends on the timebase to determine exactly when a scene changes. If you partially complete the editing of a project at 29.97 fps and then change the timebase to 25 fps, Premiere must recalculate the new timecode and decide what information to drop out to make each frame fit. This can have a negative effect on the precision of your editing and is not a recommended practice.

Frame Rate

The *frame rate* of a video is determined when you record a clip and when you export it as a movie. Although a high frame rate generally provides smoother playback, there is no advantage to recording at 15 fps and exporting at 30 fps. If you do this, Premiere simply duplicates each frame so it is displayed twice.

You should make a decision on frame rate when you are in the pre-planning stage of your movie development. If you are creating a simple animation, 15 fps is adequate to create a good sense of motion and also saves unnecessary drawing time (30 fps animation requires twice as many frames as 15 fps). For smooth motion with a video camera, choose 29.97 fps or 30 fps — the result is smooth motion without the choppiness that occurs at slower rates.

Timecode

Timecode and timebase sound similar, but they have very different meanings. *Timecode* is a code developed by the Society of Motion Picture and Television Engineers (SMPTE) to mark each frame of videotape with an absolute reference. The timecode is embedded on the tape as it is recorded.

Premiere uses timecode to find a particular frame on a tape. Device control uses timecode to advance and rewind your tape to a particular point so the system can begin and end recording at precise locations. If a tape does not have timecode on it, or there are gaps in the timecode, the computer cannot operate the camera.

Beginning videographers often make the mistake of recording a scene, advancing the tape using fast forward, and recording another scene. This technique creates gaps in the timecode and can cause time-consuming problems at the capture stage of development. We recommend putting a new tape in your camera, putting the lens cap on, and recording nothing from the beginning to end, without interruption. This technique of "laying down code" ensures the timecode on the tape will be continual. Then you can rewind the tape and use it for recording as you would a new tape.

If a tape does not have timecode on it, or there are gaps in the timecode, the computer cannot operate the camera.

Most consumer-level digital cameras record timecode on the tape; VHS models usually do not. If your tape does not have recorded timecode on it, Premiere can still find a particular point by counting frames, but this does not usually produce the same result as tape that has timecode on it. Unless you can ensure the tape started on exactly the same frame each time (which is highly unlikely), the counting method prohibits recapturing clips or transferring image position information from one device to another.

The timebase of NTSC video is fixed at 29.97 fps. SMPTE timecode counts at 30 fps. This discrepancy is small, but over time it makes a difference that can cause inaccuracies. To solve the dilemma, two versions of timecode are used: Drop-Frame and Non-Drop-Frame:

- Drop-Frame timecode counts at 30 fps, but it drops 2 frame numbers at the end of every minute unless the minute is a multiple of 10. Using this system, 20 minutes of NTSC video would create $29.97 \times 60 \times 20 = 35964$ frames. SMPTE timecode would calculate $30 \times 60 \times 20 - 36 = 35964$ frames (the 36 frames are the dropped frames). It is important to realize that the actual frames are not dropped, only the count of the frames.

- Non-Drop-Frame timecode simply counts frames at the rate of 30 frames per second. Twenty minutes of Non-Drop-Frame timecode would produce an error of 1 second and 6 frames. Most video equipment uses Non-Drop-Frame timecode. It is easy to tell which version is being used by looking at the symbol that separates the hours, minutes, and seconds. Drop-Frame code uses semicolons (01 ; 15 ; 00); Non-Drop-Frame uses colons (01 : 15 : 00).

Interlace Options

For many years, a cathode ray tube (CRT) was the only choice for video display. A CRT has a screen that is coated with phosphors. When an electron beam hits the phosphors, they glow for a short period of time (called "persistence"). If they continued to glow, the images would build up until the entire screen would turn white.

Finding a phosphor that glows for a short period and then turns dark is not an easy task. The trick is to find one that glows brightly as the electron beam scans from the top to the bottom of the screen and darkens quickly enough for the next frame to display properly.

The first CRTs could not maintain a glowing phosphor for the entire time it took the beam to trace the image all the way to the bottom. By the time the beam got to the bottom of the image, the top was too dark. To solve this problem, the image was created using two "interlaced" fields.

By dividing a video frame into two fields, and then alternately tracing those fields on the screen, the image brightness appears consistent over the entire screen. Field 1 (the upper or odd field) starts at the topmost line on the CRT and traces odd-numbered lines to the bottom. Field 2 (the lower or even field) is then traced between the odd-numbered lines. The two fields are interlaced to create a single frame that displays an even brightness from top to bottom.

Computer monitors use non-interlaced video (called "progressive scan"). Progressive scan video does not interlace fields — it scans the entire screen from the top to the bottom. This process works on a computer monitor because the monitor-display hardware is not restricted to NTSC standards.

Problems Caused by Interlacing

If a horizontal line on a screen is thin enough, it is displayed on a single field line. As the fields alternate between upper and lower, the line appears to jump up and down. If you are viewing your project on a progressive scan monitor, the jitter is not apparent unless the project is exported to an interlaced system.

There is no requirement regarding which field must be displayed first (odd or even). The dominant field (the first one to display) can vary from one piece of equipment to the next. When video is recorded on one device and played back on another, it is possible to display the lower field before the upper field. This causes the displayed image to appear very jumpy on the screen. This jumpiness is not apparent when the video is playing at full speed; but when the video is slowed down or stopped, the effect can be very distracting.

Premiere offers several options for controlling how fields are rendered. To use the options, you can select Project>Project Settings>Keyframe and Rendering. Available options are No Fields, Upper Field First, and Lower Field First.

You can use the No Fields option when you are certain your final movie will only be displayed on a computer monitor. If you encounter problems on a television screen, try switching the field that is rendered first.

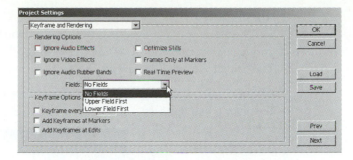

In addition to Keyframe and Rendering options, Premiere provides additional options from the Clip menu. To access the options, you can select Clip>Video Options>Field Options.

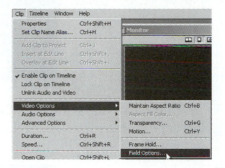

The Reverse Field Dominance option determines whether the odd-numbered field or the even-numbered field is displayed first. In the Processing Options dialog box:

- Select None if you do not want to process fields.

- Select Interlace Consecutive Frames if you want to create fields from progressive-scan video.

- Select the Always Deinterlace option to tell Premiere to keep one field and discard the other. If you also select the No Field option, the upper field is retained and the lower field is discarded. To reverse this sequence, you can select Reverse Field Dominance. Reversing the field dominance and using the Always Deinterlace option causes the lower field to be retained and the upper field to be discarded. This option is very useful for reducing flicker in freeze-frame presentations.

- Select Flicker Removal to slightly blur the two fields together so the line shows in each field.

- Select Deinterlace When Speed is below 100% to force Premiere to calculate the best field selection process for smooth motion. This is not the same as the Always Deinterlace option.

Safe Colors

Video display on a television does not have the same range of color as the RGB color model. Computer monitors use the RGB model (color space) and can reproduce many colors that a television cannot.

If you choose a color that will not reproduce properly in NTSC video (an "unsafe" color), a warning flag appears.

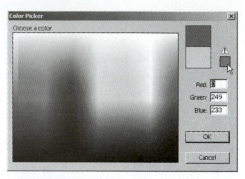

To select a color that is similar to the desired color and color-safe as well, click the color that appears under the warning flag. Premiere then selects the nearest safe color and the warning flag disappears.

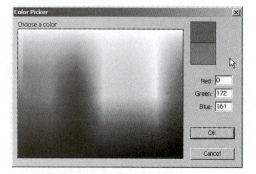

Codecs

COmpressor/DECompressor selection determines the amount of compression applied to your video. Increasing compression results in smaller (and usually faster) presentation files with a corresponding loss of quality. Compression and decompression can be produced by software or hardware. If you use software compression, Premiere provides many choices. An optional video capture card that is installed in your computer performs hardware compression. If you are using hardware compression, additional codecs appear in the selection list.

To select a compressor, you would first select Project>Project Settings>Video, and then click the down arrow located to the right of the currently selected compressor.

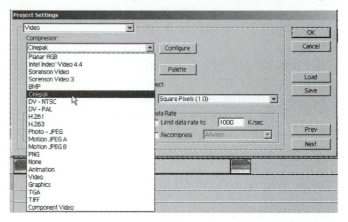

Many codecs provide additional adjustment controls in the Project Settings dialog box. Frame Size, Frame Rate, Color Depth, and Data Rate are typical adjustments. Many codecs also provide an adjustable slider to control quality. As the quality is lowered, the amount of compression is increased.

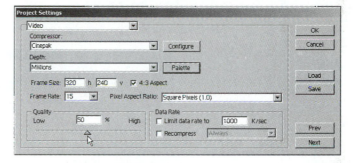

QuickTime Codecs

Many codecs are available for QuickTime video. Below are some of the most popular:

- **Animation.** When set to its best quality setting, Animation allows for an alpha channel and a color depth of millions of colors +. The Animation codec is designed for images that contain large areas of a single color.

- **Cinepak.** This is a good choice for movies that will be delivered via the Web (Macintosh- and Windows-compatible). It is also used for movies that will play directly from CD-ROMs. Cinepak is also a good choice for playback on older computers.

- **DV-NTSC and DV-PAL.** These digital video codecs are used when the output will be displayed using DV, MiniDV, and DVCpro playback equipment. They provide very good full-screen playback from a digital video camera or deck.

- **Video.** This codec should only be used for drafts that need to play back quickly. It only supports a depth of thousands of colors.

- **Motion JPEG A/B.** These compressors are primarily designed for use with hardware compression cards. They also produce very small files using software compression. The image quality is acceptable for informational purposes.

- **None.** Using no compression results in very large files with no loss of image quality. If you are using an alpha channel, it is incorporated into the final film as long as the color depth is set to millions of colors + or higher.
- **Sorensen.** The Sorensen codec is slow to compress, but does an excellent job. High compression makes this a good choice when distributing your movies via the Internet.

Audio Compression

If you are exporting your final production to videotape, audio compression is not necessary. For files that are presented on CD-ROM or over the Internet, audio compression allows the computer to process audio information at a faster rate.

There are several audio codecs available, but some are used only for engineering tests and have little value in video production. In the following list, four codecs are of particular interest:

- **IMA 4:1.** This codec is used for cross-platform multimedia projects.
- **Qdesign Music 2.** This option can deliver CD-quality audio over a 28K modem.
- **Mace 6:1.** This is a good quality, general-purpose compressor.
- **Mace 3:1.** This codec is similar to Mace 6:1, but it provides lower compression and better quality.

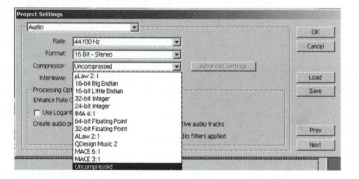

Chapter Summary

In this final chapter of the book, you learned about timebase and how it represents the individual frames on the Timeline. You learned about the difference between Drop-Frame and Non-Drop-Frame timecode. The interlace theory was discussed, and methods on how to control interlace problems were demonstrated. You learned how to avoid using colors that are not accurately reproduced in NTSC video. Finally, you learned about audio and video codecs, how to select them (based on your project needs), and how to adjust individual codec values.

Complete Project D: Central Coast Surfing

Free-Form Project #2

Assignment

Ed and Rita Smith are 82 years old. They will be celebrating 50 years of wedded bliss this year. Their family members are planning a surprise anniversary party for Ed and Rita. As a recognized local cinematographer, you were recruited to create a video that will be debuted at the party. You know most of the people who will be at the party, and you don't want to disappoint any of them. You want to apply your movie-making skills to the best of your ability to create an heirloom-quality piece.

The family members provided many still photographs of Ed and Rita's life together, as well as old movie footage and interviews with various family members. Adding appropriate background music would be an excellent way to bring all these components together in the final film.

Applying Your Skills

As you create this movie, use the following features and functions:

- Write a list of interview questions.
- Create a storyboard.
- Scan the still images.
- Tape the interviews.
- Capture the video.
- Assemble the video clips.
- Add music and voice as necessary.
- Prepare the production to play as a QuickTime movie.

Specifications

- Finished length: approximately 10-15 minutes.
- Transitions placed on all clips.
- Titles, both rolling credits and static titles, identifying the people being interviewed.
- Transitions where appropriate.
- Split screens where appropriate.
- Filters to enhance the older footage.

Included Files

There are no included files in this project. You are required to shoot all of the footage yourself.

Publisher's Comments

This is a challenging assignment because it requires you to use contemporary footage combined with stills and archived video to create the feeling of tradition. Humor is another consideration — people love to laugh at parties.

You might also watch some documentary productions from the History Channel or A&E so you can better understand how to conduct an interview — that aspect of movie making is very difficult to master. You must be objective, and ask questions while you keep your own personality out of the equation. Prepare your questions beforehand, and be ready to edit the footage to arrive at the perfect final product.

During filming, you may use members of your own family or another family that you know. A couple who is actually celebrating a 50th wedding anniversary is not required; a little bit of make-believe is always fun.

Review #2

Chapters 6 through 10

In the second half of the book, you learned that titles are an essential element of all movies. They provide the audience with necessary information as well as offer another way to entertain viewers. You found out how to create picture-in-picture movies, where the movie plays on one track and a still image is superimposed on another track. You also learned how to apply the time-honored "blue screen" technique that allows you to insert the background of your choice after the footage has been shot. You discovered the power of Premiere's filters, and how they can be used to create a wide range of effects to enhance your footage. You explored the different ways to distribute movies, and what each format requires for quality and download speed settings; knowing how to export movies to a number of different formats makes your movies accessible to a larger viewing audience. And finally, you learned many tips and techniques to increase your efficiency when working with Premiere, and how to ensure your movies are created in the most effective manner. Through this series of discussions, exercises, and projects you should:

- Be familiar with the features and functions of the Title Designer window, and be able to create interesting titles and text elements.

- Know how to apply blue screening, transparency, and alpha channels to create desired effects.

- Understand the different editing modes, and know when to use them.

- Be capable of using the Effect Controls and Video Effects palettes to apply special effects.

- Be comfortable combining multiple effects to create custom effects.

- Know how to output movies in a variety of different formats to meet the needs of as many viewers as possible.

- Understand the value of device control, and how it helps with the export process.

- Be familiar with the concepts of timecode and timebase, and know how to avoid gaps in your recordings.

Project A: The Monkey Movie

Your company's newest client is a zoo. The zoo owners are launching a fund-raising campaign and want to illustrate some of their crowd-pleasing monkeys in the midst of the antics the public finds so endearing. You are part of the team that is chartered to produce the first part of the movie. As the newest member of the team, you must set up the basic production, which will be handed off to a member of the special effects department for fine-tuning. You will make a QuickTime movie that the client can review and approve before the expensive effects are added.

In this project, you will use your new Premiere skills to assemble the initial movie. The subject of the production is a group of monkeys at play. You will combine several clips, apply transitions, and generate a QuickTime movie for the client's review.

Getting Started

1. Open Premiere and accept the default settings. Make sure the frame size is 240 × 180. If it is not, select Custom, then press the Next key until the Video menu appears, and then enter 240 × 180.

2. Select File>Import>File. When the dialog box appears, locate the **RF_Premiere>Project_A** folder, and select all of the files. Hold down the Shift/Control key, click each file name to highlight it, and then click Open. As an alternative, you can import the entire **Project_A** folder.

3. In the Project window, double-click **final_monkey.mov**. Click the Play button to preview the final project. Close the **final_monkey.mov** Clip window, but leave the Project and Monitor windows open, as well as the Timeline, to begin the project.

Assemble and Place the Clips

1. In the Project window, look through the project files. Let's place these shots in an alternating fashion on the Video 1A and Video 1B tracks of the Timeline.

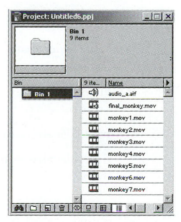

2. One at a time, drag the clips to the Timeline window and position them as indicated in the list below. Note carefully on which track they should be placed and the exact position on the Timeline:

- audio_a on Audio 1
- monkey1.mov on Video 1A at 00:00:00:00
- monkey2.mov on Video 1B at 00:00:02:13
- monkey3.mov on Video 1A at 00:00:05:23
- monkey4.mov on Video 1B at 00:00:09:16
- monkey5.mov on Video 1A at 00:00:13:15
- monkey6.mov on Video 1B at 00:00:17:26
- monkey7.mov on Video 1A at 00:00:22:26

3. Save your project as "monkeys.ppj" to your **Work_In_Progress** folder.

4. Double-check that the work area bar extends to the end of the production. Render the project, and watch the entire production play. Now you should see our special guest star monkey happily playing as music is heard in the background.

Add Transitions

1. Add the first two transitions from the folders in the Transitions palette, and position them in the overlaps of the shots as indicated below. Transitions should snap into position at the overlaps. Select Window>Show Transitions, then select:

- Iris folder>Iris Diamond transition to monkey1.mov and monkey2.mov overlap.
- Wipe folder>Clock Wipe transition to monkey2.mov and monkey3.mov overlap.

2. Press the Return/Enter key to render the production. You should see the monkey playing as transitions occur from shot to shot. Save your production again.

3. Now add the remaining transitions as indicated in the list below:

- Wipe folder>Barn Doors transition to monkey3.mov and monkey4.mov overlap.
- 3D Motion folder>Cube Spin transition to monkey4.mov and monkey5.mov overlap.
- Iris folder>Iris Cross transition to monkey5.mov and monkey6.mov overlap.
- Iris folder>Iris Round transition to monkey6.mov and monkey7.mov overlap.

4. Save your changes.

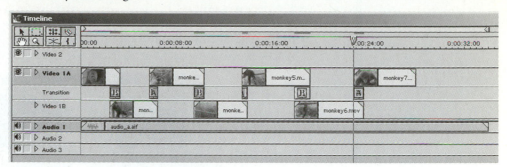

Add Color Borders to the Transitions

1. Double-click the first transition on the Timeline — the Iris Diamond. In the dialog box, check Show Actual Sources. Notice the preview of your two video clips. Drag the Border slider arrow from None to the right a little.

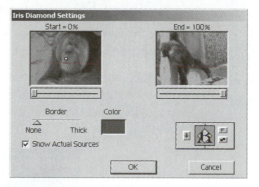

2. Click the black Color rectangle. When the Color Picker appears, set Red: 0, Green: 0, Blue: 255, and then click OK.

3. When you see a thin blue border appear on the animated preview, click OK. Double-click the second transition on the Timeline — the Clock Wipe. When the dialog box appears, check Show Actual Sources. Notice that a preview of the two video clips appears with the wipe beginning at the 12:00 mark.

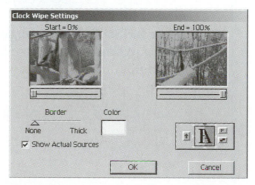

4. Click the black Color rectangle. When the Color Picker appears, set Red: 249, Green: 255, Blue: 77, and then click OK.

5. Move the Border slider arrow from None to the right a little. A thin yellow border appears in the animated preview. Click OK.

6. Double-click the third transition on the Timeline — the Barn Doors. In the dialog box, check Show Actual Sources. Notice the preview of your two video clips.

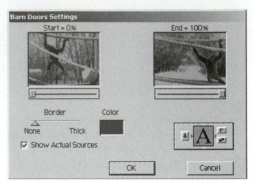

7. Click the black Color rectangle. In the Color Picker, set Red: 0, Green: 0, Blue: 255, and then click OK.

8. Move the Border slider arrow slightly to the right. You see a thin blue border appear in the animated preview. Click OK.

9. Skip the fourth transition, the Cube Spin transition. Double-click the fifth transition, the Iris Cross transition. In the dialog box, click the black Color rectangle. When the Color Picker appears, set Red: 0, Green: 239, Blue: 232, and then click OK.

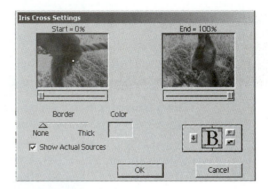

10. Move the Border slider triangle slightly to the right to create a thin, but visible, border. When a light blue border appears around the preview in the dialog box, click OK.

11. Now modify the last transition, the Iris Round transition. Move the Border slider slightly to the right. Double-click the black Color rectangle. When the Color Picker appears, set Red: 0, Green: 0, Blue: 255. Click OK, and click OK again to exit this dialog box.

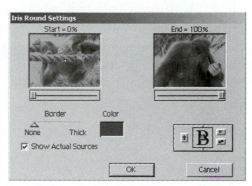

12. Render the production and watch the monkey in action with transitions between shots. Save your production.

Export as a QuickTime Movie

Now that you have all of the elements in place, let's review how to compress your work into a final movie. As you recall, a QuickTime movie compresses all elements into one complete movie. It flattens all of the project tracks into one track.

1. Select File>Export Timeline>Movie. Enter "finalmonkey.mov" as the movie Name, and then click Settings.

2. Choose the General settings dialog box. Set the File Type to QuickTime and the Range to Work Area. Click the Export Video and Export Audio check boxes.

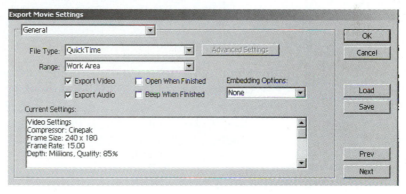

*If you think you will use
your Export Movie
Settings often, click Save
to save them for future
use. The next time you
export with the same
settings, you can simply
load them, rather than
taking the time to set
them again.*

*On most systems, double
clicking the file name of
the movie you created
opens the movie in the
system's default player.*

3. Click the Next button. In the Video Settings area, set the Compressor to Cinepak, the Depth to Millions, Frame Size to 240 h and 180 w, Frame Rate to 15, Pixel Aspect Ratio to Square Pixels, and then move the Quality arrow from 100% to 85% to reduce the file size. (You will only need to change this if the project is destined for both Windows and Macintosh systems; otherwise select Video as the Compressor.)

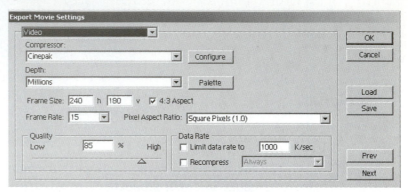

4. Click the Next button. In the Audio Settings area, select a Rate of 22050 Hz, a Format of 8-bit-Mono, a Compressor of Uncompressed, and then click OK. These settings help to keep your file size small.

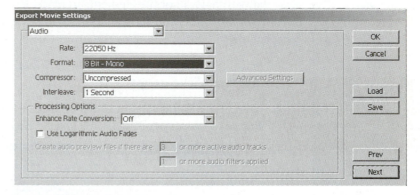

5. Premiere will return to the Timeline window. It can take several minutes to complete the rendering process, depending on the speed of your system. When the process is complete, find your movie and play it in your system's media player (Real Player, Windows Media Player, or QuickTime). Look through your Applications/Program Files folder to see which player you have on your system.

Now your project is a self-contained piece. You can delete all other files related to this project if you do not want to edit them again.

Project B: Making Spaghetti

A major software distributor hired your agency to create a multimedia cookbook for beginner cooks. The target markets are college students who are away from home for the first time and new chefs. In addition to recipes, this interactive cookbook includes a series of QuickTime movies illustrating techniques for preparing tasty dishes. Your task is to produce the movie that demonstrates the art of making spaghetti. This segment will be incorporated into the chapter on main dishes.

For this project, you will import a series of short video clips, position them appropriately, and then add transitions, music, and credits. You will create titles that explain the key points of the video. The finished movie will present a friendly face in the kitchen that will help novice cooks succeed in preparing a spaghetti dinner.

Getting Started

1. Open Premiere and accept the default settings. Double-check that your screen Size is set to 240 × 180. Select File>Import>File. A dialog box appears. Locate the **RF_Premiere>Project_B** folder. Select all the files, and then click Open. As an alternative, you can choose File>Import>Folder and import the entire **Project_B** folder. Double click **final_b.mov** to see the finished movie. When you are finished viewing, close the Clip window.

2. If you imported the entire **Project_B** folder, click on it to see the individual files. Leave all files open to begin the project.

Assemble and Place the Clips

1. Notice that there are 15 different shots (shot1.mov through shot15.mov) and the audio track (audio_b.aif) in the **Project_B** folder. Let's place the shots on Video tracks 1A and 1B.

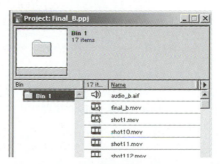

2. Begin by dragging shot1.mov to the Timeline window, positioning it at the beginning of Video 1A. Drag shot2.mov to the Timeline window and position it on Video 1B at 00:00:02:18.

3. Shot2.mov runs 00:00:06:12, which is too long. Trim two seconds from the clip, using either the Duration option in the Clip menu or the Razor tool from the Timeline toolbox.

4. One at a time, drag the remaining shots to the Timeline window and position them as indicated in the list below. Note the precise track on which they should be placed, and the exact position:

- shot3.mov on Video 1B at 00:00:06:29
- shot4.mov on Video 1B at 00:00:9:24
- shot5.mov on Video 1A at 00:00:11:12
- shot6.mov on Video 1B at 00:00:14:18
- shot7.mov on Video 1A at 00:00:16:25
- shot8.mov on Video 1B at 00:00:19:21
- shot9.mov on Video 1A at 00:00:24:17
- shot10.mov on Video 1B at 00:00:25:28
- shot11.mov on Video 1A at 00:00:30:07
- shot12.mov on Video 1B at 00:00:32:11
- shot13.mov on Video 1A at 00:00:38:18
- shot14.mov on Video 1A, directly after shot13.mov
- shot15.mov on Video 1A, directly after shot14.mov

5. Drag audio_b.aif to the Timeline window and position it on Audio 2 so it falls at the beginning of the production, directly under shot1.mov. (You must scroll to the left to move to the beginning of the production.)

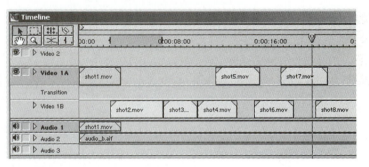

The production music is placed on Audio 2 because our chef's dialog is on the Audio 1 track.

6. The work area bar should extend to the end of the production. If it does not, extend the bar to about the one-minute mark so you can view the entire production with visible transitions.

7. Save your project as "final_b.ppj" to your **Work_In_Progress** folder.

8. Render the production so you can see how it looks so far. You should see chef Kathi making spaghetti as music plays in the background.

Add and Preview Transitions

1. From the Page Peel folder in the Transitions palette (Window>Show Transitions), drag the Page Peel transition to the Transition track. It should snap into position in the overlap of shot1.mov and shot2.mov.

2. From the 3D Motion folder, drag the Cube Spin transition to the Transition track. It should snap into position in the overlap of shot4.mov and shot5.mov.

3. Render the production and watch our chef slice vegetables. You should also see transitions (that you added in Steps 1 and 2) between the first few video clips. Don't forget to save your production again — although the production plays, the file must be saved in its most recent version.

4. Now add the remaining transitions, positioned in the overlaps between shots as indicated in the list below:

   • 3D Motion folder>Cube Spin transition to shot5.mov and shot6.mov overlap.

   • 3D Motion folder>Spin Away transition to shot6.mov and shot7.mov overlap.

   • Wipe folder>Barn Doors transition to shot7.mov and shot8.mov overlap.

   • Dissolve folder>Additive Dissolve transition to shot8.mov and shot9.mov overlap.

   • 3D Motion folder>Cube Spin transition to shot9.mov and shot10.mov overlap.

   • Slide folder>Push transition to shot10.mov and shot11.mov overlap.

   • Iris folder>Iris Round transition to shot11.mov and shot12.mov overlap.

   • Wipe folder>Clock Wipe transition to shot12.mov and shot13.mov overlap.

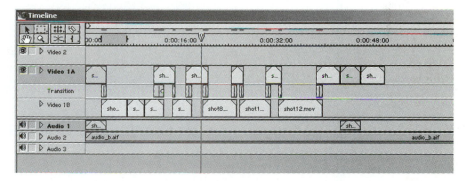

Add Color Borders to the Transitions

1. Double-click the second transition, the Cube Spin, on the Timeline. When the dialog box appears, click the Show Actual Sources button. You see a preview of your two video clips. Drag the Border slider arrow slightly to the right.

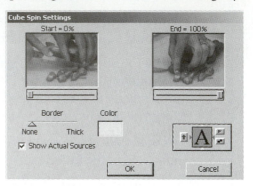

You may notice that transitions are not present between all of the clips. Too many splashy transitions can be too much of a good thing.

2. At the moment, no colored border separates the video clips. A colored border helps to define the individual sections. Click the black Color rectangle. In the Color Picker, set Red: 160, Green: 251, Blue: 255, and click OK. A thin light blue border appears to separate the images. Click OK to return to the Timeline.

3. Double-click the third transition, which is another Cube Spin transition. Click the black Color rectangle. In the Color Picker, set Red: 250, Green: 255, Blue: 108, and click OK. Move the Border slider a little to the right. A thin yellow border appears. Click OK.

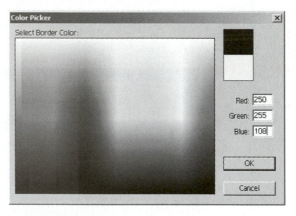

4. Double-click the fourth transition, a Spin Away transition. Click the black Color rectangle. In the Color Picker, set Red: 255, Green: 12, Blue: 48, and click OK. Move the Border slider a little to the right. When a thin red border appears, click OK.

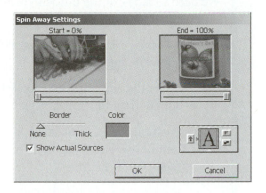

5. Double-click the fifth transition on the Timeline, the Barn Doors transition. When the dialog box appears, click Show Actual Sources. You see a preview of your two video clips.

6. Click the black Color rectangle. In the Color Picker, set Red: 0, Green: 0, Blue: 255, and click OK. Move the Border slider slightly to the right. When a thin blue border appears, click OK.

7. Skip the next transition, which is the Additive Dissolve transition. Double-click the seventh transition, a Cube Spin transition, and then click the black Color rectangle. In the Color Picker, set Red: 160, Green: 255, Blue: 188, and click OK. Move the Border slider a little to the right. When a thin light green border appears, click OK.

8. Modify the rest of the transitions. Continue to move down the Timeline and select each of the remaining transitions. Use colors of your choice to apply different borders to each in turn.

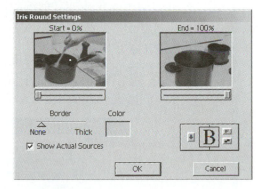

9. Save and render the production. You should see the chef cooking as transitions occur from one shot to the next.

Fade the Audio Clips

You have probably noticed that the music abruptly stops at the end of this production. We need to fade out the music in order to end the production in a more professional manner.

1. Click the triangle on the left side of the Audio 2 track. The Audio box opens to show the music.

2. Move the edit line to 00:00:48:10 and click your cursor at that point. A small red square (handle) appears.

3. Position the edit line at 00:00:49:25, and click your cursor at that point. A second handle appears. Drag that red square to the bottom of the audio area. (This is the fade-out of the music.)

4. Position the edit line at 00:00:52:00, and click to place a third handle. Drag that square to the bottom of the audio area, matching where you placed the previous handle. This keeps the music from fading in again.

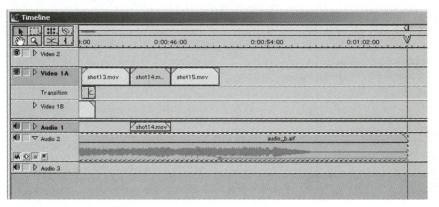

5. Click the triangle to the left of the words "Audio 2" to collapse the box. Save your work as "spaghetti.ppj" in your **Work_In_Progress** folder.

Create a Title

1. Select Edit>Preferences>Titler. Click the Show Safe Title Margins and Show Safe Action Margins check boxes (each should show a checkmark), and then click OK.

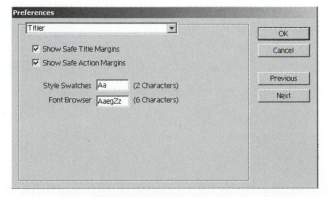

2. Select File>New>Title to display the Title Designer dialog box.

If the video will be presented only on a computer monitor, it is not necessary to stay within the safe margins.

3. The Title Designer window is the same size as the Video window. Click the Show Video check box at the top of the window.

4. Select the Text tool in the Timeline toolbox. Select a Font and Font Size from the Object Style>Properties dialog box (we used 36-pt. News Gothic), and then click on the video image. When you see a blinking I-beam, you are ready to enter some text. Type the following words, placing each on a separate line (press the Return/Enter key after each word): "How", "To", "Make", "Spaghetti". With the Selection tool, drag the text into position on the page as shown below.

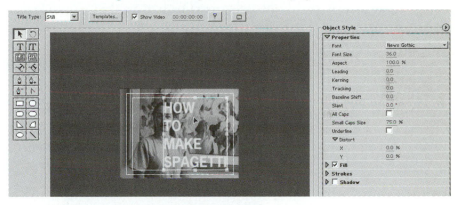

5. Click the box next to Fill and then open the Fill menu (click the triangle). Select a Solid Fill Type, set the Opacity to 100%, and then click the Color selection box. The Color Picker appears.

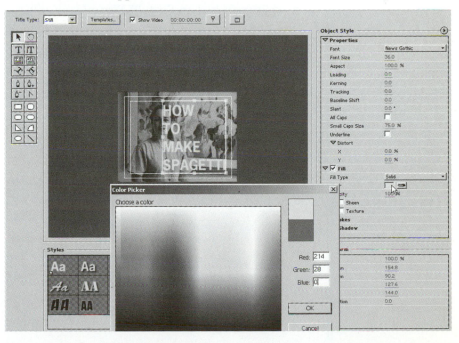

6. Set Red: 214, Green: 28, Blue: 0, and then click OK. Your title now has a bright red color. Click OK.

7. The type must be moved to the right side of the screen. Choose Title>Type Alignment>Right.

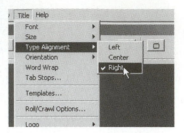

8. Add a drop shadow to the type. Click the Shadow check box in the Object Style dialog box (be sure a checkmark appears). Open the Shadow menu, and then click the Color selection box. Set the Color to Red: 180, Green: 28, Blue: 0, and then click OK.

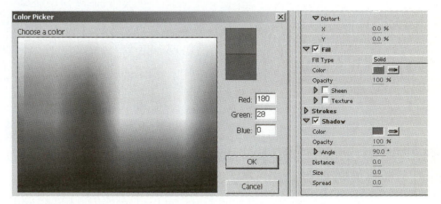

9. Adjust the final position of the text using the Selection tool. Select File>Save, and save your title as "opening.prtl" to your **Work_In_Progress** folder.

10. Once it is saved, your title automatically transfers to the Project menu. (You may need to drag it from the main project area into the same folder as your other files.) Close the Title Designer window. You should now have opening.prtl in Bin 1 (or in the **Project_B** folder of the Project window if you imported the entire **Project_B** folder). Save the file.

11. Drag opening.prtl to the Timeline and position it at the beginning of the Video 2 track. Select opening.prtl on the Timeline. Select Clip>Duration, set the Duration to 00:00:02:00, and then click OK. Your credit adjusts to two seconds in length.

Using a fade-in and fade-out creates a more professional appearance for your production.

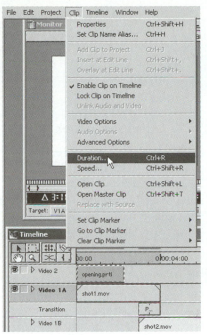

Set the Title Opacity

Press Return/Enter to view your production. As you see, the title graphic of the video starts rather abruptly at the beginning and then rapidly drops out at the end. What we would prefer is to have the graphic fade in at the beginning and fade out at the end. Premiere provides built-in controls for the opacity (fade) of the graphic.

1. Click the small gray triangle to the left of Video 2 on the Timeline. The track expands to show the opacity levels for opening.prtl.

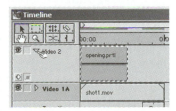

2. Notice the thin red line at the top of this window. It shows the title at 100% opacity. At the far left of the red line, notice a red handle. Move the cursor slightly to the right and click again on the red line. A second red handle appears.

3. Position your cursor over the far-left handle, and drag the handle to the bottom of the window. This is the fade-in for the title. At the far right of the red line, click once. A third red handle appears. Move the cursor slightly to the left and click again on the red line. A fourth handle appears.

4. Position the cursor over the far-right handle, and drag it to the bottom of the window. This is the fade-out for the title. Click the triangle to collapse the box.

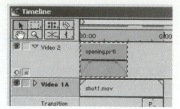

5. Save and render this production. The title fades in and fades out as the chef prepares to cook.

Create Additional Titles

Now let's create the four remaining titles that outline the steps necessary to make spaghetti. We'll show you how to create the first one; you'll create the other titles on your own. For details, review the Create a Title exercise you completed earlier in this project.

1. Select File>New>Title to display the Title Designer dialog box. Click the Text tool in the toolbox. Select a Font and Size from the Properties dialog box. When you see a blinking I-beam, type the following (without the quotation marks), pressing Return/Enter after each line:

   "Step 1:"
   "Slice the"
   "Ingredients"

2. Select a new Fill color. Click the triangle for Fill to access the menu. Click the Color selection box. The Color Picker appears.

3. Set Red: 0, Green: 9, Blue: 181, and then click OK. Your title is now a bright blue color.

4. Arrange the type by choosing Title>Type Alignment>Center, then Title>Position>Horizontal Center, and finally Title>Position>Vertical Center.

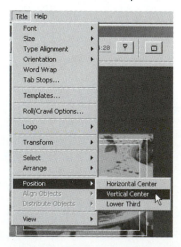

5. Place a drop shadow on the type. Make the shadow a dark blue that complements the bright blue you selected for the lettering.

6. You must save the title and add it to the Timeline. Save your title as "step1.prtl" to your **Work_In_Progress** folder. Once saved, your title automatically transfers to the Project menu. Close the Title Designer window.

7. You should now have step1.prtl and opening.prtl in the **Work_In_Progress** folder along with your other title and video clips. Save this file.

8. Place step1.prtl on the Timeline on Video 2 at 00:00:03:18. Make certain the text clip is highlighted, and click the Duration command located in the Clip window. Set the Duration to 00:00:2:15.

9. As you did with the title graphic, use the Opacity handles to make the text fade in and fade out.

10. Continue to create the titles for the rest of your production. They should resemble the preview, final_b.mov, which you viewed earlier. View this movie again if you wish. Create the following titles (without the quotation marks):

"Step 2: Add the Sauce"
"Step 3: Cook the Noodles"
"The Final Results"

The keyboard shortcut to display the Transparency Settings dialog box is Command/Control-G.

Export as a QuickTime Movie

Now that you have all of the elements in place, let's review how to compress your work into a final movie. As you recall, a QuickTime movie compresses all elements into one complete movie. It flattens all of the project tracks into one track.

1. Select File>Export Timeline>Movie. Enter "spaghetti.mov" as the movie Name, and then click the Settings button.

2. Choose the General Settings dialog box. Select QuickTime as the File Type.

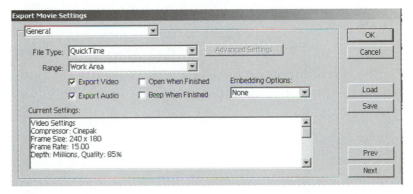

3. Click the Next button. In the Video Settings area, select Cinepak. You need to change these settings if the project is destined for both Windows and Macintosh systems; otherwise, select Video as the Compressor, set the Frame Rate to 15, and move the Quality slider from 100% to 85% to reduce the file size.

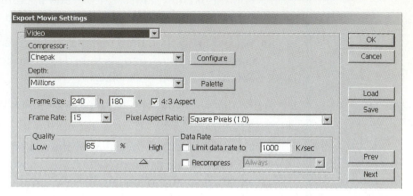

4. Click the Next button. In the Audio Settings area, select 22050 Hz as the Rate, 8-bit-Mono Format, Uncompressed as the Compressor, and then click OK. These settings help to keep your file size small.

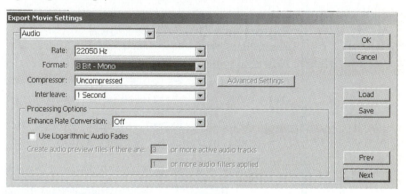

Cinepak takes longer to render, but it's an effective way to create a truly cross-platform movie.

5. Click OK to return to the Export Timeline window, and then click Save. It takes several minutes to complete the rendering process.

Now your project is a self-contained piece. Use your media viewer to see it. You can delete all other files related to this project if you do not want to edit it again.

Project C: The Gold Rush

A long-term client, the ATAA (Associated Travel Agents of America), retained your company to create a series of multimedia CDs for member travel agencies. These CDs will be used to promote desirable summer vacation destinations. Customers can use terminals in the travel agents' waiting rooms to explore vacation possibilities that the agents can then book in real-time.

Your team is developing a CD about California and Alaska vacation packages, including a cruise to Alaska with a stop at Skagway. To promote this scenic area and generate interest in the cruise, your authentic-looking old-time movie will tell a bit about the history of the gold rush, and take the viewer on a train ride along the Yukon Trail. You will create a title that explains the video and incorporates a variety of shots of the magnificent Alaska countryside.

Getting Started

1. Open Premiere and accept the default settings. Be certain you select a Size of 240 × 180.

2. Select File>Import>File. When the dialog box appears, select the **RF_Premiere>ProjectC** folder. Select all of the files (use the Command/ Control key), and then click Open.

Place, Stretch, and Trim Clips

1. Alternately place the shots contained in Bin 1 on tracks Video 1A and 1B.

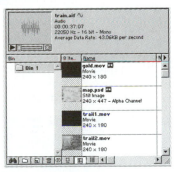

2. Drag gold.mov to the Timeline window at the beginning of Video 1B. Drag map.psd to the Timeline window on Video 1A at 00:00:02:13.

3. Map.psd runs five seconds on the Timeline, which is too short for this production. Drag the right edge of the still image and stretch it out to 00:00:31:18.

4. Drag train.aif to Audio 1. It is longer than map.psd. Fade out the music at 00:00:31:00 (use the rubberband in the Audio 1 track).

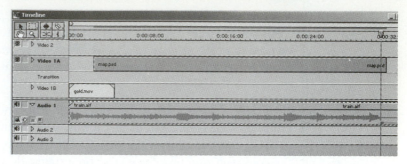

5. Drag trail1.mov to the Timeline window on Video 2 at 00:00:06:25. Drag trail2.mov to the Timeline window on Video 2 next to trail1.mov at 00:00:13:08. It stretches out to 14.10 seconds, which is too long for this production.

6. Double-click trail2.mov to open the trail2.mov Clip window. Drag the edit line marker to the right until it reads 00:00:03:04. Click the Mark Out icon. Click the Apply button. The clip shortens on the Timeline. Move it back to 00:00:13:08. Close the Clip window.

7. Drag trail3.mov to the Timeline window on Video 2 at 00:00:18:01. Shorten trail3.mov to 03:04. Drag trail4.mov to the Timeline window on Video 2 at 00:00:22:12.

8. Drag trail5.mov to the Timeline window on Video 2 at 00:00:27:17.

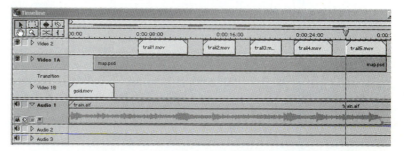

9. Save your project as "final_c.ppj" to your **Work_In_Progress** folder.

10. Render the production so you can see how it looks so far. You should see some people panning for gold, a map, and train shots as music plays in the background. Next, let's create some special effects.

Create the Effect of an Old Movie

1. On the Timeline at the beginning of Video 1B, you find gold.mov. If it is not already visible, open the Video Effects palette. From the QuickTime folder, drag QuickTime Effects onto gold.mov. The Select Effect dialog box appears.

2. Select Film Noise, accept the defaults as they appear in the dialog box, and then click OK.

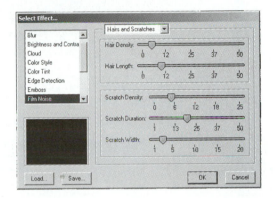

3. From the Image Control folder, drag Tint onto gold.mov. The Effect Controls palette appears. Notice that it shows the QuickTime and Tint effects are both placed on gold.mov.

4. Click the Map Black to Color Picker, and set Red: 255, Green: 120, Blue: 25, and then click OK. Click the Map White to Color Picker, and set Red: 255, Green: 242, Blue: 210, and again click OK. Click the number (0.0%) for Amount to Tint, set the Value to 30, and click OK.

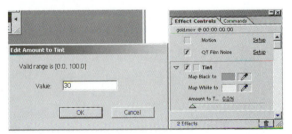

5. Render the production, and watch a seemingly old-time movie of gold diggers panning for gold. Save your production again.

Use Transparency to Create a Superimposition Effect

1. Click trail1.mov. Expand the Video 2 track on the Timeline. Select Clip>Video Options>Transparency. A dialog box appears. Change the Key Type to Multiply, and click OK.

2. We want this clip to fade in and fade out. Click and create a set of two red rubber-band handles. Pull the handles to create the fade-in and fade-out for trail1.mov. Render the production, and watch the train fade in, play, and fade out, while it is superimposed on the map.

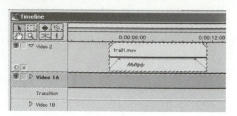

3. Add the Multiply Transparency effect to trail2.mov, trail3.mov and trail4.mov. Fade in trail5.mov, but don't fade out the clip. (Do not apply the Transparency filter to trail5.mov.) Render these new additions to the production. Each of the video clips fades in over the map and then fades out — all except the last clip, trail5.mov.

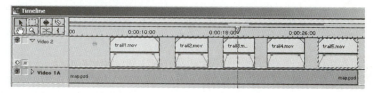

4. Save and render these changes.

Simulate Movement on a Still Image by an Image Pan

1. From the Video Effects palette Transform folder, drag Image Pan onto map.psd. The Effect Controls palette appears. Click Enable Keyframing (the box next to the words "Image Pan"). Select the first keyframe on the Timeline under map.psd. Click Setup in the Effect Controls palette. The Image Pan Settings dialog box appears.

2. Let's select a starting point for the pan. We want the pan to move from the bottom to the top. Enter a Width of 240 and Height of 180. The bounding box around the image snaps into place to keep the 3 × 4 aspect ratio of the project. Drag the box to the bottom of the Source window until the Top value equals 267 (or you can enter the value from your keyboard). Click OK.

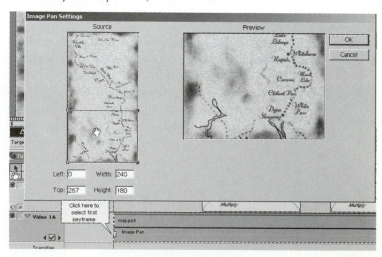

3. To complete the second half of the effect, select the second keyframe on the Timeline under map.psd at the end of the clip. Click Setup in the Effect Controls palette. The Image Pan Settings dialog box appears. Let's select an ending point for the pan. Drag the bounding box upward until the Top value is 0 (or enter a "0" in the value box). Click OK.

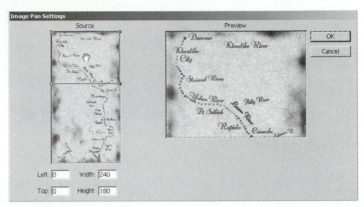

4. Save and render these changes. Be patient, as it takes a couple of minutes to complete the process.

Create the Opening Title

1. Select File>New>Title to display the Title Designer dialog box.

2. Select the Text tool from the Title Designer toolbox. Choose a Font from the Title menu (we chose News Gothic), set the Font Size to 73, and click on the drawing surface. When you see a blinking I-beam, indicating that you are ready to enter some text, type the following (without quotation marks), pressing Return/Enter after each: "The", "Gold Rush". With the Selection tool, drag the text to the center of the page (or select Title>Position>Horizontal Center, and then select Title>Position>Vertical Center).

3. Next, let's replace the current color with a new gradient color. Select Linear Gradient as the Fill type. Double-click the left gradient color indicator. The Color Picker appears.

4. Set Red: 162, Green: 36, Blue: 0, and click OK. Your title is now orange.

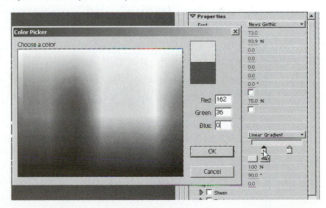

5. Double-click the right gradient color indicator. The Color Picker appears. Set Red: 255, Green: 145, Blue: 62, and click OK. Your title now has a light-to-dark rusty-orange gradient.

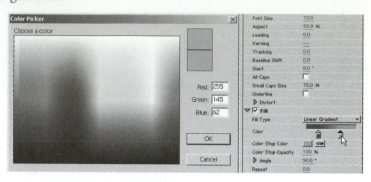

6. Set the gradient Angle to 270.0 degrees.

7. Add a drop shadow to the type. Open the Shadow dialog box, click the check box to turn on Shadow, and then select an Angle of 140.0 degrees, a Distance of 6.0, and Size of 0.0. When you have finished working with the text, save the title as "rush.prtl" to your **Work_In_Progress** folder.

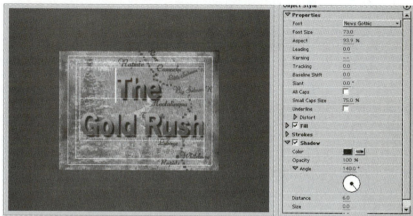

Placing a still image next to a moving video clip can be jarring to the viewer. Image Pan is an excellent way to simulate movement on a still image and make the shots work together seamlessly. The effect enables you to create the impression of a camera moving or panning across a wide scene.

8. After it is saved, the file should automatically appear in the Project window. If not, choose File>Import>File. Close the rush.prtl Title window. Save this file again.

Use Alpha Channels and Opacity to Generate Fades

The title graphic starts abruptly and rapidly drops out at the end. We actually want the graphic to fade in and fade out more subtly. We also want to ensure the title is superimposed on the video of the people panning for gold. We'll use Premiere's built-in controls to direct the opacity of the graphic.

1. Drag rush.prtl to the Timeline window at the beginning of Video 2, and click to highlight it. Select Clip>Video Options>Transparency.

2. When the Transparency Settings dialog box appears, rush.prtl is displayed in the Sample box. Double-check that Key Type is set to White Alpha Matte. If it is not, change the Key Type option from None to White Alpha Matte. Click OK to close the Transparency Settings dialog box.

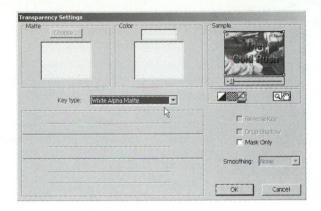

3. Your credit should run for five seconds. If it does not, expand the clip until it runs for that length of time.

4. Expand the Video 2 track on the Timeline to show the opacity levels for rush.prtl.

5. You should see a thin red line at the top of this window, indicating the title is at 100% opacity. At the far left of the line, notice a red handle. Move the cursor slightly to the right, and click again on the red line. A second handle appears.

6. Position the cursor over the far-left handle and drag it down to the bottom of the window. This is the fade-in for the title. At the far right of the red line, click once. A third handle appears. Move the cursor slightly to the left, and click again on the red line. A fourth handle appears.

7. Position the cursor over the far-right handle, and drag it to the bottom of the window. This is the fade-out for the title. Collapse this box.

8. Save and render the production. Your title fades in and fades out as the video plays.

Add a Transition

This old-time movie needs an old-time transition. Let's add one now.

1. From the Transitions palette Page Peel folder, drag Page Peel onto the Transition track on the Timeline. It should snap into place between gold.mov and map.psd.

2. On the Timeline, double-click the Page Peel transition. A dialog box appears. Let's make the page peel diagonally upward, from lower right to upper left. Click the red directional arrow in the lower-right corner (at about 5 o'clock, as shown below). Check to ensure that Forward ("F") is selected. Click OK.

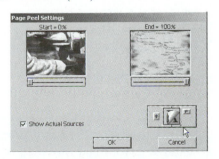

3. Save and render this file.

As an alternative to dragging the viewport (the box that shows the image view), you can get more precise results by manually entering the settings. The correct settings for this effect are Left: 0, Width: 240, Top: 267, and Height: 180.

It generally takes three to five seconds for viewers to read a credit. If you can read it aloud, at a normal pace, the display time is correct.

Export as a QuickTime Movie

Now that all of the elements are in place, let's review how to compress your work into a final movie. As you recall, a QuickTime movie compresses all elements into one complete movie. It flattens all of the project tracks into one track.

1. Select File>Export Timeline>Movie. Enter "goldrush.mov" as the movie Name (you will save it in your **Work_In_Progress** folder), and then click the Settings button.

2. Choose the General settings dialog box. Select QuickTime as the File Type.

3. Click the Next button. In the Video Settings area, select Cinepak. You must change this if the project is destined for both Windows and Macintosh systems; otherwise, select Video as the Compressor. Set the Frame Rate to 15. Move the Quality slider from 100% to 80% to reduce the file size.

4. Click the Next button. In the Audio Settings area, select a Rate of 22050 Hz, 8-bit-Mono Format, Uncompressed as the Compressor, and then click OK. These settings help to keep your file size small. Set the Interleave setting to 1 Second (a value of 1/2 to 1 Second offers the best performance on most computer systems).

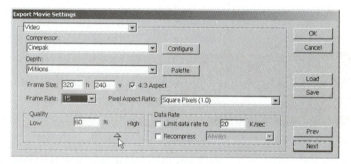

5. Click OK to return to the Export Timeline window, and then click Save. It takes several minutes to complete the rendering process. Find the movie in your **Work_In_Progress** folder and play it.

Now your project is a self-contained piece. You can delete all other files related to this project if you do not want to edit it again.

The ATAA and your team will be very pleased with your production. Now customers can get a taste of Alaska's history, prompting them to book exciting vacations to the area you featured in your new travel video.

Project D: Central Coast Surfing

Your client, the visitor's bureau of a small town on the Central Coast, wants to include a surfing video on their promotional Web site. The bureau director supplied you with a CD-ROM with several footage files of surfers in action and some out-takes of the ocean. The footage files consist of unedited clips. You are not required to use all of them. The bureau agreed to purchase one needle drop (a single continual sound clip that includes negotiated usage rights) of cleared music that you already acquired via the Internet.

Your job is to edit the clips into an interesting video that is designed to attract beginning and intermediate surfers to your client's town. You are also responsible for creating the titles (the copy is supplied). The people in the video are not recognizable, so model releases are not required. The development team has allotted 1.5 to 2.0 minutes on the final CD-ROM for your contribution.

Getting Started

1. Open Premiere and accept the default settings. Be sure you have selected 240 × 180 as the Size. Select File>Import>File. When the dialog box appears, select the **RF_Premiere>Project_D** folder, and import all the files (**surfl1.mov** through **surfl9.mov** and **audio.mov**).

2. Double-click audio.mov and play the audio track to get a feeling for the music. Close the audio.mov Clip window, but leave everything else open to begin the project.

Place, Select, and Trim the Clips

1. Place each clip, in sequence, on the Timeline, alternating between the Video 1A and Video 1B tracks.

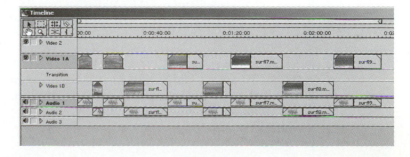

2. Press the Return/Enter key to render and preview the untrimmed clips as a rough cut. Some clips are not needed and others are too long.

3. Click surfl2.mov in the Timeline, and then press the Delete key. Click surfl5.mov in the Timeline, and then press the Delete key. These clips are redundant and not needed.

4. Double click surfl3.mov on the Timeline. In the Clip window, drag the edit line marker to 00:06:11, click the Mark In button at the bottom of the window, and click Apply.

5. Repeat Step 4 to trim the rest of the clips as follows: (Some clips are exactly the right length. Check them to be sure.)

Clip	In	Out
surfl4.mov	00:00:00	00:11:29
surfl5.mov	Deleted	
surfl6.mov	00:00:12	00:13:20
surfl7.mov	00:00:00	00:20:29
surfl8.mov	00:12:09	00:25:03
surfl9.mov	00:00:00	00:23:22

6. Drag each clip to the correct position on the Timeline as follows:

Clip	Track	Start Point
surfl1.mov	Video 1A	00:00:00
surfl2.mov	Deleted	
surfl3.mov	Video 1B	00:06:15
surfl4.mov	Video 1A	00:09:15
surfl5.mov	Deleted	
surfl6.mov	Video 1B	00:20:14
surfl7.mov	Video 1A	00:32:23
surfl8.mov	Video 1B	00:52:24
surfl9.mov	Video 1A	01:04:04

7. If you show only two audio tracks, create another (Audio 3). To do this, select Timeline>Add Audio Track. Drag audio.mov to the Audio 3 track at 00:00:00. Position the edit line marker to 00:00:00. Save your project as "surfl.ppj" to your **Work_In_Progress** folder.

8. Press Return/Enter to render and play your project. As the complexity of the project increases, the render time also increases. Notice that the audio of the surf is too loud.

9. Select Window>Audio Mixer. The simulated Audio Mixer appears. All of the surf sounds are on tracks Audio 1 and 2.

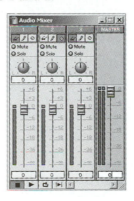

10. Control/right click the bar at the top of one of the slider controls, and then select Audio Mixer Window Options. Click the Write radio button in the Automation Write Options section. This option allows you to make a change that affects all of the tracks without having to move the slider during the recording phase of development.

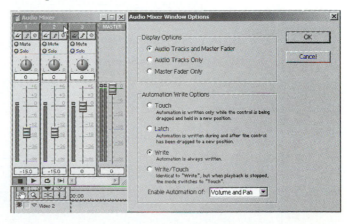

11. Click OK, then select the Automation Write tool at the top of tracks Audio 1 and 2. Drag the slider controls for tracks Audio 1 and 2 to –15, or manually enter the value at the bottom of the track controls (click the existing value before entering a new one).

12. Be sure the edit line marker is at 00:00:00, then click the Play button at the bottom of the Audio Mixer window. This records the desired change to the audio tracks. Be sure to play the audio all the way through to the end of the Timeline. Close the Audio Mixer, then press the Return/Enter key to render the project. Do not save the project. If you are not satisfied with the changes, Select File>Close (do not save the project), then select File>Open, find the project that you saved in Step 7 of this exercise, and then click Open. Try again using new values for tracks Audio 1 and 2 (this is an easy way to undo audio changes). When you are certain the changes are correct, save your project.

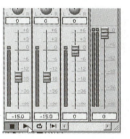

Add Transitions

1. Open the Transitions palette. Select Window>Show Transitions.

2. Select the Dissolve transition, and then drag Cross Dissolve to the Transition track. Place one Cross Dissolve between the end of surfl1.mov and surfl3.mov, and another between the end of surfl3.mov and the beginning of surfl4.mov (remember that surfl2.mov was deleted from the project). Continue adding transitions (your choice) to each of the remaining clips.

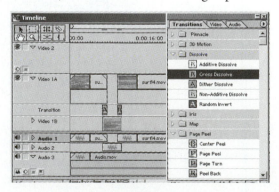

Correct a Clip

1. Clip surfl7.mov is too dark as a result of the extensive compression required to fit the clip on the CD-ROM. Add a Brightness & Contrast correction to lighten it. Select Window>Show Video Effects. Drag and drop Brightness & Contrast (from the Adjust folder) onto the surfl7 clip in the Timeline. Set the Brightness value to +16.0, and then close the Effect Controls palette.

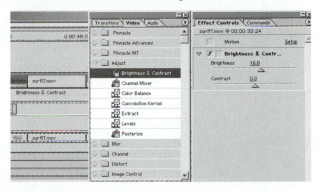

2. Press Return/Enter to render and preview the effect, and then save the project.

Create and Add a Still Image

1. Currently, the movie simply ends. You need to capture a still frame from the end of the movie and extend it long enough to add a title. Move the edit line marker to 01:21:00. Select File>Export Timeline>Frame, click Settings, and choose TIFF as the File Type. Name the file "endshot.tif", and save it in your **Project_D** folder.

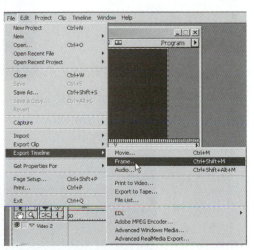

2. Move the edit line marker to 01:26:15. Choose File>Import>File, and then select **endshot.tif**. Drag endshot.tif to the Timeline and place it at 01:26:15 on track Video 1B. Select Clip>Duration, and set the Duration to 00:06:00 (the endshot.tif clip must be selected to do this). You can also set the duration when you save the still shot, if you know the required duration at the time you save it.

3. Open the Transitions palette, and select Additive Dissolve. Drag it to the beginning of endshot.tif.

Add a Closing Title

1. Move the edit line marker to 01:26:00. Select File>New>Title. When the Title Designer window appears, select Title>View>Text Baselines. Then select Title>View>Safe Title Margin (be sure there is a checkmark in front of it).

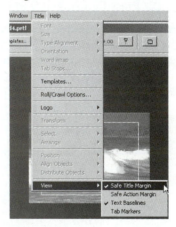

2. Create two lines of text using Arial-Italic as the Font. Set the Font Size to 50 and the Color to a sea blue. Move each line of text into position within the Safe Title margins.

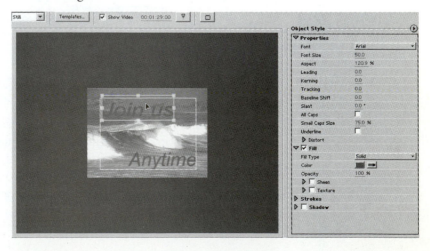

3. Save the title as "joinus.prtl", then close the Title Designer window. Place the title on Video 2 at 01:26:00. Set the Duration of the title to 00:06:00. Open the bottom half of the Video 2 track and adjust the transparency so the title appears at full intensity as surfl9.mov ends.

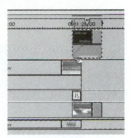

4. Select the Audio 3 track. Drag the right end of audio.mov to the left until it lines up with the end of the movie. Fade the sound to 0 using the rubberband at the bottom of the track. If it is not there already, drag the right end of the work area to line up with the end of the movie. Save your work.

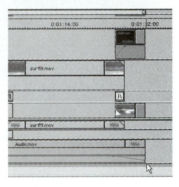

5. Move to the beginning of the movie and create a title that reads (without the quotation marks):

> "Central Coast"
> "Surfing"
> "Association"

6. Center the title by selecting Title>Type Alignment>Center, and then choose a font and font size that allows the title to remain entirely inside the Safe Title margins (we used 36-pt. News Gothic). Add a White Shadow with a Distance of 2.0 at an Angle of 180.0 degrees.

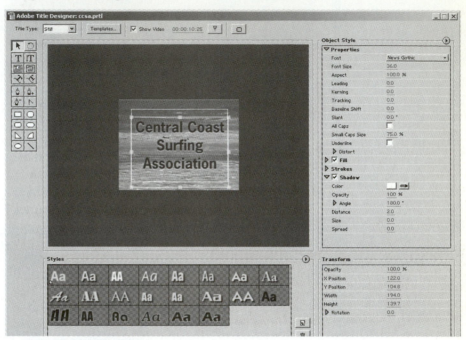

7. Save the title as "ccsa.prtl". Drag the title from the Project window to the Video 2 track at the beginning of the movie. Set the Duration to 00:06:00. Open the bottom of the Video 2 track and use the rubberbands to make the title fade in and fade out. Save your work, and then press Return/Enter to preview the movie. If all is correct, export the Timeline as a QuickTime movie, and then open it and view it as you did after completing the first three projects.

You have completed the final project of the book. By using the Safe Title margins, you can be sure this promotional piece will look as good on television as it does on your computer screen.

A/B Editing Mode

An editing mode that uses two video tracks, usually designated as "A" and "B" to assemble video clips.

Achromatic

By definition, having no color, therefore, completely black, white, or some shade of gray.

Acrobat

This program from Adobe Systems, Inc. allows the conversion of any document from any Macintosh or Windows application to PDF format, which retains the graphics, color, and typography of the original document. It is widely used for distributing documents online.

Action Safe Zone

The image area of a television screen that assures the action will not disappear off the edges (also Action Safe Margin).

Actor

A person who performs or plays a role, typically in a dramatic presentation or commercial production.

Adaptive Palette

A sampling of colors taken from an image and used in a special compression process, usually to prepare images for the Web.

Additive Color Process

The process of mixing red, green, and blue light to achieve a wide range of colors, as on a color-television screen.

Adjacent Color

An adjoining color. Since the eye responds to strong adjoining color, its perception of a particular color is affected by any nearby colors. This means that a color with adjacent colors may look different than it does in isolation.

Algorithm

A specific sequence of mathematical steps to process data. A portion of a computer program that calculates a specific result.

Alpha Channel

A fourth channel in an RGB image that defines what parts of the image are transparent or semitransparent.

Programs such as Adobe Illustrator, Photoshop, Premiere, and After Effects use alpha channels to specify transparent regions in an image. If a Photoshop file uses an alpha channel for transparency, Premiere finds and interprets it.

Analog

A signal that fluctuates exactly the same as the original, both in audio and video.

Animated GIF

A series of GIF graphics that functions like a film loop, giving the appearance of animation. See GIF.

Archival Storage

The process of storing data in a totally secure and safe manner. Archiving differs from backup in that it's meant to be used to restore entire systems or networks, rather than providing quick and easy access to specific files or folders.

Art

Illustrations and photographs in general. All matter other than text that appears in a mechanical.

Artifact

By definition, something that is artificial or not meant to be there. An artifact can be a blemish or dust spot on a piece of film, or unsightly pixels in a digital image.

Aspect Ratio

The width-to-height proportions of an image.

Audio

The electronic reproduction of audible sound.

Back Light

Lighting from behind the subject and opposite the camera.

Backing Up

The process of making copies of current work or work in progress as a safety measure against file corruption, drive or system failure, or accidental deletion. Backing up work in progress differs from creating an archive (see Archival Storage) for long-term storage or system restoration.

Bit (Binary Digit)

A computer's smallest unit of information. Bits can have only two values: 0 or 1. This number can represent the black-and-white (1-bit) pixel values in a line-art image. In combination with other bits, it can represent 16 tones or colors (4-bit), 256 tones or colors (8-bit), 16.8 million colors (24-bit), or a billion colors (30-bit). These numbers are derived from counting all the possible combinations (permutations) of 0 or 1 settings of each bit.

Bitmap Image

An image constructed from individual dots or pixels set to a grid-like mosaic. Each pixel can be represented by more than one bit. A 1-bit image is black and white because each bit can have only two values (for example, 0 for white and 1 for black). For 256 colors, each pixel needs eight bits (2^8). A 24-bit image refers to an image with 24 bits per pixel (2^{24}), so it may contain as many as 16,777,216 colors. The file must contain information about the color and position of each pixel, so the disk space needed for bitmap images is usually quite significant.

Bitmapped

Forming an image by a grid of pixels whose curved edges have discrete steps because of the approximation of the curve by a finite number of pixels.

Black

The absence of color; an ink that absorbs all wavelengths of light.

Bleeding

A key whose edges are not sharp and let the background show through.

Blocking

Carefully worked-out movement and actions by the talent and for all mobile television equipment.

Blue Screen

A colored backdrop (not always blue) used to create transparency using color key or chroma key effects.

Boom

1. A type of microphone or video support. 2. To move the camera via the boom of the camera crane.

Brightness

1. A measure of the amount of light reflected from a surface. 2. A paper property, defined as the percentage reflection of 457-nanometer (nm) radiation. 3. The intensity of a light source. 4. The overall percentage of lightness in an image.

Byte

A unit of measure equal to eight bits (decimal 256) of digital information, sufficient to represent one text character. The standard unit measure of file size. (See also *Megabyte*, *Kilobyte*, and *Gigabyte*).

Cable Television

Distribution device for broadcast signals via coaxial or fiber-optic cable.

Calibration

Making adjustments to a color monitor and other hardware and software to make the monitor represent as closely as possible the colors of the final production.

Camcorder

A small portable camera with a built in video tape recorder.

Camera

1. A light-tight photographic device that records the image of an object formed when light rays pass through an aperture and fall on a flat, photo-sensitive surface. 2. The overall name for the camera head, which is made up of the lens, the main imaging device, electronic accessories, and the viewfinder.

Camera Graphics

Graphics specifically designed for the television camera.

Cassette

A video or audiotape recording or playback device that uses tape cassettes.

Cause-to-Effect Model

The concept of moving an idea from a production to the effect it has on the viewer.

CD-ROM

A device used to store approximately 600 MB of data. Files are permanently stored on the device and can be copied to a disk but not altered directly. ROM stands for Read-Only Memory. Equipment is now available on the consumer market for copying computer files to blank CD-ROMs.

Chroma Keying

Special key effect that uses color (usually blue or green) for the background. This color is replaced by another picture during the key. (See *Color Key*.)

Clip

A piece of video, still, or audio footage.

Cloning

Duplication of pixels from one part of an image to another.

Close-Up (CU)

The overall name for viewing an object at close range, framed tightly.

CODEC

COmpressor/DECompressor algorithm used to compress and decompress visual and audio data. Enables smaller storage requirements and faster data transmission.

Color Bars

A color standard used by the television industry for the alignment of camera and videotape recordings.

Color Cast

The modification of a hue by the addition of a trace of another hue, such as yellowish green, pinkish blue, etc. Normally, an unwanted effect that can be corrected.

Color Correction

The process of removing casts or unwanted tints in a scanned image, in an effort to improve the appearance of the scan or to correct obvious deficiencies, such as green skies or yellowish skin tones.

Color Gamut

The range of colors that can be formed by all possible combinations of the colorants of a given reproduction system, such as colors that can be displayed on television.

Color Key

The process of electronically replacing a color, such as green or blue, with a graphic or live video. This allows one piece of video to be keyed or superimposed upon another.

Color Model

A system for describing color, such as RGB, HLS, CIE LAB, or CMYK.

Color Picker

A function within a graphics application that assists in selecting or setting a color.

Color Space

A color must be represented by three basic characteristics, depending on the color model, so the color space is a three-dimensional coordinate system in which any color can be represented as a point.

Color Temperature

1. The temperature, in degrees Kelvin, to which a blackbody would have to be heated to produce a certain color radiation. (A *blackbody* is an ideal body or surface that completely absorbs or radiates energy.) The graphic arts viewing standard is 5,000 K. (The degree symbol is not used in the Kelvin scale.) The higher the color temperature, the bluer the light. 2. Relative to light, the red or blue cast, as measured in Kelvin degrees. The norm for TV lighting is 3,200 K, and for outdoors is 5,600 K.

Colorimeter

An optical measuring instrument designed to measure and quantify color. It is often used to match digital image values to those of cloth and other physical samples.

Compression

A digital technique used to reduce the size of a file by analyzing occurrences of similar data. Compressed files occupy less physical space, and their use improves digital transmission speeds. Compression can sometimes result in a loss of image quality and/or resolution.

Compression Utility

A software program that reduces a file's size for storage on a disk. If a compressed file is too large to fit onto a single disk, the compression utility copies it onto multiple disks.

Continuity Editing

The preservation of visual continuity from one shot to the next.

Contrast

The relationship and degree of difference between the dark and light areas of an image.

Control Track

The area of a videotape used for recording the synchronization information. It provides a reference point for the editor by giving frame counts.

Copyright

Ownership of a work by the originator, such as an author, publisher, artist, or photographer. The right of copyright permits the originator of material to prevent its use without express permission or acknowledgment of the originator. Copyright may be sold, transferred, or given up contractually.

CPU

Stands for Central Processing Unit, the main part of a computer that routes all of the system information.

Crane

A camera dolly that resembles an actual crane in appearance and operation. The crane can lift the camera from just off the video floor to more than 10 feet above it.

Crawl

A title that moves horizontally across the screen.

Cropping

The elimination of parts of a photograph or other original that are not required for printing.

Cue

Signal for various production activities, or to select a section of a videotape.

Cue Card

A large hand-lettered card that contains copy. It is usually held next to the camera lens to ensure easy reading.

Cursor

A small symbol that can be moved around a video screen. Used to indicate position where data will be entered or an action taken.

Default

A specification for a mode of computer operation that occurs if no other is selected. The default font size might be 12 point, or a default color for an object might be white with a black border.

Demographics

Audience research factors concerned with such items as age, sex, marital status, and income.

Densitometer

An electronic instrument used to measure optical density. Reflective (for paper) and transmissive (for film).

Depth of Field

The area in which all objects located a different distances from the camera appear in focus. Depth of field depends heavily on the lens type selected.

Desktop

1. The area on a monitor screen on which the icons appear, before an application is launched. 2. A reference to the size of computer equipment (system unit, monitor, printer) that can fit on a normal desk, thus, desktop publishing.

Diffused Light

Light that illuminates a relatively large area and creates soft shadows without the use of a key light.

Digital

The use of a series of discrete electronic pulses to represent data. In digital imaging systems, 256 steps (8 bits, or 1 byte) are normally used to characterize the gray scale or the properties of one color.

Digital Camera

A camera that produces images directly into an electronic file format for transfer to a computer.

Digital Video (DV)

Video information stored on tape or disk in digital format.

Dimmer

A device that controls the intensity of light.

Dingbat

1. A font character that displays a picture instead of a letter, number, or punctuation mark. There are entire font families of pictographic dingbats. Dingbats exist for everything from the airplanes that represent airports on a map, to telephones, stars, balloons, and more. 2. Also, a printer's typographical ornament.

Directional Light

Light that illuminates a relatively small area with a strong light beam. Creates harsh, well-defined light areas.

Dissolve

A gradual transition from shot to shot, where the two images overlap.

Dolly

1. Camera movement that uses both the camera and the base of the camera, causing the entire unit to move in or out of a shot. 2. The portable platform that supports the camera equipment and permits such movement.

DPI (Dots Per Inch)

The measurement of resolution for page printers, phototypesetting machines, and graphics screens. Currently graphics screens use resolutions of 72 to 96 dpi, standard desktop laser printers work at 600 dpi.

Draw-Type Pictures

Pictures created from a series of instructions that tell the computer to draw lines, curves, rectangles, and other objects. Also called "object-oriented images" or "vector graphics." See Bitmap Image.

Drop

Large, painted piece of canvas used for scenery backing.

Drop Shadow

A duplicate of a graphic element or type placed behind and slightly offset from it, creating the effect of a shadow.

Dry Run

Rehearsal without equipment during which the basic actions of the talent are worked out.

Dub

A duplication of a videotape. Digital dubbing produces copies almost identical to that of the original.

Editing

The selection and assembly of shots in a logical sequence.

Element

The smallest unit of a graphic, or a component of a page layout or design. Any object, text block, or graphic might be referred to as an element of the design.

ENG

Stands for electronic news gathering. The use of portable cameras to cover stories that are not planned.

EPS

Acronym for encapsulated PostScript, a single-page PostScript file that contains grayscale or color information and can be imported into many electronic layout and design applications.

Essential Area

The section of the television picture that contains the most needed information. It is based on the average consumer television.

Establishing Shot

Extreme long shot. Used to establish location or place.

Export

To save a file generated in one application into a format that is readable in another.

Extension

1. A modular software program that extends or expands the functions of a larger program. A folder of Extensions is found in the Macintosh System Folder. 2. A suffix used on a file name to indicate the application in which the file was created.

Fade

The gradual appearance (or disappearance) of a picture to or from black.

Feed

Signal transmission from one program source to another, such as a network feed or a remote feed.

Field

One of two images that make up a frame. Fields can be referred to as Top/Bottom, A/B, or Odd/Even.

Field Log

A record of each take during the videotaping session.

File

A specific collection of information stored on the computer disk separately from all other information. Can be randomly accessed by the computer.

Fill Light

Additional light on the opposite side of the camera from the key light to illuminate shadow areas and thereby reduce hard shadows.

Filter

In image-editing applications, a small program that creates a special effect or performs some other function within an image.

Flat Color

Color that lacks contrast or tonal variation. Also, flat tint.

Floor Plan

A plan of the studio floor, showing the walls, the main doors, and the location of the control room, with the lighting grid superimposed over it.

Flow Chart

A block diagram representing the major steps of an event. It is used by computer programmers to translate events into computer logic.

Folder

The digital equivalent of a paper file folder, used to organize files in the Macintosh and Windows operating systems. The icon of a folder looks like a paper file folder. Double-clicking it opens it to reveal the files stored inside.

Font

A font is the complete collection of all the characters (numbers, uppercase, and lowercase letters and, in some cases, small caps and symbols) of a given typeface in a specific style; for example, Helvetica Bold.

Font Substitution

A process in which Windows or your printer uses a font similar to the one you used in your publication to display or print your publication. Although the substitute font may be similar to the original font, your publication will not look exactly as you intended; line breaks, column breaks, or page breaks may fall differently, which can affect the appearance and effectiveness of the publication.

Footage Item

An image, video, composition, or sound clip used in a production.

Format

Type of television script indicating the major programming steps. Generally contains a fully scripted show opening and closing. Example: the nightly news.

Frame

In desktop publishing — 1. An area or block into which text or graphics can be placed. 2. A border on such an area.

Frame Rate

The number of successive images that are displayed in one second, designated fps (frames per second).

Freeze-Frame

Continual replaying of a single frame, which is perceived as a still shot.

F-Stop

The calibration on the lens indicating the aperture or diaphragm opening. Controls the amount of light that can pass through the lens.

Gain

1. In audio, level of amplification for audio signals. 2. In video, electronic amplification of the video signal. 3. To "ride the gain" means to keep the levels at a proper level.

Gamma

A measure of the contrast, or range of tonal variation of the midtones in a photographic image.

Gamma Correction

1. Adjusting the contrast of the midtones in an image. 2. Calibrating a monitor so midtones are correctly displayed on screen.

Gang

Refers to changes made to multiple tracks simultaneously. For example, if you want to change the audio volume levels in tracks 1, 3, and 4 simultaneously, gang those three tracks together.

Generated Graphics

Graphic material that is generated and/or manipulated by a computer and used directly on the air or stored for use at a later time.

GIF (Graphics Interchange Format)

A popular graphics format for on-line clip art and drawn graphics. Graphics in this format look good at low resolution. See *JPEG*.

Gigabyte (G)

One billion (1,073,741,824) bytes (230) or 1,048,576 kilobytes.

Global Preferences

Preference settings that affect all newly created files within an application.

Gradient Fill

See Graduated Fill.

Graduated Fill

An area where two colors (or shades of gray or the same color) are blended to create a gradual change from one to the other. Graduated fills are also known as blends, gradations, gradient fills, and vignettes.

Graphics

All visuals specially prepared for the television screen, such as title cards, charts and graphs.

Grayscale

1. An image composed in grays ranging from black to white, usually using 256 different tones of gray. 2. A tint ramp used to measure and control the accuracy of screen percentages on

press. 3. An accessory used to define neutral density in a photographic image.

Green Screen

A colored backdrop (not always green) used to create transparency using color key or chroma key effects.

Grid

A division of a page by horizontal and vertical guides into areas where text or graphics may be placed accurately.

Group

To collect graphic elements together so an operation may be applied to all of them simultaneously.

GUI

Acronym for Graphical User Interface, the basis of the Macintosh and Windows operating systems.

Hard Drive

A rigid disk sealed inside an airtight transport mechanism that is the basic storage device in a computer. Information stored may be accessed more rapidly than on floppy disks and far greater amounts of data may be stored.

Hardware

The physical components of a computer and its auxiliary equipment.

Headroom

The space left between the top of the head and the upper edge of the screen.

High-Definition Television (HDTV)

The use of special cameras and recording equipment for the production of high-quality pictures. The pictures have a higher resolution than regular television pictures. The aspect ratio of HDTV is 16 by 9.

Highlights

The lightest areas in a photograph or illustration.

HSL (Hue, Saturation, Luminosity)

A color model that defines color as it is displayed on a video or computer screen. See *HSV*.

HSV (Hue, Saturation, Value)

A color model based on three coordinates: hue, saturation and value (or luminance).

Hue

The wavelength of light of a color in its purest state (without adding white or black).

Icon

A small graphic symbol used on the screen to indicate files, folders or applications, and activated by clicking with the mouse or pointing device.

Import

To bring a file generated in one application into another application.

In the Can

A term borrowed from film, which refers to when the finished film was finally completed and placed in a storage can. Now means a finished television recording; the show is preserved and can be used any time.

Indexed Color Image

An image that uses a limited, predetermined number of colors; often used in Web images. See also *GIF*.

Insert Editing

Inserting shots in an existing recording without affecting shots on either side.

Intensity

Synonym for degree of color saturation.

Interlace

A method of combining two video fields to make up a video frame.

Internet

An international network of computer networks that links millions of commercial, educational, governmental, and personal computers.

Internet Service Provider (ISP)

An organization that provides access to the Internet for such things as electronic mail, bulletin boards, chat rooms, or use of the World Wide Web.

Intershot Movement

The movement that occurs during one shot regardless of length. Examples: a pan or tilt.

Jaggies

Visible steps in the curved edge of a graphic or text character that result from enlarging a bitmapped image.

JPG or JPEG

A compression algorithm that reduces the file size of bitmapped images, named for the Joint Photographic Experts Group, an industry organization that created the standard. JPEG is a "lossy" compression method, and image quality is reduced in direct proportion to the amount of compression. JPEG graphics produce better resolution for color photographs than those in the GIF format.

Jump Cut

Cutting between shots that are identical in subject yet slightly different in screen location. The subject seems to jump from one screen location to another for no apparent reason.

Justified Alignment

Straight left and right alignment of text — not ragged. Every line of text is the same width, creating even left and right margins.

Kerning

Moving a pair of letters closer together or farther apart, to achieve a better fit or appearance.

Key

1. Principal source of illumination. High- or low-key lighting. 2. Also an electronic effect; example: chroma key.

Kilobyte (K, KB)

1,024 (210) bytes, the nearest binary equivalent to decimal 1,000 bytes. Abbreviated and referred to as K.

Laser Printer

A high-quality image printing system, using a laser beam to produce an image on a photosensitive drum. The image is transferred to paper by a conventional xerographic printing process. Current laser printers used for desktop publishing have a resolution of 600 dpi. Imagesetters are also laser printers, but with higher resolution and tight mechanical controls to produce final film separations for commercial printing.

Layout

The arrangement of text and graphics on a page, usually produced in the preliminary design stage.

Leading ("Ledding")

Space added between lines of type. Usually measured in points or fractions of points. Named after the strips of lead that used to be inserted between lines of metal type. In specifying type, lines of 12-pt. type separated by a 14-pt. space is abbreviated "12/14," or "twelve over fourteen."

Left Alignment

Straight edge of text with a ragged or uneven right edge.

Lens

Optical device, essential for projecting an optical (light) image of a scene in front of the surface of the camera. Lenses comes in various fixed focal lengths, or in variable focal lengths and with various aperture (iris) openings.

Letterspacing

The insertion or addition of white space between the letters of words.

Level

1. Audio: sound volume. 2. Video: signal strength measured in volts.

Library

In the computer world, a collection of files having a similar purpose or function.

Lightness

The property that distinguishes white from gray or black, and light from dark color tones on a surface.

Line Art

A drawing or piece of black-and-white artwork with no screens. Line art can be represented by a graphic file having only 1-bit resolution.

Linear Editing

Non-random editing that uses tape-based systems.

Linking

An association, through software, of a graphic or text file on disk with its location in a document. That location may be represented by a placeholder rectangle, or a low-resolution copy of the graphic

Lip-Sync

Synchronization of sound and lip movement.

Location Survey

Written assessment, usually in the form of a checklist, of the production requirements for a remote.

Log

The daily diary that tracks shots taken during a video shoot. Records the usefulness of the material.

Long Shot (LS)

Object seen from far away or framed very loosely.

Lossy

A data compression method characterized by the loss of some data.

Luminosity

The amount of light or brightness in an image. Part of the HLS color model.

Lux

European standard unit for measuring light intensity: 1 lux is the amount of 1 lumen (one candlepower of light).

M, MB (Megabyte)

One million (1,048,576) bytes (220) or 1,024 Kilobytes.

Macro

A set of keystrokes that is saved as a named computer file. Macros are used to efficiently perform repetitive tasks.

Medium

1. A physical carrier of data, such as a CD-ROM, video cassette, or floppy disk. 2. A carrier of electronic data, such as fiber optic cable or electric wires.

Medium Shot

Object seen from a medium distance. Covers any framing between a long shot and a close-up shot.

Megabyte (MB)

A unit of measure of stored data equaling 1,024 kilobytes, or 1,048,576 bytes (1020).

Megahertz

An analog signal frequency of one million cycles per second, or a data rate of one million bits per second. Used in specifying computer CPU speed.

Memory

The storage device in a computer. Its capacity is given in numbers of bytes. See *RAM* and *ROM*.

Menu

A list of choices of functions or items, such as fonts. In contemporary software design, there is often a fixed menu of basic functions at the top of the page that have pull-down menus associated with each fixed choice.

Microphone

A small, portable assembly for the pickup and conversion of sound into electric energy.

MIDI

Stands for musical instrument digital interface: a standardization device that allows various digital audio equipment and computers to interface.

Midtones or Middletones

The tonal range between highlights and shadows.

Modem

An electronic device for converting digital data into analog audio signals and back again (MOdulator-DEModulator). Primarily used for transmitting data between computers over analog (audio frequency) telephone lines.

Monochrome

An image or computer monitor where all information is represented in black and white, or with a range of grays.

Montage

A single image formed by assembling or compositing several images.

Morphing

Short for metamorphosis. Using a computer to animate the gradual transformation of one image into another.

Multimedia

The combination of sound, video images, and text to create a moving presentation.

NAB

Acronym for the National Association of Broadcasters.

Network

Two or more computers that are linked to exchange data or share resources. The Internet is a network of networks.

Neutral

Any color that has no hue, such as white, gray, or black.

Neutral Density

A measurement of the lightness or darkness of a color. A neutral density of zero (0.00) is the lightest value possible and is equivalent to pure white; 3.294 is roughly equivalent to 100% of each of the CMYK components.

Noise

Unwanted signals or data that may reduce the quality of output. On television it looks like snow.

Nonlinear Editing

Using a computer for instant random access to and easy rearrangements of shots. The video and audio information is stored in digital form on high-capacity computer hard drives or read/write laser videodiscs.

Normal Key

A description of an image where the main interest area is in the middle range of the tonal scale or distributed throughout the entire tonal range.

NTSC

Stands for National Television System Committee. Normally designates the composite television signal, using RGB color model.

Nudge

To move a graphic or text element in small, preset increments, usually with the Arrow keys.

Object-Oriented Art

Vector-based artwork composed of separate elements or shapes described mathematically rather than by specifying the color and position of every point. This is in contrast to bitmap images, which are composed of individual pixels.

Oblique

A slanted character (sometimes backward, or to the left), often used when referring to italic versions of sans-serif typefaces.

Off-Line Editing

Produces an EDL (edit decision list) or a videotape that is not intended for broadcast.

Omni-Directional

Pickup pattern where the microphone can pick up sounds equally well from all directions.

On-Line Editing

Produces the final high-quality edit-master tape for broadcast or program duplication.

Opacity

1. The degree to which paper will show print through it. 2. The degree to which images or text below one object, whose opacity has been adjusted, are able to show through.

Optical Disks

Videodisks that store large amounts of data used primarily for reference works, such as dictionaries and encyclopedias.

Output Device

Any hardware equipment, such as a monitor, laser printer, or imagesetter, that depicts text or graphics created on a computer.

Over-the-Shoulder Shot (O/S)

Camera looks over one person's shoulder at what that individual would see.

Palette

1. As derived from the term in the traditional art world, a collection of selectable colors. 2. Another name for a dialog box or menu of choices.

Pan

Horizontal turning of the camera during shooting. The base remains stationary.

Pasteboard

In a page-layout program, the desktop area outside of the printing-page area, on which elements can be placed for later positioning on any page.

PCX

Bitmap image format produced by paint programs.

PDF (Portable Document Format)

Developed by Adobe Systems, Inc. (read by Acrobat Reader), this format has become a de facto standard for document transfer across platforms.

Pedestal

Camera dolly that permits raising and lowering the camera while shooting.

Performer

A person who appears on-camera in nondramatic shows. The performer plays him or herself and does not assume any other role. Example: a game show host.

Perspective

The effect of distance in an image, achieved by aligning the edges of elements with imaginary lines directed toward one to three "vanishing points" on the horizon.

PICT/PICT2

A common format for defining bitmapped images on the Macintosh. The more recent PICT2 format supports 24-bit color.

Pixel

Abbreviation for picture element. One of the tiny rectangular areas generated by a computer or output device to constitute images. If a pixel is "turned on," it has color or shading. If it is "turned off," it looks like a blank space. Pixels can vary in size from one type of monitor or printer to another. A greater number of pixels per inch results in higher resolution on screen or in print.

Plot

1. The sequence of events in a story.
2. To plan out such a sequence.

Point

A unit of measurement used to specify type size and rule weight, equal to (approximately, in traditional typesetting) 1/72 inch. Note: font sizes are measured differently from leading, even though they're both specified in points. The only way you can verify font size on your hard copy is by measuring it against the designated sizes you'll find on an E-scale.

Point of View (POV)

The perspective of an individual.

Polygon

A geometric figure, consisting of three or more straight lines enclosing an area. The triangle, square, rectangle and star are all polygons.

Posterize, Posterization

1. Deliberate constraint of a gradient or image into visible steps as a special effect. 2. Unintentional creation of steps in an image due to a high LPI value used with a low printer DPI.

Postproduction

Any production activity that occurs after the production. Usually refers to either videotape editing or audio sweetening.

Postproduction Editing

The assembly of recorded material after the actual production.

PostScript

1. A page-description language, developed by Adobe Systems, Inc., that describes type and/or images and their positional relationships on the page. 2. An interpreter or RIP (see Raster Image Processor) that can process the PostScript page description into a format for laser printer or imagesetter output. 3. A computer-programming language.

Pot

Short for potentiometer, a sound-volume control.

Preferences

A set of modifiable defaults for an application program.

Premultiplied

Alpha (transparency) information that is precombined with the red, green, and blue channels of an image.

Preproduction

Preparation of all production details.

Preroll

To start a videotape and let it roll for a few seconds before it is put in the playback or record mode so the electronic system has time to stabilize.

Primary Colors

Colors that can be used to generate secondary colors. For the additive system (i.e., a computer monitor), these colors are red, green, and blue. For the subtractive system (i.e., the printing process), these colors are yellow, magenta, and cyan.

Printer Driver

The device that communicates between your software program and your printer. When you're using an application, the printer driver tells the application what the printer can do, and also tells the printer how to print the publication.

Producer

Creator and organizer of films or television shows.

Production Bundle

An add-on package supplied by Adobe, at additional cost, containing extensive controls and effects used in professional productions.

Production Schedule

A plan that shows the time periods of various activities during the production day. Also called a "timeline."

Program

1. A specific television show.
2. A sequence of instructions, encoded in a specific computer language, for performing predetermined tasks.

Program Proposal

Written document that outlines the process message and the major aspects of a television presentation.

Project

A single Premiere file that describes a video. It stores references to all clips in that file as well as information about how they are arranged. It also includes details of any transitions or effects applied.

Props

Short for properties. Furniture and objects employed for set decoration. Used by actors or performers.

Queue

A set of files input to the printer, printed in the order received unless otherwise instructed.

RAM

Random Access Memory, the "working" memory of a computer that holds files in process. Files in RAM are lost when the computer is turned off, whereas files stored on the hard drive or floppy disks remain available.

RAM Preview

Rendering and displaying a movie directly from computer memory rather than disk.

Raster

A bitmapped representation of graphic data.

Raster Graphics

A class of graphics created and organized in a rectangular array of bitmaps. Often created by paint software, fax machines, or scanners for display and printing.

Rasterize

The process of converting digital information into pixels at the resolution of the output device. For example, the process used by an imagesetter to translate PostScript files before they are imaged to film or paper.

Remote

A large television production shot outside the studio.

Render

A real-time preview of clips and all effects as your production plays.

Resolution

The density of graphic information expressed in dots per inch (dpi) or pixels per inch (ppi).

Reverberation

Technically, reflections of a sound wave after the sound source has ceased vibrating. Perceived as audio echo.

RGB

1. Acronym for red, green, blue — the colors of projected light from a computer monitor that, when combined, simulate a subset of the visual spectrum. When a color image is scanned, RGB data is collected by the scanner and then converted to CMYK data at a later step in the process. 2. Also refers to the color model of most digital artwork.

Right Alignment

Text having a straight right edge and a ragged or uneven left edge.

Ripple Edit

Trims a specific clip, keeping all of the other clips intact. The additional clips are pushed or pulled into position.

Roll

1. Graphics (usually credit copy) that move slowly up the screen. 2. The command to start a videotape.

ROM

Read Only Memory, a semiconductor chip in the computer that retains start-up information for use the next time the computer is turned on.

Rotation

Turning an object at some angle to its original axis.

Rough Cut

The first tentative arrangement of shots and shot sequences in the approximate order and length. Done in off-line editing.

RTF

Rich Text Format, a text format that retains formatting information lost in pure ASCII text.

Rules

Straight lines, often stretching horizontally across the top of a page, to separate text from running heads.

Running Time

The duration of a program or a program segment.

Run-Through

Rehearsal before a shoot.

Safe Title Margin (Zone)

See *Essential Area*.

Sans Serif

Fonts that do not have serifs. See Serif.

Saturation

The intensity or purity of a color; a color with no saturation is gray.

Scaling

Within a program, to reduce or enlarge the amount of space an image will occupy by multiplying the data by a factor. Scaling can be proportional, or in one dimension only.

Scanner

A device that electronically digitizes images point by point through circuits that can correct color, manipulate tones, and enhance detail. Color scanners usually produce a minimum of 24 bits for each pixel, and 8 bits each for red, green, and blue channel.

Scene

Event details that form an organic unit, usually in a single place and time. A series of organically related shots that depict these event details.

Scenery

Background flats and other pieces (windows, doors, pillars) that simulate a specific environment.

Schedule Time

Shows the clock time at the beginning or the end of a program or program segment.

Scoop

A scoop-like television floodlight.

Screen Shot

A printed output or saved file that represents data from a computer monitor.

Scrim

1. Lighting: a spun-glass material that is put in front of a light to diffuse the brightness. 2. Scenery: a soft material placed behind the actors to give a uniform background.

Script

Written document that tells what the program is about, who is in it, what is supposed to happen, and how the audience will view the event. The text of a production.

Scrub

Advancing or reversing a clip manually. Enables you to precisely identify and mark events.

Select

Place the cursor on an object and click the mouse button to make the object active.

Sequencing

The control and structuring of a shot sequence during editing.

Serif

A line or curve projecting from the end of a letterform. Typefaces designed with such projections are called serif faces.

Set

Arrangement of scenery and properties to indicate the locale and/or mood of a show.

Shade

A color mixed with black. A 10% shade is one part of the original color and nine parts black. See Tint.

Sharpness

The subjective impression of the density difference between two tones at their boundary, interpreted as fineness of detail.

Shortcut

1. A quick method for accessing a menu item or command, usually through a series of keystrokes. 2. The icon that can be created in Windows to open an application without having to penetrate layers of various folders. The equivalent in the Macintosh is the "alias."

Shot Sheet

List of every shot a particular camera has to obtain. It is attached to the camera to help the camera operator remember a shot sequence.

Shotgun Microphone

A highly directional microphone for picking up sounds over great distances.

Show Format

Lists the show segments in order of appearance. Used in routine shows, such as daily game or interview shows.

Silhouette

To remove part of the background of a photograph or illustration, leaving only the desired portion.

Single-Track Mode

A video-editing mode that uses a single video track to edit clips.

Skew

A transformation command that slants an object at an angle to the side from its initial fixed base.

Slate

1. Visual and/or verbal identification of each videotaped segment. 2. A little blackboard upon which essential information is written, such as the show title or take number. It is recorded at the beginning of each take.

Slow Motion

A scene where the objects appear to be moving more slowly than normal. In television, slow motion is achieved by slowing down the playback speed of the tape, which results in multiple scanning of each television frame.

Small Caps

A type style in which lowercase letters are replaced by uppercase letters set in a smaller point size.

SMPTE/EBU Timecode

An electronic signal recorded on the cue or address track of the videotape or on an audio track of a multi-track audiotape through a timecode generator. It provides a time address for each frame in hours, minutes, seconds, and frame numbers in elapsed time.

Sound Bite

Brief portion of someone's on-camera statement.

Source Videotape

The tape with the original footage in an editing operation.

Special-Effects Controls

Buttons on a switcher that regulate special effects. They include buttons for specific functions, such as wipes and key effects.

Split Screen

Multiple-image effect caused by stopping a directional wipe before its completion. Both shots are on the screen for a period of time.

Spotlight

A lighting instrument that produces directional, relatively undiffused light with a fairly well-defined beam.

Stand-By

A warning cue for any kind of action in television production.

Stock Shot

A shot of a common occurrence: clouds, crowds, cars, etc. They are generally generic and are usually available for rental or purchase from agencies.

Storyboard

A series of sketches of the key visualization points of an event along with audio information. Often includes camera angles, any camera movement, and key phrases from the script.

Style

A set of formatting instructions for font, paragraphing, tabs, and other properties of text.

Sub-Pixel

A point based on a calculated distance that is less than the size of a single pixel.

Subscript

Small-size characters set below the normal letters or figures, usually to convey technical information.

Subtractive Color

Color that is observed when light strikes pigments or dyes that absorb certain wavelengths of light. The light that is reflected back is perceived as a color.

Super

Short for superimposition. The simultaneous showing of two pictures on the same screen.

System Folder

The location of the operating system files on a Macintosh.

S-VHS

Stands for Super Video Home System. A high-quality 1/2 inch VHS system that meets broadcast standards.

Sweetening

Variety of quality adjustments of recorded sound in postproduction.

Switcher

1. Technical crew member working the video switcher (usually the technical director). 2. A panel with rows of buttons that allow the selection and assembly of various video sources through a variety of transition devices, and the creation of electronic special effects.

Switching

A change from one video source to another during a show or show segment with the aid of a switcher. Also called instantaneous editing.

Sync

Electronic pulses that synchronize the scanning between the origination source (live cameras, videotape) and the reproduction sources (monitor or television receiver), and other vital electronic functions between electronic equipment, such as video tape recorders.

Take

1. Signal for a cut from one video source to another. 2. Any one of similar and repeated shots taken during videotaping and filming. 3. Sometimes take is used synonymously with shot. A good take is the successful completion of a shot, a show segment, or the videotaping of the whole show. A bad take is an unsuccessful recording, requiring another recording.

Talent

Collective name for all performers and actors who appear regularly on television or in a production.

Target Audience

The audience selected or desired to receive a specific message.

Telephoto Lens

An optical device that gives a narrow, close-up view of an event relatively far away from the camera. Also called long-focal-length lens or narrow-angle lens.

Teleprompter

A prompting device that projects the moving (usually computer generated) copy over the lens so the talent can read it without losing eye contact with the viewer.

Text

The characters and words that form the main body of a publication.

Texture

1. A property of the surface of the substrate, such as the smoothness of paper. 2. Graphically, variation in tonal values to form image detail. 3. A class of fills in a graphics application that give various appearances, such as bricks or grass.

Theme

1. What the story is all about; its essential idea. 2. The opening and closing music in a show.

Three Shot

Framing of three people.

Thumbnails

1. The preliminary sketches of a design. 2. Small images used to indicate the content of a computer file.

TIFF (Tagged Image File Format)

A popular graphics format.

Tile

1. A type of repeating fill pattern. 2. Reproduce a number of pages of a document on one sheet. 3. Printing a large document overlapping on several smaller sheets of paper.

Tilt

The up and down movement of the camera, the base remains stationary.

Time Cues

Cues to the talent about time remaining in the show.

Timecode

Electronic signal that provides a specific and unique address for each electronic frame.

Timeline

An editing window indicating how clips are arranged and how they change over time. Also includes special effects and transitions.

Tint

1. A halftone area that contains dots of uniform size, that is, no modeling or texture. 2. The mixture of a color with white: a 10% tint is one part of the original color and nine parts white.

Title Safe Zone (Margin)

The area on a television screen that assures that text will not disappear off the edges.

Toggle

A command that switches between either of two states at each application. Switching between Hide and Show is a toggle.

Tracking

Adjusting the spacing of letters in a line of text to achieve proper justification or general appearance. You may want to squeeze letters closer together to fit into a frame, or spread them apart for a special effect.

Transformation

A change in the position, velocity, or opacity of an object.

Transition

The change from one video clip to another. Premiere provides an extensive assortment of transitions, including cuts, dissolves, blurs, blends, wipes, zooms, and more.

Treatment

Brief narrative description of a television program or other production.

Trim

To refine or make adjustments to the In and Out points of a clip.

Tripod

Three-legged camera mount, usually connected to a dolly for easy movement of the camera.

Truck

To move the camera laterally by means of a mobile camera mount.

TrueType

An outline font format on both Macintosh and Windows systems that can be used on the screen and on a printer.

Two Shot

Framing two people in a shot.

Type 1 Fonts

PostScript fonts, based on Bézier curves and encrypted for compactness, that are compatible with Adobe Type Manager.

Type Family

A set of typefaces created from the same basic design but in different weights, such as bold, light, italic, book, and heavy.

Typo

An abbreviation for typographical error. A keystroke error in the typeset copy.

Uppercase

The capital letters of a typeface as opposed to the lowercase, or small, letters. When type was hand composited, the capital letters resided in the upper part of the type case.

Utility

Software that performs ancillary tasks, such as counting words, defragmenting a hard drive, or restoring a deleted file.

Vector Graphics

Graphics defined using coordinate points and mathematically drawn lines and curves that can be freely scaled and rotated without image degradation in the final output. Fonts (such as PostScript and TrueType), and illustrations from drawing applications are common examples of vector objects. Two commonly used vector-drawing programs are Adobe Illustrator and Macromedia FreeHand. A class of graphics that overcomes the resolution limitation of bitmapped graphics.

Vertical Justification

The ability to automatically adjust the interline spacing (leading) to make columns and pages end at the same point on a page.

VHS

Stands for video home system. A consumer-oriented 1/2-in. VCR system. Now used extensively in all phases of television production for previewing and off-line editing.

Video

1. Picture portion of a television program. 2. Non-broadcast production activities.

Video Tracks

Most videotape formats have a video track, two or more audio tracks, and a separate timecode track.

Videocassette

A plastic container in which a videotape moves from supply to take-up reel, recording and playing back program segments through a videotape recorder.

Videotape

A plastic, iron-oxide coated tape of various widths for recording video and audio signals as well as additional technical code information.

Videotape Recorder (VTR)

Electronic recording device that records video and audio signals on videotape for later playback or post-production editing.

Viewfinder

An electronic device at the back of a camera that gives a representation of the shot being taken.

Visible Spectrum

The wavelengths of light between about 380 nm (violet) and 700 nm (red) that are visible to the human eye.

Visualization

Mentally converting a scene into a number of key images. The mental image of a shot. The images do not need to be sequenced at that time.

Volume

The relative loudness or softness of a sound.

Walk Through

A rehearsal without taping. The director explains to both the talent and the camera operators what will take place during the actual shoot.

White Light

Light containing all wavelengths of the visible spectrum. Also known as 5000 K lighting.

White Space

Areas on the page that contain no images or type. Proper use of white space is critical to a well-balanced design.

Window

In Premiere, a self-contained area of the screen where various editing, viewing, or file organization takes place.

Wipe

Transition where a second image, framed in some geometrical shape, gradually replaces all or part of the first one.

WYSIWYG

An acronym for "What You See Is What You Get." (Pronounced "wizzywig.") Means that what you see on your computer screen bears a strong resemblance to what the final product will look like.

Zooming

The process of electronically enlarging or reducing an image on a monitor to facilitate detailed design or editing and navigation.

INDEX

Resource CD-ROM

ADOBE® PREMIERE® 6.5

Digital Video Editing

AGAINST THE CLOCK

System Requirements

Windows:

- Intel® Pentium® III 500MHz processor (Pentium 4 or multiprocessor recommended)
- Microsoft® Windows® 98 Second Edition, Windows Millennium Edition, Windows 2000 with Service Pack 2, or Windows XP
- 128MB of RAM (256MB or more recommended)
- 600MB of available hard-disk space for installation
- 256-color video display adapter
- CD-ROM drive
- QuickTime 5.0 recommended
- For DV: Microsoft DirectX certified IEEE 1394 interface, dedicated large-capacity 7200RPM UDMA 66 IDE or SCSI hard disk or disk array, and DirectX compatible video display adapter
- For third-party capture cards: Adobe® Premiere® certified capture card
- For Real-Time Preview: Pentium III 800MHz processor (Pentium 4 dual processors recommended)

Macintosh:

- PowerPC® G3 or faster processor (G4 or G4 dual recommended)
- Mac OS 9.2.2 or Mac OS X v.10.1.3
- 64MB of RAM (128MB or more recommended)
- 600MB of available hard-disk space for installation
- 256-color video display adapter
- CD-ROM drive
- QuickTime 5.0.2
- For DV: QuickTime compatible FireWire® (IEEE 1394) interface, large-capacity hard disk or disk array capable of sustaining 5MB/sec, and FireWire 2.7
- For third-party capture cards: Adobe Premiere certified capture card
- For Real-Time Preview: G4 processor (G4 dual recommended)

To use the additional resource ... the appropriate applications installed on your system and enough free space ... s product does not come with the application software required to use the da...